Leo Barić and Lorraine F. Barić

HEALTH PROMOTION AND HEALTH EDUCATION

Module 3

EVALUATION, QUALITY, AUDIT

Foreword by
Dr Ilona Kickbusch
WHO Geneva

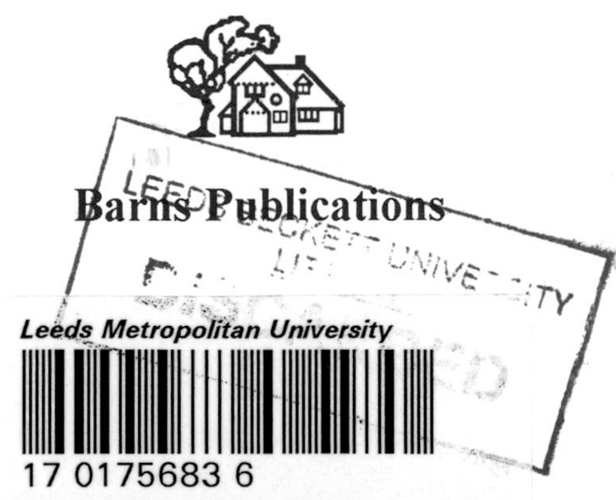

Also by Leo Barić:

Health Promotion and Health Education
Module 1: Problems and Solutions

Health Promotion and Health Education
Module 2: The Organisational Model

First Edition 1995

ISBN 0-95-16973-2-3

Published by Barns Publications, 14, High Elm Road, Hale Barns, Altrincham, Cheshire, WA15 OHS, England. FAX: 0161-980-7446

CONTENTS

PLANNING AN INTERVENTION 107

FOREWORD

Dr ILONA KICKBUSCH
Director Divison of Health Promotion, Education & Communication
WHO HQ GENEVA

This is the third book by the Author in the trilogy on Health Promotion and Health Education. The first book aimed at redressing the balance from emphasising the study of the problems to giving equal emphasis to the selection of health promotion and health education solutions. The second book traced the historical developments of health promotion and health education up to the point of the introduction of the organisational model and provided examples of implementing this model in practice. The third book draws the whole subject matter to its logical conclusion by providing an overview of the methods necessary for the assessment of the processes and outcomes of health promotion and health education interventions in terms of evaluation, quality assessment and auditing.

To appreciate the important contribution of this trilogy it will be necessary to remind ourselves about the radical changes which have taken place in promoting health and delivering health care in the world during the last few decades.

One of the most important changes was the consequence of the *Alma Ata Declaration* (1978) initiated by the World Health Organisation, which stated that health is one of the basic human rights and that governments should undertake the responsibility for the provision of necessary conditions for people to exercise this right. It resulted in setting as its aim the achievement of "Health for all by the Year 2000" for the purpose of emphasising the urgency of solving health problems in the world. During the years the Declaration has served as the basis for the reform of the health care delivery systems in many countries. It has, however, also met with certain amount of criticism, mainly due to the "over-optimistic" setting of goals within a limited time-scale. Accepting the fact that the whole world will not be "healthy" by the year 2000, the importance of the Declaration cannot be questioned. As an example one can take the slogan "liberté, egalité, fraternité" supposedly shouted from the barricades during the French revolution. Although the likelihood of achieving these aims was very slight at the time to say the least, the slogan has swept throughout the world and today we take it for granted, it is a part of our value system. In the same way the Alma Ata Declaration has become a part of our value system concerning health and the delivery of care.

The implications of the Alma Ata Declaration for the future of health education and the newly recognised health promotion have been considerable. These are best expressed in the *Ottawa Charter* (1986) which defined the new approaches and developments and lay the foundations for the present "organisational model".

One of the more important principles includes the emphasis on the settings in which people live, work and play and within which health promotion and health education should tackle the health problems and risks. It shifts the emphasis from medical problems to people and their needs and in this way represents a shift of emphasis from a medical to an organisational model of health promotion and health education and answers the critics of the dominant role of the medical profession in matters of health as well as disease. This resulted in shifting the responsibility for health promotion and health education from the "specialists" and in some cases even "professional health promoters" to all the members of each setting who deal directly or indirectly with clients or consumers. This answered the criticism some time directed towards the "bureaucratisation" of health promotion and health education, implying that the limited resources available are being spent on supporting the bureaucracy with only a small proportion actually reaching the consumers. A good example is the reform of the National Health Service in UK with the differentiation between the "purchasers" and "providers" of the services including health promotion and health education services. The health promotion officers who have been in the past "providers" of the services are now a part of the "purchasing" system and the "providers" are the various members of different settings in direct contact with consumers.

It also helped in clarifying the relationship between health promotion (influencing environmental factors) and health education (influencing personal factors). The organisational model is applied to settings which are mainly a part of the service industry and, therefore, primarily concerned with the needs of the consumers. Within an organisational model the contribution of health promotion is concerned with the creation of an environment (physical and social) conducive to healthy lifestyles, whereas health education is concerned with enabling individuals to adjust to these demands and make best use of these services. Following the Ottawa meeting, the developments took different paths with health promotion being developed in Europe, whereas in the USA they continued to develop health education, since they identified health promotion with "social engineering". The presently applied organisational model depends on the contributions of both health promotion and health education as two parts of the same process. This differentiation has, therefore, become artificial since health promotion (European model) included health education and health education (the USA model) included the social as well as personal factors in their approaches.

Another important consequence of the Ottawa Charter has been the definition of the methods used in health promotion and health education as "enabling, mediating and advocating". At present there has been some criticism raised against health promotion and health education as interpreted by some critics, who have been accusing certain agencies of promoting "healthism". The so-called "healthists" bully people into behavioural changes, deprive them of their rights or the opportunity to exert their rights by a set of proscribed practices and by applying sanctions to the "non-conformists" to the rules governing a "healthy lifestyle". Some of the examples quoted are the restrictions of smoking in certain places, the refusal of heart operations to heavy smokers, the refusal to treat children's teeth if they do not give up eating sweets, increased insurance premiums for certain risk categories, loss of employment because of being HIV positive, etc. The Ottawa Charter has been the best answer to all these criticisms, because it states that the approved method is that of "enabling" people to make their choices, which one hopes will be conducive to their health and expressed in a healthy lifestyle, and which does not detract from the individual's right to make any choice he/she prefers as long as it is an educated choice and not made out of ignorance and is in agreement with prevalent social expectations or norms.

The introduction of the organisational model of health promotion and health education emphasises the need for accountability and control over the interventions aimed at individuals and/or populations. The Module 3 of the book on Health Promotion and Health Education dealing with the topics of Evaluation, Quality Assessment and Auditing should, therefore, be considered as a major contribution to the achievement of this accountability. The application of the assessment approach should answer many of the critics of health promotion and health education by showing whether the resources are used for the benefit of the consumers, whether the enabling process has increased the decision-making abilities of the consumers, whether the mediating and advocating processes have contributed to the resolution of conflicts of interest and whether they have extended the area of rights for underprivileged, deprived or discriminated population groups. The detailed description of the requirements related to evaluation, quality assessment and auditing should be reflected in the policy and strategy aspects of planning health promotion and health education, taking into account the different needs and possibilities of different population groups and different countries within the WHO definition of health, which is much wider than a medical intervention directed towards diseases.

INTRODUCTION

What is this book about?

This book sets the scene for anyone who intends to measure the various aspects of a health promotion and health education intervention or activity. It deals with a number of sophisticated and specialist topics, which are relevant to any objective and scientifically credible assessment. It is not intended to replace the large number of existing handbooks related to specific topics such as statistics, quality assessment and evaluation. It is, rather, intended to acquaint the reader with the issues involved in each of these specialised topics and help him/her to become 'literate' in the field of measurement and assessment.

Hired help

Someone involved in health promotion and health education activities, who wishes to assess what is happening and with what consequences, will probably require the help of experts or consultants. The selection, contracting and utilisation of experts or consultants is a complex process in its own right and needs background knowledge and considerable preparation. The decision about hiring expert help will depend on the awareness of the processes involved in the assessment of health promotion and health education and the availability of helpers with special expertise. This will be of special relevance for any activity in the context of the organisational model, where the responsibility for taking action will be in the hands of the members of various settings, who may not necessarily have knowledge and skills in the field of health promotion and health education.

A variety of experts could be considered relevant to and necessary for the assessment of a health promotion and health education intervention or activity. These include:

- *health promotion and health education specialists,* who can provide expertise in planning, in execution, and in setting preconditions for subsequent assessment; they can help in the process of transforming a setting into a 'health promoting setting', with its specific commitments and procedures;

- *medical experts,* who may be required to provide expertise in the field of preventive and curative medicine in cases where those involved in the process of assessment do not have such expertise; they can be very useful in helping to set specifications and in the choice of appropriate indicators and criteria for the assessment of processes and outcomes;

- *experts in research methods*, whose expertise lies in the area of planning and execution of the intervention and evaluation studies required for the assessment process; their special expertise will be in data collection through helping in the design of the instruments and collection of information; they may, however, require additional expertise in the statistical methods necessary for the analysis of information and drawing of inferences;

- *experts in quality management,* who deal with this new aspect of the assessment procedure, which requires experts in setting up a quality management system, in helping to establish mechanisms for meeting the requirements set by standards defined by some body recognised for certifying the quality system and in designing the specifications for the product(s), which will serve as a benchmark for similar assessment exercises in that field;

- *experts in evaluation,* who can fulfil the demand for evaluation in health promotion and health education, which has focused the attention of various institutions and organisations on experts who will be able to apply their general expertise to health promotion and health education projects; this activity has gained recognition in the USA as a profession with professional organisations, such as the American Evaluation Association; in Europe, this expertise is not so clearly defined and those active in the area of health promotion and health education are expected to be able to plan and carry out evaluation as a part of their expertise.

It seems obvious that different settings may require a different mix of expert help. When choosing the necessary experts it will be necessary to keep in mind the following issues:

- proof of the required expertise;
- past track record of the expert;
- cost of the expert;
- duration of the help needed;
- evaluation of the expert's contributions.

When an expert able to satisfy the needs of the setting's management has been selected, it will be necessary to draw up a contract with the expert or with the expert's organisation. The contents of such a contract should provide a guarantee for both signatories and should be specific enough to serve as a specification for services rendered. This can be used as a basis for the evaluation of the expert's contribution to the activity in question.

The fact that health promotion and health education activities have now become the responsibility of a number of different 'agents' and not limited to HE/HP specialists, has resulted in the need for expert advice in this field as a temporary measure until other professions and occupations acquire the necessary knowledge and skills.

Off-the-shelf programs

In addition to buying in expert advice for assessment and evaluation, there are now available a number of ready-made programs for data collection and analysis including the sophisticated statistical manipulation of data. These programs have been developed for use with personal computers.

These programmes are user friendly and are increasingly covered in books on methodology. Even early books, such as Babbie's (1989), book on research methodology, discusses SPSS PC+, the Statistical Package for Social Sciences, which is available in many universities in the UK. It analyses data and provides the researcher with ready-made statistical tests. It is important, however, that users should not be misled by the ease with which these programs are used; it is necessary to understand the underlying statistical tests.

The WHO has produced a special computer programme, the Epi Info (see Appendix 2), which is appropriate for data analysis in the fields of epidemiology and health promotion. The program has been produced by the Epidemiology Program Office, Centers for Disease Control and Prevention, and the Global Programme on AIDS, and the disks are readily available. It includes word processing, development of questionnaires, data analysis and statistical tests, together with extensive tutorials on research skills.

The structure and contents

This is the third book in the trilogy of handbooks covering the theoretical, methodological and practical aspects of health promotion and health education.

Module 1: Problems and Solutions published in 1991 gives a general overview of health promotion and health education, accompanied by a set of examples in the form of case studies.

Module 2: The Organisational Model published in 1994 gives a detailed description of the developments in health education and health promotion which have led to the currently popular "organisational model". This is accompanied by a set of case studies of different settings in which this model can be applied. The Appendices include the most important policy documents related to historical developments.

Module 3: Evaluation, Quality, Audit has been designed to acquaint the reader with the theories and practical requirements for the assessment of health promotion and health education interventions. These can be carried out in the form of special programmes or projects, or can be an integral part of the activities of a setting.

The three Modules have been structured using a 'building block' design, which aims to deal comprehensively with aspects of the theory and practice of health promotion and health education, and which allows for different combinations of various building blocks to be used when and where appropriate. It picks up detailed aspects of the evaluation of health education and health promotion, parts of which have been described in the other two Modules in more general terms.

The content of the book is divided into sections, including the *background information* about health promotion and health education; it outlines the *methodological issues* related to any investigation about the processes and outcomes; it also deals with the *evaluation* of programmes, the *quality assessment* of processes and outcomes, and *auditing* of the health promotion and health education activities.

The book provides the reader with examples of application of different methods of assessment in different settings and is intended to provide knowledge and the basis for developing skills to both purchasers and providers of health promotion and health education services.

Appendix 1 gives a summary of the evaluation report concerning the present state of progress in achieving Health for All by the Year 2000 in the European Region.

Appendix 2 includes the description of a particulary useful computer program, Epi Info, mentioned earlier.

HISTORICAL BACKGROUND

INTRODUCTION

This section deals with the present situation concerning the promotion and maintenance of health as well as the prevention and management of disease and discusses the new demands and expectations from the health care delivery system and the consumers. It summarises the various models and approaches, which have been described in detail elsewhere (Baric, 1991, Baric, 1994), and concludes with the most recent organisational model, which has emerged from these developments. It gives an overview of the existing criticisms of the current approach and offers an answer to the critics. The section includes a critical examination of the health promotion and health education intervention methods which are vital for any assessment exercise.

In this section the historical developments are summarised, to provide an appropriate introduction to the organisational model that has developed as a logical consequence of adopting a settings approach. It also summarises current criticism directed towards the new approach and provides answers which are intended to justify the use of health promotion and health education.

TRACING THE CHANGES

The need for assessment of health promotion and health education is closely linked with the development of these activities. In the past and in some cases even at present, these activities have been the domain of "experts", "professionals" or "special agents", depending on the country, their location within the system and their educational background. This conceptualisation of health promotion and health education (HP/HE) as a special activity carried out by some specialist agents brought about the need for accountability and the demands for evaluation have been growing ever since.

The main change in the practice of health education occurred in 1978 when the Alma Ata Declaration introduced the concept of health promotion and defined the differences between health education and health promotion. The Ottawa Charter (1986) later shifted the emphasis from problems to settings. The logical consequence of these two changes has been the understanding that health promotion deals with environmental factors and health education with personal factors, although they are two aspects of the same activity. It also implies that the new approach needs to be based on an organisational model since the concept of settings includes most features of organisational theory. Looking at settings as organisations demands consideration of the organisational structure, including the managerial and the consumer (client) aspects. The new approach is not "just another model" as some would like to believe, but a profound change in conceptualisation (Baric, 1991,1994). The UK Government (1992), like others, has applied these new principles and approach in its recent documents and policies. The next step is to provide a theoretical explanation for this approach as well as the means of implementing it in daily practice.

Within the organisational model a distinction has been made between HP/HE that is integrated into a setting and a 'health promoting setting'. This differentiation will have important consequences for the choice of approaches concerning the assessment of the activities and outcomes.

HP/HE in settings

The integration of health promotion and health education into a setting usually implies the provision of information about health matters to the members of staff or the clients (e.g. doctors, nurses and patients, teachers and pupils, etc.) located within that setting. This integration of health promotion and health education is currently carried out in a great number of different settings, in some cases without the existence of any specific programmes. Most schools have some health promotion and health education lectures or activities for the pupils. The same applies to hospitals and general practices, where the staff carry out health promotion and health education as a part of their normal activities. This is also the case in most enterprises, which have certain health promotion and health education activities connected with other issues of occupational health or prevention of accidents at work.

The contents of these activities will depend on the area of interest deemed appropriate by the management or the staff in such a setting. In schools, the contents are at present mostly concerned with sex education and the enhancement of the personal and social skills of the pupils, whereas in the health care settings, the contents are concerned with topics relevant to the medical speciality of the staff and the acute needs of the patients. In industrial and commercial enterprises the contents are largely related to occupational health issues. In general, it can be said that the contents of health promotion and health education integrated into a setting are 'setting specific' and usually do not address the more general topics of interest for the population as a whole.

The integration of health promotion and health education into a setting is usually carried out by the members of staff or by 'farming out' the activity to some specialist in the relevant topic. In a hospital health promotion and health education will be carried out by a member of staff (doctor or nurse), whereas in schools, health promotion and health education is rarely carried out by teachers and the most common pattern is to invite some representative of the health care system to provide the information on the chosen subject to the pupils. This is frequently a nurse who is employed by the local Health Authority and who specialises in school health education. Within the health care system it is the doctors and nurses who have direct contact with the patients and in various enterprises it is the members of the occupational health service. They are all experts in the contents and, therefore, have credibility in providing the relevant information.

The main problems faced by the various agents of health promotion and health education are those of effective communication with the clients. In most cases, they are not specifically trained in the communication process and follow 'common sense' rules. They are not aware of the existing theoretical background to health communication, such as: socialisation, various communication models, different types of readiness of the clients to understand and implement the information received, learning theory, patterns of normative behaviour, the decision-making process, the nature of social support, as well as the processes of empowerment and self-reliance.

The integration of health promotion and health education into various settings can result in unpredictable outcomes, depending on the intervention methods used. Certain settings will require an individual approach whereas others may benefit from a group or a mass media approach. If the approaches are not adjusted to the needs of the people in the setting, there may be some undesirable side-effects. Using mass media when dealing with smoking in pregnancy is an example. Publicising the fact that smoking during pregnancy may affect the size and the mental ability of the unborn child may be considered a strong motivation for pregnant women to stop smoking. The unforeseen side-effect when using mass media could be the stigmatisation of women who smoked during their pregnancy in the past and conceived a handicapped baby. Similarly, using group methods in dealing with smoking amongst school children may not reduce smoking but increase the group cohesion of smokers and reduce the likelihood of changing the group norms related to smoking. To avoid such and similar side-effects it will be necessary to base the choice of methods on a differential diagnosis of the needs of the clients, for which the health promotion and health education agents should be specially trained.

Integrating health promotion and health education into a setting is very rarely evaluated and, therefore, does not provide an opportunity for formative feedback and modification of the intervention programmes. In the past, the excuse was that health promotion and health education are built in without requiring the implementation of a specific intervention programme and, consequently there are no specific aims and objectives, and thus no evaluation is possible.

The Health Promoting Setting

A 'health promoting setting' represents a new concept in health promotion and health education, arising from the Ottawa Charter and the introduction of an organisational model. The main difference between this and the integration approach lies in the way a health promoting setting needs to change to accommodate the new requirements. Guidance here is offered by an international or a national network of health promoting settings.

A setting aiming to be health promoting needs to take on the commitment to meet the requirements of a health promoting setting, which include the acceptance of the Ottawa Charter and involvement in the following activities:

- creating a healthy working environment;
- integrating health promotion and health education into daily activities;
- outreach into the community.

Since, in such a setting, all the members should be involved, there will be a need to create a mechanism for participation of the members of the setting in health promotion and health education activities. This mechanism should also include the training facilities for the members of a setting to become competent in carrying out their work.

At present, there is no empirically tested universal model of how to transform a setting into a health promoting setting and it will be necessary for the setting to design its own transformation based on a set of intervention studies. These studies should enable the staff to develop and test their own methods of integrating health promotion and health education into the daily activities of a setting. These intervention studies should comply with accepted research standards, which include the definition of aims and objectives, choice of indicators and criteria, as well as the development and testing of instruments.

The outcomes of such an exercise, especially if it is a pilot health promoting setting, should be the development of a model which is relevant to the context of its own setting, and which may be tested in other similar settings.

The role of agents

The changes in health promotion and health education are being reflected in the roles of the agents who are carrying it out. At present the main agents are health promotion "specialists", although their role is now being questioned. The new settings approach depends on the health promotion and health education activities of the various members of these settings. These can be integrated into the work of the agents or they can be carried out as separate programmes.

The role of the specialist, as one of the agents, needs to be redefined. One way of doing this is to stress its links with the training programmes for the members of various settings. This new role entails developing a knowledge-based training curriculum, which can only be derived from research and intervention studies in this field.

Thus, one can describe the potential role of the specialists as:

- carrying out research to establish new ways of enabling consumers to improve their health;

- carrying out intervention studies to develop a theoretical base and test the various methods of approach;

- developing curricula for training programmes on various levels of sophistication;

- organising training programmes concerning research methods and the practical application of health promotion and health education;

- acting as consultants to various settings to help them to integrate and operationalise health promotion and health education into their regular activities and carry out evaluation;

- initiating and participating in discussions concerning the ethical aspects of health promotion and health education.

The role of other agents within different settings, who are responsible for carrying out health promotion and health education within these settings, is also at present not clearly defined. It is for this reason that these agents are expected to carry out health promotion and health education within a "pilot intervention" approach, which implies that they should explore and decide which of the various health promotion and health education methods are most suitable for the structure of their setting and the needs of their clients.

CRITICISMS AND REACTIONS

It would be wrong to give the reader the impression that the present situation regarding health promotion and health education is clear and that there is general agreement about what and how they should be done and who should do them.

The first set of controversies relates to the application of health promotion and health education. Following the Alma Ata Declaration, which differentiated between health promotion as the process influencing social factors, and health education as the process influencing personal and group factors, these two activities have had a different history of development and application. Health education has been predominantly applied in the USA, whereas in Europe the emphasis has been on health promotion, although this can also include health education as one of its constituent parts (Baric, 1994).

This difference in the application of the two approaches in different parts of the world has also been reflected in the criticism directed towards them.

The paper entitled "The Singer or the Song" (Baric, 1995) deals with the most recent criticism of health promotion and health education. It provides some answers by examining existing changes in the delivery of health care and the role of health promotion and health education and their implications, and translating them into the "new" approaches of health promotion and health education, based on the Ottawa recommendations. This is then related to the main points of the existing criticism.

There are some critics of the pace and direction of these changes. Although not great in number, these critics have been influential in spreading doubt about the implementation of the new approaches that have introduced health promotion, which in some cases has replaced health education. They confuse the situation by criticising the past practices of health promotion, which may still persist in the present, instead of providing constructive suggestions based on the potential for improvement provided by the planned changes embodied in the "new" organisational model.

The critics

In the past, there have been many criticisms of health care delivery and the practice of health professionals. One of the more powerful attacks on the way health care was developed and delivered was that of Ivan Illich (1975), who argued that the medical profession were overstepping their remit of curing illness and were taking over the responsibility for ensuring people's health. The decade following the publication of Illich's book can be characterised as a period of conflict, with the medical profession trying to discredit Illich either by denying the accusations or dismissing him as an amateur, a Marxist or a former Jesuit priest, whose attack had a hidden agenda of a religious nature, rather than concentrating on the issues. Some, however, accepted the criticism and acted upon it, which resulted in a movement that is sometimes called "doctor bashing".

Following Illich's attack, another was launched in the 1980 BBC Reith Lectures delivered by Ian Kennedy (1981), an economist, who attacked the medical profession and especially psychiatrists. He, however, made the mistake of trying to be "constructive" by offering advice on how the health of the public could be improved in an "acceptable", way by means of health promotion. By doing this, Kennedy fell foul of both sides, being rejected both by the medical establishment as well as by all the other critics of health promotion.

Some subsequent critics agreed with Illich, or directed their criticism specifically at health promotion (Williams, 1984; Becker, 1986; Kurtz, 1987).

One of the most recent criticisms of the medical establishment and the health care system has been made by Petr Skrabanek (1994), who has also directly criticised health promotion. The author uses a three-pronged attack, directed against "healthism", "lifestylism" and "coercive medicine".

Healthism

Healthism, as defined by Skrabanek, is a movement which is the consequence of the change of emphasis from individual endeavours to stay healthy to a state ideology, which may lead to "political sickness". In extreme cases it may lead to "health fascism", which justifies racism, segregation and eugenic control (see Rufford, 1995 : "China moves to ban babies with defects"). In its milder forms (as in Western democracies) it may extend state intervention beyond education and information to propaganda and various forms of coercion, expressed in the establishment of the norms of a "healthy lifestyle" for all. Skrabanek criticises healthism by describing it as follows:

> *"Human activities are divided into approved and disapproved, healthy and unhealthy, prescribed and proscribed, responsible and irresponsible. Irresponsible behaviour includes activities dubbed by moralists as 'vices', such as 'immoral sex' and the use of drugs, both legal (alcohol, tobacco) and illegal, but it can be extended to not going to regular medical check-ups, eating 'unhealthy' food, or not participating*

in sport. The proclaimed aim of healthism is the 'health of the nation' with an implicit promise of a greater happiness for all." (pp. 15-16)

The theoretical justification for healthism is derived from the developments in medicine, especially public health. A world renowned epidemiologist, Geoffrey Rose (1992), put forward the idea that most people lead an unhealthy life and that we are a 'sick population'. He suggests as a solution that the whole society must be re-educated to understand what is normal and what is socially acceptable. This implies a change in the role of the medical profession to include also the responsibility for the healthy population by teaching them what is 'normal'.

Another well-known epidemiologist, Thomas McKeown (1976), provided additional justification, by being highly critical of the general claim that medicine is an important contributing factor to the general health of people, which, in his opinion, is in fact the result of improved social and environmental factors such as nutrition, hygiene, housing, family size, clean water, etc., improvements that occurred even before the discovery of the relevant treatment procedures.

The spread of similar ideas brought about changes, which are reflected in the state's taking over an increased responsibility for people's health. The politicians discovered that the promotion of health is a very attractive area, especially if one can put the responsibility for health maintenance on the people themselves. Some such 'healthist' documents were published in 1974, including the Lalonde Report "A New Perspective on the Health of Canadians", and the US Department of Health document "Forward Plan for Health". The general idea expressed in these and other similar documents was that health depends on individual behaviour. This resulted in the 'blame the victim' approach since, according to these documents, most diseases are 'self-inflicted'. Consequently, the right of an individual to health should be matched by the individual's duty to be healthy. To be healthy is thus 'politically correct'.

In summary, healthists are accused by Skrabanek of identifying a whole range of concepts and labels as 'politically correct' including:

- the treatment of patients as 'consumers';
- the 'needs' of people are defined by the medical profession;
- the patient is handled by a 'health-delivery team';
- 'proactive' or 'anticipatory' medicine insists on preventive screening and regular check-ups;
- health has become a marketable commodity delivered to the consumer by the health care delivery system;
- non-attendance at preventive screening is labelled as 'non-compliance';
- advertising health by playing on people's guilt;
- the complexity of the health services producing a rapid increase of a new profession of 'health managers', interposed between the doctor and the patient;
- a rapid increase in the production and selling of health-related products (health foods and supplements, trainer-shoes, exercise equipment and videos, etc.) as a direct result of advertising health based on the guilt feelings of healthy people.

According to Skrabanek, the character of preventive medicine has changed to become 'anticipatory care', as a part of 'pro-active' medicine. This implies that doctors do not wait to be 'summoned' but go out into the community and solicit healthy people to make use of such services as 'check-ups' or various 'screening' tests. The idea of 'health maintenance' is analogous to car maintenance, with individuals having to present themselves at a certain point in their life for examinations, vaccinations, screening, etc. Skrabanek quotes a statement by the American College of Physicians concerning the official recommendations for preventive care of *'a healthy woman between 20 and 70 years of age: she should visit her doctor annually, and have 278 examinations, tests and counselling sessions during that period of her life'*. (p.33)

The most relevant criticism of healthism for us is associated with the attack on health promotion as a part of this new pro-active medicine. The preoccupation of individuals with their health and fear of dying has been, according to Skrabanek, used by health promotionists to "seek enrichment and power". Skrabanek is most critical of "promoting positive health" which is, using health promotion rhetoric, defined as:

> *"Health must be more than absence of disease, it must be exuberant health, super-health. Health is happiness and happiness is health. All healthy people must be under constant supervision. It does not omit to mention the 'economic value of the individual' and the nonsense of the 'inherited right' of everyone to supper-health.......The idea of super-health was incorporated into the Constitution of the WHO in 1946, where health is defined as 'not merely the absence of disease or infirmity but a state of complete physical, mental and social well-being',"* (which can, according to Skrabanek be achieved only fleetingly during orgasm or when high on drugs. p.42).

Skrabanek is derisive of the idea of 'health for all by the year 2000' and states that even the ever-optimistic Christians were more realistic by deferring the promise of complete happiness to the afterlife. Skrabanek also gives short shrift to the Alma Ata Declaration because it declared 'health as a basic human right' in a repressive political situation in the (then) Soviet Union, and was supported by Brezhnev (USSR), Baby Doc (Haiti), Idi Amin (Uganda) *"besides scores of representatives of other murderous regimes, totalitarian states and military dictatorships"* (p.43). His criticism of the Ottawa Declaration, however, is based on the fact, that

> *"The signatories included Ceaucescu's Rumania and other Communist dictatorships......In the 1993 Annual Report of Amnesty International, 110 governments were accused of using torture in their prisons and police stations, but WHO documents naturally never mention this drawback in their health declaration, as the same governments who sponsor torture also sponsor WHO health declaration"* (p.45).

Skrabanek quotes Carlyon (1984), Director of the Department of Health Education of the American Medical Association, who accused health promoters *'of pursuing glittering vagaries of human happiness and medicalising mankind's yearning for Utopia'* (p.46). Some of the accusations include:

- it (wellness) gives health promoters a carte blanche to meddle in any area of private or public life;
- it allows them to manipulate the various aspects of everyday life (habits, attitudes, sexuality, beliefs);
- they hide the real objective, which is acquisition of power;
- they use 'half truths', wishful thinking, and unsupported claims;
- they have extremely limited evidence of effectiveness in reducing mortality and morbidity;
- the preventive measures increase the cost of health care;
- it is a big business with the proliferation of university posts, consultants, health shops, publications, health farms, holistic centres and screening clinics;

- they are engaged in empire building by staking claims on all kind of activities related to health (education, organisation, management, psychology, sociology, behavioural and environmental adjustments, etc.)

How far this interference with civil liberty can go, can be seen from an extreme example of health promotion ("Flush of Health in Japan", Guardian, 26.10.1989). This is the development of an 'intelligent toilet' in Japan, which analyses the constituents of the stool and urine with the addition of a special device into which the occupant can insert a finger while using the toilet to obtain a record of pulse rate and blood pressure. The hope of the inventors is that such toilets will be linked to a health centre.

Answering accusations about 'healthism'

One can accept the fact that the international community as well as the U.K. government have in recent years increased their involvement in creating positive conditions for health promotion and health education, as a means of preventing diseases and improving national health. The intention to help people become healthier would widely be regarded as desirable. Governments were, nevertheless, dependent on the existing health promotion and health education services at their disposal at the time and on the competence of the practitioners to carry them out.

The main problem with recent changes in HP/HE lies in the diversity of models and approaches coexisting in present practice; the most recent developments are not, therefore, generally implemented. Much of the criticism of HP/HE is valid for only some of the former practices, which do not reflect updated approaches. HP/HE current policy is characterised by the recognition of two different areas of activity (interventions on the environmental and on the personal level) and by the following changes from the old approaches:

- a shift from problems to settings, which implies that the efforts and resources are concentrated on the various settings within which people experience health-related problems;
- a multisectoral approach, which implies the involvement of various agents within different settings and not an exclusive dependence on "specialists", as well as a differentiation of roles between the researchers and teachers on the one hand and the practitioners on the other;
- a methodology based on the Ottawa Charter;
- the accountability of HP/HE actions based on evaluation, quality assessment and auditing.

As already mentioned, this approach is not "just another model", but has emerged from the recent developments, which have been translated into a "new" HP/HE approach (or organisational model).

This new approach does not envisage government interference in individual life but, on the contrary, aims at *empowering individuals* to take the responsibility for their own health and the health of those to whom they have a duty (parent/child, teacher/pupil, foreman/worker, doctor/patient, etc.). The methods endorsed are based on the Ottawa Charter and include:

- enabling individuals to take on the responsibilities for their own health and the health of their dependents;
- mediating between individuals and the external system to enable individuals to fulfil these responsibilities;
- advocating on behalf of individuals to be able to exercise their rights and fulfil their duties.

These endeavours of the government and their agencies, aimed at empowering individuals, need to be evaluated, their quality needs to be assessed and the resulting activities need to be audited as a part of the government accountability to the electorate. This new approach cannot be in any way identified with crude 'healthism', as described by the critics.

Health promotion has been attacked for taking a "healthist" approach and for using agents to produce a whole range of prescriptive and proscriptive measures. My view is that attacking an approach that should already be considered out of date does not contribute to the improvement of health, for the following reasons:

- the new HP/HE makes provision for different agents in different settings to take over the responsibility for HP/HE as a part of their regular activity; it is necessary, however, to recognise the fact that the mode of delivery of health promotion and health education services in the UK is unusual, with its system of health promotion specialists in charge of health promotion and health education; it does not represent a general pattern since in the rest of Europe this activity is distributed among a number of different agents and institutions;

- the new approach takes into account the UK situation, and is being gradually implemented through the change of the role of HP Units from providers to purchasers of services, provided by members of each setting as a part of their normal activities; thus, health promotion in general cannot be criticised for something that some health promotion agents may have been doing in the past, in one country, and without taking into account the contribution of health education;

- even in the present UK situation, there exist various self-correcting mechanisms in the form of a free press and the activities of self-help and consumer protection groups, which can react to any excesses of official representatives who attempt to reduce the free choice of individuals.

The general accusations aimed at HP/HE, as representing a "healthist" movement, are not, therefore, justified since the new HP/HE approach, now widely being adopted, aims at **empowering individuals** by enabling, mediating and advocating for them to take responsibility for their health.

Lifestylism

Skrabanek argues that health promotion has also been accused of being 'healthist', in that it is concerned with the general idea of **postponing death,** even if this cannot be avoided. Its concern has been to postpone the effects of growing old and keep the body as young as possible for as long as possible. Healthists are criticised for the use of health promotion jargon such as 'lifestyle', 'unhealthy behaviour' and 'risk factors'. These focus on what an individual should do to stay young and live long. This kind of healthism can be traced through history, and Skrabanek quotes a number of authors from two thousand years ago up to the present time who offer advice about how this can be achieved.

A further result of the healthist movement, according to the critics, is the *fitness craze* which is expressed in people's participation in sport and exercise to the extent that it can become addictive. A number of studies have shown that people's addiction to exercise is associated with the chemicals produced by the body as a by-product of exercise. The "fitness craze", on the other hand, is a social movement, and can be condemned as a source of exploitation by those producing and selling various types of equipment, clothing and shoes, which have become fashion articles with expensive labels and a part of a multi-billion dollar industry.

Another outcome of healthism, according to Skrabanek. is people's concern with diet, which has also become obsessive in the western world and is known as *'foodism'*. Throughout history a number of foods have been condemned as inappropriate or unhealthy. This has been re-emphasised by people's concern with obesity and attempts to lose weight. Expert opinion about the desirable composition of a diet has gradually changed through history and many of the foods recommended in the past are today condemned as contributing to early death. In some countries, such as the UK, there are government bodies concerned with dietary problems, which produce guidelines and reports intended to give the weight of authority to recommendations produced by health promotionists. These reports are sometimes contradictory and can entail different messages about the same habit. Critics of these reports question the evidence on which the statements made in them are based. An example, quoted by Skrabanek (p.95), is the 'mystery' of the Framingham study. During the past thirty years, this intervention was successful in reducing 'risk factors' (smoking, blood pressure, blood cholesterol) in a group of middle-aged men and yet morbidity and mortality from heart disease increased. One can, therefore, agree that "foodism" as a means of reducing risk from coronary heart disease can be a sign of unhealthy preoccupation with one's diet without any expected results. A recent journalist critic of government attempts to improve people's diet is Nigella Lawson (1995) who attacks the government's "messages" about a healthy diet for their "hypocrisy" because they spend millions on propaganda instead of ensuring that people are able to afford a healthy diet. The writer objects to being told what is good or bad for health because it smacks of "political correctness", is "bullyingly intrusive" and sounds like "cultural imperialism", which does not take into consideration the cultural differences and preferences.

Healthists are thus blamed by critics for corrupting medicine by a form of lifestyle-related morality, which treats any 'risky behaviour' as sinful, implying that it should be negatively sanctioned by society. This is especially the case with *sexuality,* which has been the subject of health promotion messages related to the kind and methods of practice, e.g. homosexuality and condom use. There are widespread arguments about sanctioning contraception and including lectures on homosexuality in school curricula. Sometimes enthusiasm can go too far and incur government condemnation, as in the Health Education Authority booklet "Your Pocket Guide to Sex", which had to be withdrawn due to government pressure. A more recent and positive result of healthists' concern with sex has been the introduction of the concept 'sexual harassment', used as the basis for litigation and claims for compensation. Another problem area is 'child molesting', which has been recently in the news due to a number of court cases aiming at protection of children from 'child abuse'.

According to critics of healthism, *alcohol* is also a very popular topic to promote moral as well as preventive messages. Concepts are used to describe people's drinking habits, such as 'moderate', 'social', 'occasional' etc. drinking, which may justify the consumption of alcohol. With a lack of conclusive evidence about the causal relationship between alcohol and certain diseases (with the exception of alcoholism as a disease) the healthists' lobby against drinking has been exposed to criticism. This has been especially reinforced by the fact that non-drinkers are more likely to die from coronary heart disease than moderate drinkers. A most fertile ground for healthists, according to the critics, is *tobacco* consumption and smoking. Strong lobbies have exerted pressure on governments to introduce legislation which prohibits smoking in certain places, as well as the regular increases in the taxation of tobacco. A less influential group of critics who claim to be speaking in the name of smokers tries to counteract the health promotion campaigns against smoking.

Answering the accusations of 'lifestylism'

In the criticism of health promotion approaches concentrating on different risk factors as a part of a 'life style' two issues need some consideration: the 'lifestyle' approach and the advice about various risk factors.

It is necessary to recognise the fact that all these labels represent theoretical constructs and must be interpreted within the appropriate context. Lifestyle is one such convenient construct. It denotes the attempt to treat human behaviour as a system within which a number of different actions take place. Since part of a system cannot be changed without affecting the whole, a lifestyle approach is promising because it takes into consideration the totality of achievements, as well as possible negative side effects, of any HE/HP intervention.

The criticism about the way HE/HP treats various risk factors is more complex and should be examined in the light of two questions: should one take certain 'normal daily activities' (eating, movement, etc.) and turn them into medical issues; and, if so, should one use often unsupported evidence about their contributions to health? For example, there is evidence that sedentary occupations and lack of exercise can reduce the feeling of well-being. Addiction to exercise is an abnormality and requires treatment. Does this then justify the condemnation of exercise in general?

The fact that some people have become obsessed by their diet is an exception, and cannot be used as a justification for completely neglecting the benefits of a balanced diet for health and well-being. The fact that there are different opinions about what exactly makes up a balanced diet does not imply that there are no general indications about which parts of a diet could be deleterious to health. The critics do not dwell on the variety of diets (cultural, religious, social class or age specific). Their condemnation of the pathological obsession with diet does not justify withholding information and affecting the people's right to know more about a healthy diet and be able to make an educated choice.

'Sexuality' as a potential source of disease is also a topic for the critics of HP/HE. They cannot disprove the fact that this activity can have many consequences society considers undesirable (child molesting, teenage pregnancy, pre- and extra-marital promiscuity, sexually transmitted diseases, prostitution, etc.). Whereas some sexual practices have been socially defined as sin or deviance long before the invention of health promotion, the individual has a right to know about recently emerging risks and their possible avoidance. This information should not be confused with proscriptions, since each is an aspect of a completely different set of social forces.

Nevertheless, both drinking alcohol and smoking tobacco are habits that do have a direct influence on health. Critics who oppose governmental and social interventions aimed at reducing the incidence of these habits are expressing a specific political orientation with respect to action. Whether one is in favour of an intervention or not, one cannot negate the risk to health caused by these habits nor the right of individuals to be informed about them.

In summary, it can be said that many of the 'risk factors' picked on by the critics as being 'healthist', when translated into aspects of a 'lifestyle', have been attacked for expressing a new morality as a means of enhancing the power of health promotion. Even the most severe critics, however, cannot justify their objections to the use of terms such as 'lifestyle', 'unhealthy behaviour' and 'risk factors'. These are just convenient labels to indicate the possible threats to the health of an individual or a population.

Drawing a person's attention to a potential risk is a normal part of human relationships and cannot reasonably be condemned. This risk can be specific or, if one uses a systems approach, it can be seen as a part of a lifestyle. It is an exaggeration to see this as a misguided attempt to achieve immortality or eternal youth.

Coercive medicine

Skrabanek is also critical of the new public health and health promotion and identifies it with other totalitarian or fascist movements as yet another form of coercion:

> *"Today's epidemiology has become the bottomless spring of such dubious truths converted by statistical sleight-of-hand to required certainties.......the ways of implementing healthist politics include the substitution of health education by health promotion propaganda; the introduction of regular 'health' screening for all citizens; the coercion of general practitioners, through financial incentives, to act as agents of the state; the presentation of the politically corrupt science of healthism as objective knowledge; the taxation of goods deemed to be 'unhealthy'; interference with the advertising of legal products; and introducing legislation which is 'nothing better than the hurried botching of short-sighted interests and blind passions'. Healthist authorities are not directly accountable to the public. They operate in a moral vacuum. Their power is, in practice, uncontested because of the legitimacy*

they have spuriously borrowed from medicine and science and their concerned beneficience. Their potential for harm is unassessed."(pp. 138-139).

An extreme example of this kind of healthist activity is quoted by Skrabanek, who received a clipping from a local Singapore newspaper (Straits Times 6/12/91) according to which *"the Senior Minister of State for Education announced a new government strategy to combat obesity amongst school children - they were to be given marks for their weight in their report books, so that their parents when checking on their academic progress would also see their grade for health and fitness"* (p.141).

Medical practitioners are sometimes responsible for advising the government and influencing it to support a type of coercive medicine that can be recognised by its paternalistic approach. Some critics go even further and label such an approach as a typical example of undesirable 'social engineering', which has found its expression in various strategies for behavioural modification of individuals by using methods of conditioning. This kind of criticism has been extended to general practitioners *"who are willing to become agents of the state and take on 'health promotion' for payment"* (p.146).

"Coercive medicine" is sometimes identified by its critics with 'totalitarian medicine', the extreme expression of which can be found in the example of the 'pregnancy police' at one time active in some totalitarian countries.

Lifestyle surveillance is considered by its critics to be closely related to healthism and coercive medicine. According to them, many of the tests now available may influence the range of choices given to individuals, so they are condemned as being an expression of certain political, moral or religious movements. A very important aspect of so-called 'health screening' is, according to critics, its hidden danger of labelling people due to certain characteristics or habits. Although this labelling may not improve their chance of staying healthy and living longer, it certainly can be misused for the purpose of discrimination in terms of employment, health insurance or other types of social stigmatisation. With the introduction of genetic screening this danger has become even greater and there is no indication what kind of consequences it will have on the future of individuals and whole societies.

Answering the accusations of 'coercive medicine'

The importance given to preventive medicine is due to an increase in the body of knowledge reflected in the introduction of such preventive services as screening clinics. There are two opinions concerning the utilisation of screening services: one is that most of the people who could benefit from it do not use it, and the other is that doctors carry out too many unnecessary tests on unwilling patients or healthy members of the population. Both opinions are true to some extent. Nevertheless, this does not mean that we should abandon screening opportunities for those individuals who need them, want them and could benefit from them. The role of HE/HP is to enable people to make educated choices and not suffer from ignorance. This view of its functions is radically different from 'coercive medicine' and the deployment of state health police.

The participation of GPs in HP/HE, attacked by some critics, is a good example of the introduction of an effective and comprehensive health care system. GPs have always to some extent been involved in comprehensive care. The difference today is that they will be paid in the recognition of their work and will have an opportunity to become more competent in fulfilling this role. Labelling them as "the agents of the state" explains nothing, since all civil servants and many others depending on the payment from the state could be similarly labelled.

SUMMARY

This review of historical development has offered an insight into the various changes in the practice of health education and subsequently health promotion during recent decades. The main changes occurred following the Alma Ata Declaration, in the form of the introduction of the concept of health promotion, and the later Ottawa Charter, where the methods and the concepts of health promotion and health education were clearly defined. The shift from disembodied problems to settings in which problems are located resulted in the acceptance of the relevance of an organisational model, implemented in a settings approach. These changes can be summarised in the following table:

	HEALTH PROMOTION			HEALTH EDUCATION		
	Settings	Networks	Alliances	Individual	Family	Group
Enable						
Mediate						
Advocate						

It is important to note that these changes have mainly been implemented in Europe, whereas in the USA the emphasis remained on health education. This can be easily understood (Etzioni, 1993) if one takes into consideration the Fourth Amendment of the US Constitution, which basically assumes that no government action should target groups but only individuals. Individuals are theoretically protected, and any intrusion should be based on 'reasonable doubt' about a misdeed being committed or contemplated and by strict adherence to the Miranda rule (police must read suspects their rights). According to the Constitution any population screening programmes, random checks or examinations directed towards a population group (women of certain age, drivers of cars, passengers at airports, etc.) are against the basic rights guaranteed by the Constitution. This has been widely used as an argument against public health measures and health promotion preventive actions by various groups such as American Civil Liberties Union, Radical Individualists and others.

The changes which are taking place in Europe have been met by criticism from a number of sources basing their objections on general human rights, since there is no limitation in most of the national constitutions which would correspond to the USA Constitution. Some of them have criticised the changes in the health care delivery in general, whereas others were more specifically critical of health promotion. The accusations ranged from the introduction of healthism, lifestylism and coercive medicine to a general rejection of professional interventions in 'private' aspects of a person's life.

In answer to the 'anti-healthists', it can be said that the concept of 'rights and duties' can be represented as a continuum with two extreme points: total state control on the one extreme and total individual freedom on the other. All the countries in the world can be located on the continuum somewhere between these two extreme points. Whether they will be located closer to the one or the other will be defined by the political system and values in each country. One of the expressions of each political system will be the health care available to the citizens. The reform of the NHS has tried to move the UK health care system some way towards the 'individual freedom' end of the spectrum. This fact has not been taken into account by the 'anti-healthists' who still believe that the system promotes 'coercive medicine', which would place it considerably nearer to the 'state control' end of the spectrum. In view of the existing situation, this criticism is outdated and does not fit present-day attempts to introduce greater individual responsibility and choice into health care. It also does not reflect the fact that mechanisms of social support still exist for those who cannot benefit from the market economy and still depend on state support.

The importance of an activity can sometimes be measured by the amount of attention it attracts. This is true for criticism as well as praise. Health promotion and health education are becoming increasingly recognised as the main instruments for the expression of human rights in the field of health.

In the (even recent) past, there were cases which could justify some of the arguments presented by the critics. At the same time, one should be aware of the direction in which the activity is moving. The move is in the right direction although it can be criticised for the pace with which the changes are being implemented.

The new HP/HE is in many ways so progressive that it will require some radical changes before it can be fully implemented. It requires some basic cultural changes and readjustments of the existing value system. These take time, are painful and will be exposed to opposition, criticism and many barriers. When listening to the critics, one should ask oneself whether the criticism is related to 'the singer or the song'? This article maintains that the 'song' is developing in the right direction but that there are many 'singers' who need to catch up with the new developments, re-train and become competent in fulfilling their new roles.

In this section a summary of the latest developments in health promotion and health education activites has been presented together with the criticisim directed towards new health promotion. The reason for this has been to bring the readers up to date with the 'state of the art' in this field and make them aware of the existing criticism which they may have to face during their work. The main assumption, however, has been that it is necessary to be clear about the processes involved in health promotion and health education for the purpose of defining aims as required by any effective evaluation.

RESEARCH METHODS

Introduction
Conceptualising the Activities
The Systems Approach
Areas of Enquiry
Summary

INTRODUCTION

The previous description of the new developments in health promotion and health education provides the necessary framework for any planned assessment. The application of research methods to the assessment of a health promotion and health education intervention will depend on meeting a number of requirements.

The first such requirement will be to clarify the conceptualisation of the health promotion and health education interventions. If one accepts that health behaviour is a function of external influences and personal characteristics, then for research purpose it is possible to visualise a tripartite system, each one being dependent on specific disciplines with an accompanying set of theories and practices:

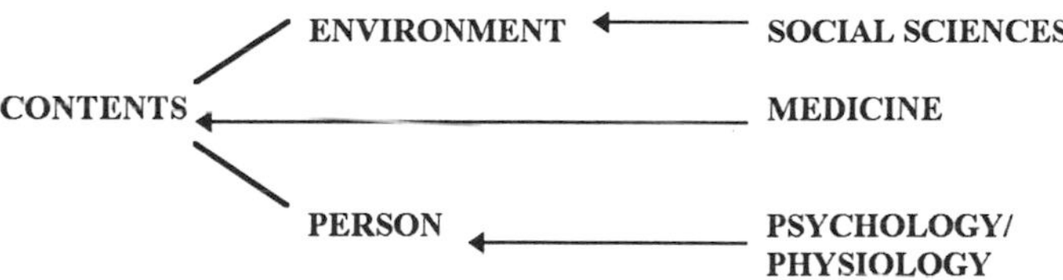

The main concern of a health promotion and health education intervention will be the medical content of the envisaged health threat or disease; consequently the contents will depend on the theories related to the medical sciences. The effects of a health threat on a person will depend on the environmental and personal factors. The study and measurement of the influence of environmental factors will need to employ the theories of the social sciences, whereas the measurement of the contribution of personal factors will use the theories developed by psychology, physiology and the most recent developments in genetics.

The interrelationship among these three factors should be considered as a part of a system of interaction. The study of systems requires the use of methods appropriate for studying complex systems, such as the relationships among the contributing factors and the settings in which a study is taking place.

This section also deals with areas of enquiry and the various techniques for data collection and data analysis.

CONCEPTUALISING THE ACTIVITIES

The choice of appropriate methods of measurement for the purpose of assessing health promotion and health education processes and outcomes raises a number of important questions.

What went on in the past?

It is vital to realise that any health promotion and health education intervention represents a social process in its own right and does not occur in a vacuum. Therefore, it is necessary to find out what went on in the past, in terms of background information about the various needs and potentials in a population. The same also applies to the needs and potentials of individuals. The method of approach can be described as 'historical research' into the context.

What is going on now?

Once the intervention is set into motion it will be necessary to find out what is going on. This will require taking into consideration the health promotion and health education approach used within the framework of an organisational model which can be represented in the following matrix:

	HP/HE IN SETTINGS	**HEALTH PROMOTING SETTINGS**
EVALUATE		
QUALITY		
AUDIT		

This will require the monitoring of the intervention in terms of evaluation, quality assessment and auditing.

What could happen?

It is difficult to anticipate the effects of an intervention and the outcome it can have on an individual or a population. To find out more about it, one can use a quasi-experimental research approach (Campbell & Stanley, 1968), case studies or population studies. Within a 'pilot' situation the experience gained from such an ongoing enquiry should ensure that the possible negative side-effects are dealt with in time and that the documented final approach will make a contribution to planning wider implementations.

What are the future trends?

An experimental approach within a pilot situation should produce results which can be generalised as appropriate to other settings and to other problems within certain settings. Generalisation can even have a predictive quality and ensure that the approach when implemented in different settings which have common features will produce comparable results.

Research approaches

To find answers to the questions raised during a health promotion and health education intervention, it will be necessary to use different research strategies which include the following useful approaches:

Historical research

A great deal can be achieved through the collection and examination of existing information which is essentially historical research. If this is a re-analysis of existing data, it is known as secondary data analysis. This is distinct from the revealing of traces from the past as yet unknown, such as the archaeologists digging and examining of artefacts, or the identification through 'unobtrusive methods' (Webb et al., 1971) of evidence from the past. A third aspect is the encapsulation of an interpretation of the past in people's beliefs, norms and values. In the case of health promotion and health education , we need both an enquiry into past events and people's perception of them.

A Systems Approach

A systems approach is appropriate for studying the health promotion and health education activities within an organisational model in the context of a setting. This approach allows for the examination of complex processes within a system and provides a comprehensive insight into what is involved in the interventions and outcomes. An early form of systems model already adopted in health promotion and health education is a version (non-mathematical) of operational research (Baric, 1968).

Evaluation

This can be described as the assessment of the achievement of the defined aims of a programme; one can differentiate between a general or a specific evaluation. Evaluation may cover products, projects or programmes. Formative evaluation asks 'are we on course?' while summative evaluation asks 'what did we do, and was it worth doing?'

Quality assessment

This includes the monitoring and examination of the various stages of a process and comparing it with the defined specifications relevant to the expected outcome; here, one can differentiate between quality management and total quality management as two distinct approaches in quality assessment.

Audit

This is the assessment of processes and outcomes according to some generally accepted norms (professional, legal, religious etc.) or expectations (based on stakeholder's specifications, value system etc.).

Experimental research

This examines the causes and consequences of an intervention, based on testing certain hypotheses, carried out under controlled conditions, usually in laboratory settings. In a social context, it is more likely to be quasi-experimental.

Case studies

These examine individual cases for certain associations between possible causes and recorded outcomes; they provide us with the possibility of an event taking place but do not attempt to predict the probability of such an event occurring in a population.

Population studies

These use survey methods, which explore an event in a population, which is often represented by a sample, and aim at defining the probability of an event occurring; they allow for the generalisation of the probability of an event occurring in comparable populations; they can also include simulation methods for the prediction of future trends.

The methods

The methods used in such approaches include:

Case study method

Case studies deal with individual instances for which extended interview or participant observation methods are appropriate. The data produced is largely qualitative (descriptive), and is associated with research approaches such as ethnomethodology and semiotics.

Survey

A survey deals with whole populations or samples from such populations and involves different instruments for collection of information, such as questionnaires and tests.

Data analysis

Data analysis will depend on the conceptual framework of the inquiry and the approach used, which yields the following type of data:

Qualitative ('soft', descriptive) data

There are various means of analysing these data, which are derived from people's opinions and descriptive material. The most powerful methods of analysis require the handling of descriptive text and ordering it, for example in matrix form.

Quantitative ('hard') data

Analysis here describes associations between variables, distributions in a population, general norms and other predictive characteristics; it utilises a number of approaches such as statistical descriptions and inferences, games theory, queuing theory, simulations, and quantitative causal analysis.

THE SYSTEMS APPROACH

The health education practitioner is mainly interested in applied or "action" research which aims at providing specific answers to specific problems. The action always takes place within a complex system. One extremely valuable systems-oriented technique used in applied research is operational research. It is not identical with/or a substitute for applied research, nor is it an alternative to the classic statistical approach: operational research may employ statistical analysis and interpretation of data but it has, in addition, a number of other techniques at its disposal (Baric, 1968).

Operational research has been defined in different ways. For our purposes, the definition given by Churchman, Ackoff and Arnoff (1957) is appropriate: *"Operational research is the application of scientific methods, techniques and tools to problems involving the operations of a system so as to provide those in control of the system with optimum solutions to the problems."* The most important aspect of this definition is the statement that operational research looks at systems as a whole and tries to establish how and where events under examination fit into that system.

The term 'operational research' was popular in the 1960s, and has been overtaken in popularity by the more general concept of 'systems research', within which operational research acquired a specific meaning.

Let us take road accidents as an example. Records do not always give a full picture of the causes; they may even distort them or present them in a partial form. One reason for this is that registration of such accidents is closely linked with court requirements for the prosecution of the culprit. The first thing the police do in some countries is to conduct a breathalyser test. If the test is positive it usually suffices for a prosecution. If it is negative, the next question may be whether the driver was speeding. If this can be proven, then the driver may be prosecuted for the speeding alone. In this way, according to the existing laws of the country and the practice of the police, accidents may be registered under the first cause which provides the legal basis for prosecution, and any other cause, however important, may be omitted from the records. For instance, a valid driving licence implies that the sight of the driver is "normal" and does not take into account the possibility of a recently developed impairment of sight, or any other illness which could reduce the concentration or reflexes.

A systems research approach would, on the other hand, look at the system as a whole, in an attempt to understand the interaction of various elements within the system at the time the accident happened. In this example, the interacting factors could be the driver, the car, the road and the pedestrian. Once all the factors involved have been established, the next step is to give them proper weighting so as to establish the combination of the predominant factors - which may be different from the cause registered in official records.

This is a simplified version of a research approach and it is obvious that a number of other factors would have to be taken into consideration.

The concept of systems research

In its application systems research usually follows certain steps of procedure: (a) defining the system; (b) setting up a model of the system; and (c) choosing and applying appropriate techniques of analysis and interpretation of findings. In the following sections each of those steps will be examined in general terms.

At the outset, it is necessary to stress one of the main advantages of systems research: it does not experiment with the system itself but enables us to experiment with a conceptual model of the system. It can be followed by action, informed by knowledge of the outcomes of manipulating the model.

The advantages of a systems research approach have been extensively exploited in industry and commerce as well as other fields. The reason is obvious when one thinks of the risk of changing an organisational process without first exploring the possible outcomes.

Defining the system

Before launching into any research we must attempt to limit the area of investigation. This begins with defining the system under study; making sure that the system is appropriately circumscribed and accepting the fact that the optimal solution will be relevant only to the system under study.

To explain what is understood by a system we can use the definition give by the Concise Oxford English Dictionary: *"System, n. Complex whole, set of connected things or parts, organised body of material or immaterial things,........method, organisation, considered principles of procedure, (principles of) classification........"*

In health education and health promotion, a system can refer to the structure and/or function of an organisation such as a hospital, local health department, etc.; it can be an interaction between two roles such as those of doctor and patient, etc.

A 'soft system' analysis is a preliminary method of conceptualising the parts of the system and the relationships among them. The results are often expressed in the form of a diagram, sometimes called a 'bubbles and arrows' diagram, which maps these relationships (Patching, 1994). Operational research can build on this analysis by looking for the action to apply for an 'optimal' solution to a specific problem.

But if we cannot define the system and draw its boundaries, then the operational research approach may not be applicable and other approaches may be more appropriate. If, however, we decide that operational research is an appropriate method, then we must bear in mind that the optimal solution derived at, will be 'optimal' only for that system, and that, as a solution, it may have deleterious effects on other interrelated systems. It all depends where the boundary is drawn.

Let us take an example. If we are interested in the problem of why patients must wait sometimes for hours to see a doctor for perhaps two minutes, we may find that the optimal solution for the reduction of waiting time of the patients would be to increase the number of doctors. This may be the optimal solution for the "doctor-patient" system. If, however, we examine the relationship between this system and the system of health services, we may find that an increase in the number of doctors is impossible. Therefore, an apparently optimal solution need not always be applied, and certain value judgements may have to be made to see whether it is practically possible or even advantageous overall. However, if we are ignorant of the optimal solution, we may make a wrong choice and unwittingly create further problems.

Setting up a model

If we want to experiment with a system, as was mentioned before, we will have to set up a model of the system. A model is a simplified physical or symbolic representation of an object (or a system) designed to incorporate or reproduce those features of the real object (or system) that the researcher deems significant for the research problem. It is usually derived from an amalgam of empirical observations, theory and assumptions. It takes pieces of information about parts of the system and assembles them into a representation of the whole system.

From this follows that there are different kinds of models: for example, they may be small replicas of new buildings such as the town planners or architects use to explain their ideas or to experiment with different traffic systems; they may be flow charts or diagrams as in the case of soft systems models mentioned earlier, or they may be completely abstract and expressed in mathematical terms.

For health education and health promotion research, the most appropriate approach is through an "operating model". This is a representation of behaving systems, which attempts to reproduce processes in action. As such, operating models provide information about variable, component, and relationship changes within a system over time.

There are two important characteristics of models which need to be stressed. One is that a model is a simplified representation of the system, containing only those factors which the researcher supposes are relevant to the problem. The other one is that models are neither true nor false: they may represent the reality well or less well, may be less or more appropriate, but are only a conceptual framework designed by the researcher to represent the system under study. Models should be understood for what they are and used with discretion.

However, models enable us to study the relationships between elements within a system and to formulate findings in terms of theories which can be tested and possibly disproved. But, in themselves, models are not theories (Willer, 1967). Nevertheless, there exists a tendency to confuse models and theories and to use models to explain some form of behaviour, as if they were proven theories.

A very good example is the widely used behavioural model of preconditions needed for a health action (Becker, 1974). The model suggests that for a health action to take place, a person must: (a) be aware of the health threat; (b) perceive his/her own susceptibility to the threat; (c) perceive the severity of the threat; and (d) see an acceptable way out.

This model has been used by a number of researchers in the field of health education (Meltzer, 1953; Glasser, 1958; Hochbaum, 1958, 1960; Kegeles, 1959; Rosenstock et.al, 1960, 1960, 1969; Heinzelman, 1962) as a conceptual framework within which to study the decision-making process related to a health action. It is also unfortunately indiscriminately used in vague explanations of how a health action occurs. In the first instance, it is rightly used as a conceptual framework for a research project, whereas in the second instance it is wrongly taken as a proven theory, explaining how certain processes occur in general.

This brings us to the next question, of whether a model can be used or tested by the same or by other research workers in a variety of situations. It can, so long as it uses the same conceptual framework, but to reproduce it in order to test the theories derived from it, we require standardised measurements of each of its attributes. In brief, as long as the explanations of the terms used, such as "severity", "susceptibility", etc., are the same, then we work within the same conceptual framework; but if the terms are measured in different ways, they may become different attributes with the same names. To examine theories derived from a model in different situations we would need standardised measurements of attributes and comparable populations.

After this brief discussion of the place of models in health education research in general, let us return to their more specific use in operational research. As an example, we may compare the effectiveness of the approach used by a health visitor (interview) with that used by a health educator (group discussion). In this example, for reasons of simplification, only one factor will be examined, namely the exposure to a health message, assuming that all the other factors, such as effectiveness, etc., are held constant.

This exposure can be measured with respect to its direct (face-to-face) and indirect (diffusion) opportunities. The direct exposure can be measured by timing the interaction between the transmitter (health visitor) of a message and his/her target. The indirect exposure (health educator) can be measured by using a network analysis of the extent of the communication links and thus looking at the possible amount of diffusion of a message.

Let us say, for argument's sake, that a health visitor can in one working day visit 5 women in their homes, spending 15 minutes with each one, while a health educator can in one day hold a group discussion with 10 people (say a women's club), spending on average 6 minutes per person, if the meeting lasts one hour.

Now the obvious conclusion is (supposing that both workers are equally successful) that the health educator's approach is more economical because he spends on average 6 minutes per person whereas the health visitor spends on average 15 minutes or nearly 3 times as much with a supposedly same effect. Now let us introduce an additional element into the model, i.e. the diffusion effect, and suppose that each woman has a communications network composed of 2 neighbours, 1 relative and 1 colleague or friend.

From travelling time spent by the health visitor one can suppose that the women visited by that health visitor are relatively far from each other. The model assumes that the women talking to their networks will cause the health visitor's message to be diffused to each separate network. In this way the health visitor will reach 25 women with five visits. The health educator interacts with 10 women in a group. One can assume that those women have similarly composed networks. Theoretically the health educator should be able to reach 50 women with a meeting (taking into consideration the diffusion element). However, the chances are that, since it is a social gathering of a women's club, the women attending can be interrelated or friendly to start off with. In other words, they can be part of each other's network and therefore the number of women reached through this diffusion effect may not reach 50. Let us suppose that because of overlap of networks, the total is 22.

From this follows that a health visitor spends 75 minutes to reach not 5 but 25 women (3 minutes on average per woman), whereas the health educator spends 60 minutes to reach not 10 but 22 women (2.7 minutes on average per woman) which does not represent such a great difference considering the effectiveness of the interaction.

One could introduce many refinements and modifications in the model used. For example, one could consider the difference in the number of contacts within each network: let us suppose that the audience at club meetings is mainly composed of 'middle class' women, whereas the health visitor concentrates on 'working class' women. This not only affects the chances of reaching high-risk groups but will also influence the number of contacts within the network since research has shown that traditional 'working class' women have a closer knit network and the diffusion element may consequently be much stronger.

A word about the indices used: exposure is considered as necessary precondition for a health action, and therefore, could reasonably be used as one of the processes to be measured. Another process to be measured could be the understanding and retention of the message and the action that should follow. An additional part of the process is commitment for action. We can divide this process into several stages: (1) information about the opportunity for an action; (2) request for additional information; (3) expression of doubts, fears; and (4) commitment: in this case, making an appointment.

In favour of the health educator is the fact that in his meeting with 10 women, all the 10 of them have an opportunity to make a commitment, whereas in the case of the health visitor only 5 women have that opportunity. In favour of the health visitor, on the other hand, is the fact that each woman is seen separately and, therefore, has an opportunity of discussing only her own doubts or fears, whereas in a group meeting the number of fears could multiply by spilling over from one woman to the others. To enable each member to verbalise her fears (existing or acquired) more time could be necessary than anticipated.

This example illustrates that even such a simple factor as exposure to a health message reveals its complex nature if we consider it within a systematic framework of networks of interaction. It further demonstrates the danger of making "common sense" assumptions, and the value of a systems approach and an operational research analysis in this instance.

Techniques of analysis in operational research

As any other research approach, operational research uses a number of techniques for the collection, analysis and interpretation of findings. We will limit ourselves to a general description of a few techniques. Most of these, however, require specialised knowledge and if research-minded health education and health promotion practitioners decide to use any of them, they should seek expert help and advice from the relevant professionals, who have been up till now mainly used by industry, government and commerce.

Statistical analysis

This is the most widely used technique of describing and interpreting data collected, and will, therefore, be mentioned here only briefly. Some of the main fields of mathematical statistics used in operational research are: tests which enable us to make a distinction between real and chance occurrences; calculation of the probability with which certain events will occur in particular situations; measurement of correlation between different attributes; and estimating errors which may occur in our measurements and inferences.

Linear programming

If we can express a relationship in a linear equation then we can use graphical presentation of such an equation to find the optimal solution (Lapin, 1988). For the less mathematically minded readers we can use a simple example of planning a party with £10 to spend. Suppose that we have decided to spend more on drinks than on food. This example is derived from Duckworth (1965).Let X represent drinks and Y the food:

$$X + Y = 10 \qquad X > Y$$

This means that X (drinks) and Y (food) can cost 10 or less, and that the amount spent on drinks will be higher than the amount spent on food. From this we can calculate all the possible values for those two equations:

X + Y = 10	X	0	1	2	3	4	5	6	7	8	9	10
	Y	10	9	8	7	6	5	4	3	2	1	0

The next step is to present it in a graphical form locating all the values of X on the axis X and all the values of Y on the axis Y:

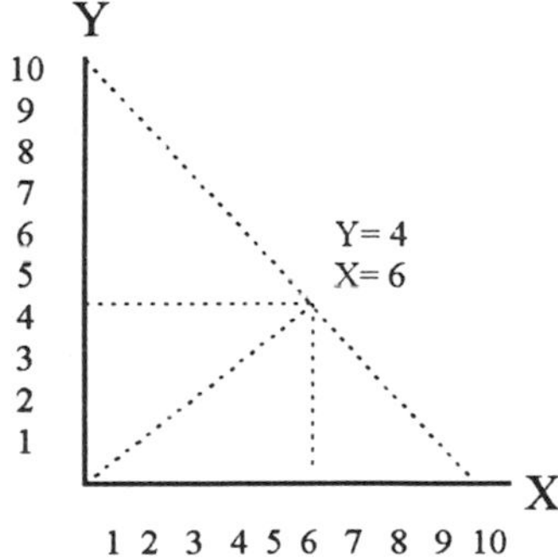

By drawing the lines for the two equations we get the optimal solution at the interception of those two lines. In this simple example it is £6 for drinks and £4 for food. One thing soon becomes obvious when using this method of analysis: the more elements there are in an equation, i.e. the more conditions on a relationship we impose, the more limited the choice of solutions will be.

This kind of analysis is widely applied in industry to find an optimal solution to a production process where for example, output and cost are functionally related. In health education and health promotion it has many uses, including planning a budget for programmes, costing audio-visual aids, distributing resources and so on.

Game theory

This is a branch of mathematics which deals with situations of conflict, involving decisions where the outcome will be affected by two or more (N) decision-makers. Game theory deals with games of strategy, as opposed to probability theory, which deals with games of chance. An important aspect of this theory is that the players must know the rules of the game.

A simple example of the two-person game theory application is the chess game, in which the players are constantly faced with a set of possible moves out of which they must make what they consider the best choice. N-person game theory can be used in the study of political decisions, with reference to coalitions and movements of members between different parties.

As such an approach has not been applied in the field of preventive medicine, let us invent a very simplified instance. Health education and health promotion is relevant to the problem of the rising divorce rate, since this is a health problem if we interpret health in its wider context as defined by WHO. There are certain laws and social norms (rules of the game) which the husband and the wife (two players) know and which will influence their decisions as related to the optimal choice of behaviour. We can build a model of possible decisions and actions, depending on the prevalent value system in a country and trace the decision-making process based on an imaginary case:

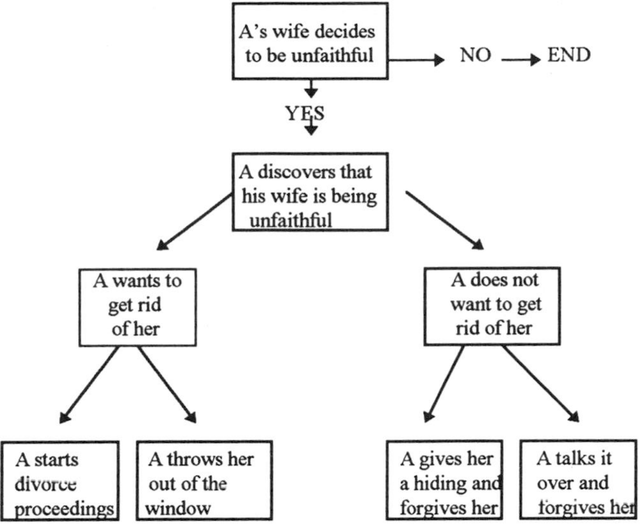

If the husband knows the "rules of the game" he will make a decision which will be optimal for him. The "rules" are different for different countries and different cultures. For example, if A lives in England, where the 'crime passionnel' is not fully recognised, if A wants to get rid of his wife, he is more likely to start divorce proceedings than throw her out of the window. As for A's wife, the chance of her deciding to be or not to be faithful will depend on the "rules of the game" and on the expected optimal strategy of her husband.

If a country decides to revise the existing divorce laws (changes the rules of the game), it may result in a confusion at first, until the new rules become a part of social norms. To come back to health education and health promotion: in this case it could play an important part in explaining the existing laws (rules) to the public.

As can be seen, game theory is very useful for model building because it offers a framework of interaction that enables us to consider possible decisions in a formal way.

Queuing theory

This mathematical theory serves to calculate for any given situation what kind of a queue will result, how long people (or items) will have to wait before service, and to work out the optimal solution, taking into account all the restrictive elements within the system. This approach has been successfully applied in industry and transport. In the field of health, attempts have been made to use it for the analysis of the usage of hospital beds, medical care in general, and waiting time in clinics (Bailey, 1951, 1952; Goodall, 1951, 1951).

The problem with queues is that they have a cumulative effect which can end up in bottle-necks. Irregular arrival of consumers or understaffed services can add to the waiting time. This can very often be a reason for the failure of a health measure which could be attributed to health education. Therefore, this factor must not only be taken into consideration in the evaluation of a health education activity, but additional research using queuing theory may help to solve the problem as well.

Let us take a simplified example (adapted from Duckworth) of one place where one doctor is engaged in vaccinating children. For solving queuing problems mathematically an expression known as the traffic intensity is used. It means dividing demand by capacity. Since neither the demand nor the capacity are constant (women do not come at equal intervals and the doctor does not spend the same amount of time for each child) it will be necessary to calculate the mean service time and divide it by the mean interval time between successive arrivals.

The intervals between the arrival of mothers is measured and the average of these intervals determined. To avoid distortion through a few very long intervals it is best to calculate a cumulative average interval. Let us suppose that we measured the intervals of time between the arrival of mothers and that we got the following values (in minutes):

5, 4, 10, 6, 3, 2, 6, 4, 8, 15, 2, 5, 4, 6, 8, 7, 3, 5, 2, 6, 8, 7, 4, 3, 2, 6, 7, 5, 3, 4, 6, 5, 8, 4.

Now we calculate cumulative totals by adding the first interval to the second, then the first three intervals, then the first four intervals, etc:

9, 19, 25, 28, 30, 36, 40, 48, 63, 65, 70, 74, 80, 88, 95, 98, 103, 105, 111, 119, 126, 130, 133, 135, 141, 148, 153, 156, 160, 166, 171, 179, 183.

The cumulative averages are obtained by dividing all the cumulative totals by the number of intervals making up each total, as follows:

9/2; 19/3; 25/4; 28/5; 30/6; 36/7; 40/8; 48/9; 63/10; 65/11; 70/12; 74/13; 80/14; 88/15; 95/16; 98/17; 103/18; 105/19; 111/20; 119/21; 126/22; 130/23; 133/24; 135/25; 141/26; 148/27; 153/28; 156/29; 160/30; 166/31; 171/32; 179/33; 183/34.

or in decimal notations:

4.5; 6.3; 6.2; 5.6; 5.0; 5.1; 5.0; 5.3; 6.3; 5.9; 5.8; 5.7; 5.7; 5.9; 5.9; 5.8; 5.7; 5.5; 5.6; 5.7; 5.7; 5.6; 5.5; 5.4; 5.4; 5.5; 5.5; 5.4; 5.3; 5.3; 5.3; 5.4; 5.4.

Now we plot those cumulative averages against the number of intervals and get the average cumulative arrival interval time which is around 5.4 minutes.

Now we do exactly the same for the average service time (time the doctor on average spends with each child). Since it is exactly the same operation, there is no need to repeat it here. Let us, therefore, assume that it is calculated to be 4.5 minutes.

In this instance, we can calculate the traffic intensity by dividing the two average values:

$$\frac{4.5}{5.4} = 0.833$$

The traffic intensity is usually given the Greek symbol ξ. We can now calculate the mother's average waiting time (including the time spent with the doctor) by using the following formula:

$$\frac{1}{1 - \xi} \text{ x mean service time, or}$$

$$\frac{1}{1-0.833} \text{ x } 4.5 = 27 \text{ minutes}$$

This applies only in the case of one doctor, one queue and random variations between servicing and arrival times. This situation could be tolerable, but if the mean arrival interval time decreases to 5 minutes, then the average waiting time will rapidly increase to 45 minutes.

Knowing the distribution of average waiting times and average service times we can anticipate bottle-necks and provide extra help to be on call and avoid the forming of queues that are too long.

Systems approach

Recent developments in systems thinking offer a set of useful tools for the conceptualisation and evaluation of health promotion and health education activities. We have already noted that solutions for one part of the system may in fact create problems for another part. The reasons why such shifted problems may go undetected is that those who dealt with the first problem may be different from those who are experiencing the transferred problem (Senge, 1990, 1993, p.58). The important contributions of the systems model include the means of identifying the points in a system where the greatest 'leverage' can be exerted. Instead of trying to influence a whole system, with all its complex relationships, the dynamics of the system are analysed and the point of best focus chosen. This depends less on trying to conceptualise the parts of the system, which is an initial preoccupation, and more on understanding the internal processes (the 'arrows' rather than the 'bubbles'). This is always complicated by the fact that in human systems, there are long delays between cause and effect. Nevertheless, the aim is to find an element of the reinforcing process in a system not subject to limits to growth, that is, a system that is not self-balancing.

Systems thinking, especially when the thinker becomes familiar with using the diagrams that are fundamental to seeing how the elements hang together, allows one to incorporate all the key components of a system, which may include norms, beliefs and values, as well as groups, parts of organisations and flows of goods and services. Without an explicit picture of the nature of the system involved, interventions cannot be properly evaluated.

Simulations

This is an experimental treatment of processes through manipulation of models; it can be applied to teaching and research. The application in teaching is common and we may remember experiments on physical models from our school days. A simulation takes place when a systems model is embodied in some form and 'run forward' to test outcomes.

In research it has also been widely used in the fields of geography, hydrodynamics, aeroplane construction (wind tunnels), etc. Its application in the study of social processes occurring in preventive medicine is rare. It has received great encouragement through computer simulation and its main advantage is in predicting the direction in which the system as a whole moves.

Some effective simulations can be simpler. An example is given by Guetzkow (1962) who carried out a simulation experiment in a number of schools to find out to what degree a boy's or a girl's aspirations and attitudes are affected by the attributes of the person he/she looks up to, and in what way changes in aspirations and attitudes affect the schools as systems in their own right.

A questionnaire was administered to school children at the beginning and end of a school year. One of the pertinent questions was: "If you could be remembered in high school in any of these ways, which would it be: (1) brilliant student; (2) athletic star; or (3) most popular?" The substantive question was: To what extent does a boy who wants to be seen as a brilliant student have an effect on shaping the aspirations of a boy who holds him as a point of reference? The answer can only be provided by using computer analysis, since not only must the two answers of one boy (beginning and end of school year) be considered, but also the answers of the boy(s) mentioned as reference points. Computer analysis makes it possible to quantify the structures of relationships between people.

The second step in this example is to find out how changes in relationship between the children (due to conflicts in aspiration) affect the system and its changes. We can ask now about the direction in which the system is moving (i.e. reasons for which some schools become known for their academic or athletic achievements). To do this we take the two kinds of answers (at the beginning and end of school year) and work out the probability of any observed shift. Then we can simulate subsequent shifts for a number of years ending with the overall shift expected for the system as a whole.

In practice, we start with the first referring individual, find his reference person and compare their attitudes, taking as given the actual data at time 1. But now, if the reference person wants to be, say, a star athlete, and the referring person wants to be a brilliant student, then the referring person's attitude may change or he may drop the reference person. Which of those two possibilities will occur can be found from data at time 2. When all the persons have been analysed in this way, the proportion of various changes are calculated. Up to this moment the computer has been using data from time 1 and time 2. Using the probabilities of the proportions of change, it calculates the new hypothetical distribution of attitudes, then replaces the old ones with the new ones, and starts out again in a new cycle. This new cycle treats the hypothetical attitudes as data and calculates change in them, giving rise to a second, "new distribution" of attitudes. It then replaces the old ones with the new ones and again cycles through a new time period. This can be repeated for any amount of years we want to look ahead.

The program obtains the probabilities of change from data at two points in time, which give us the "weights" or the probabilities which serve as parameters in the system simulation.

This kind of approach can be very useful in the analysis of various possible consequences in health promotion and health education. It provides a way of developing scenarios, which can contribute to the practical planning process.

A systems approach, including its use in planning, as in operational research, can be useful in looking for solutions to many problems in health promotion and health education, where the action often does not depend solely on individual decisions but to a great extent on the structure of the system as a whole.

Introduction of such formal methods from the behavioural sciences requires that certain preconditions should be met. This in itself should bring about an improvement in health education research, through introducing an element of greater precision in defining the problem area and collection of data. This required precision may take us out of the realm of simple "counting heads" and enable us to become aware of the consequences of the decisions of health promotion and health education practitioners as well as of the decisions of the consumers of health services.

Only some of the possible techniques have been mentioned here. The main issue is the sharpening of perception about systems and how they may be examined as wholes. Any researcher would do well to precede any study or action by at least a soft systems analysis of the situation. Public health as a system is undergoing constant changes, many of which are induced by legislation or by changes in the training of its professional as well as by changes in the character of threats to health. There are many questions which need to be answered.

These and many other problems cannot be answered on the basis of personal impressions, since they involve choice and decisions which individuals make as members of groups in a certain social context and as a part of a certain culture. Available methods of evaluating health education and health promotion have been too simple to be fully successful and new ways of dealing with these problems will have to be found.

AREAS OF INQUIRY

The measurement of health promotion and health education interventions requires the choice of measures considered indicative of changes which occur as a result of a specific intervention. These indicators can be described as attributes or variables, which should be used in the measurement and which will differ according to the problem and the type of intervention which is taking place.

Any measurement of a health promotion and health education intervention will primarily depend on the type of problem which is being addressed and only secondarily on the type of intervention carried out.

The type of problem or health threat can be defined by using the definitions arising from medical studies, which can include the aetiology (cause-effect relationships) as well as epidemiological data on the distribution of a disease or health threat in a population.

The type of intervention, carried out within an approach based on an organisational model, will be defined by the characteristics of the disease or the health threat as well as attributes or variables related to the two aspects of the intervention, the health promotion and the health education activities. These are the two dependent parts of an intervention. The health promotion variables will reflect the characteristics of the environmental influences (physical and social), whereas the health education variables will reflect the individual characteristics (personality and competence).

Medical definitions

The definition of a medical problem or a health threat relevant to a health promotion and health education intervention should include the description of what causes the problem (aetiology) as well as where the problem is most prevalent (epidemiology) in a population (Baric, 1990 pp. 25-37).

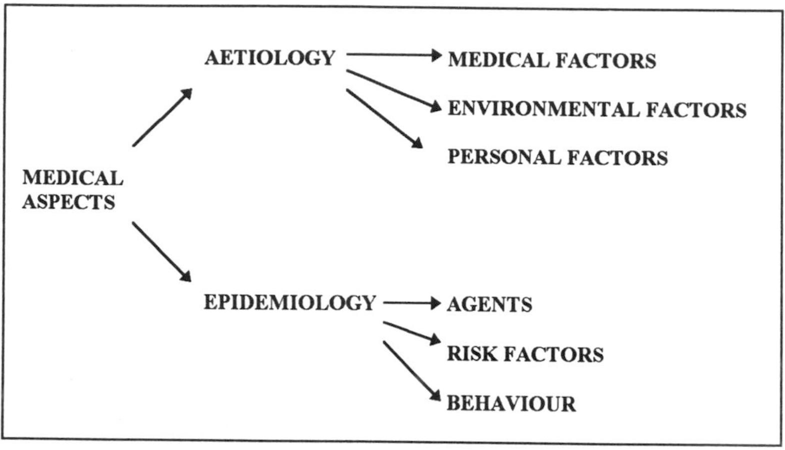

The medical definition of a problem is dependent on medical research, which is guided by a strict ethical code of practice. The results of such research may clearly establish a cause-effect relationship or may be based on a higher than expected probability of the relationship between certain factors and the disease. Towards the end of last century, when there were many discoveries of causes of infectious diseases, many clear relationships were established. In the present situation, we are faced with diseases of complex causality or with diseases for which we can only estimate the causal probability.

As this relates to a medical intervention, a differential diagnosis and monitoring carried out by doctors will provide safeguards even in situations of uncertainty. The outcome of such situations will be acceptable since the doctor can be in continuous contact with the patient and make use of feedback, which will ensure the avoidance and correction of possible negative side-effects.

In general terms the aetiology of a health problem is acceptable as an important base for any health promotion and health education intervention, since it will include information about the causal agent(s), symptoms, the processes and the expected outcome. All these will affect the lifestyle of a potential consumer of health promotion and health education services and interventions.

Aetiology

The definition of the causation of a health problem is based on medical research, which includes laboratory tests and experiments, as well as the verification of the findings, using trials on animals and humans. This is a highly sophisticated process carried out by highly trained researchers. There are cases when the cause of a disease cannot be established by laboratory tests and experiments. In that situation, researchers are limited to population studies of the distribution of a disease. By establishing some shared characteristics of the people with that disease, it is possible to define the factors contributing to the increased probability of the association between a disease and certain personal or population characteristics.

There are many examples of the discovery of a specific cause of a disease, most notably the discovery of the causes of infectious diseases, many of which are clearly identifiable (e.g. malaria, cholera); but there are cases where the sole cause of the disease has not been established; a good example is coronary heart disease. The reason for complexity could be that there is no single cause and that the disease is the outcome of an interaction of a number of factors.

Studies of the causation of lung cancer illustrate the point. Ever since Bradford Hill and Doll (1951) established an association between cigarette smoking and lung cancer, a large number of researchers have been attempting to elaborate on this initial finding.

Dunn (1973) provides a comprehensive review of the then existing research approaches. They can be roughly divided into the following groups:

1. Comparison of smokers with non-smokers: The assumption is that the difference between these two population groups will explain why some people smoke and others do not smoke. To find out this difference the researchers looked at:

- *personality traits:* smokers were more likely to be independent, active and energetic, extroverts, high on 'orality', happy-go-lucky, of poorer mental health, less rigid, less orderly, more impulsive, relied more on external controls, emotional, chance oriented, emotional, less agreeable, had less strength of character, higher anxiety levels and had personality type 'A' which means that they were more time-conscious and competitive;

- *life-style characteristics*: smokers were more likely to be business-oriented, had poorer academic performance, used more alcohol, attended religious services less frequently, were more likely to change jobs and marital partners: parents were more likely to smoke, smokers were more active in sports, had more auto accidents and drank more coffee or tea;

- *morphological traits*: smokers had greater body weight, were taller, thinner, had thinner skin folds;

- *demographic characteristics*: men smoked more, the smokers were proportionately between 25 and 45 years of age, on average belonged to a lower socio-economic class, they were proportionately fewer college men and were more likely to be urban residents.

2. *Models using the direct interrogation approach:* The assumption of researchers using the direct interrogation approach is that it is not possible to find the cause of acquisition and/or maintenance of the smoking habit by means of indirect or derived measurements. They assume that the best and simplest way of finding out the relevant facts is by direct questioning of the relevant population. The methods and techniques of doing this may vary, as may the methods of analysing the findings, but the main assumption still remains: "one can find out why a man smokes by asking him". Answers are grouped to give certain composite categories of reasons given by people as to why they smoke, which permits the identification of different types of smokers. An example of this approach quoted by Dunn is the study carried out by Ikard, Green and Horn (1969). They administered a 23-item questionnaire which contained statements of subjective conditions or affective states associated with smoking. The results were subjected to a multiple factor analysis, which identified the six most prominent factors: 'habitual', 'addictive', 'reduction of negative effects', 'pleasurable relaxation', 'stimulation' and 'sensory motor manipulation'.

3. *Models concentrating on the discrete smoking act and the attendant phenomena:* These models disregard the motivational aspects and are mainly concerned with the biochemical and physiological aspects of smoking. They are characterised by more sophisticated methods of measurements including laboratory experiments. Most of the studies, however, have been carried out on animals, which were induced to inhale

cigarette smoke in test situations rather than humans. The findings of these studies reflect the effects of smoking on animal activities such as: reduction in free activity level in rats; increased lever pressing activity in rats and cats; reduced aggression in rats; increased speed in learning in rats; inhibition of the extinction of an avoidant response in rats; improved memory, increase in EEG activity.

4. Synergistic models: The investigators also found a great variety of responses to the effects of nicotine in the organism among different animals or humans. McArthur, Waldron and Dickinson (1958) attempted to extract meaning from the great mass of highly variable data obtained on smoking among Harvard students. They concluded that "we may hypothesise that starting to smoke is largely brought about by one's social environment but that the reactions to smoking, once it has started, seemed to depend in good part on the personal needs that the newly acquired habit is able to gratify." They conclude that probably the most critical mechanism in the maintenance of the smoking habit will be a synergistic effect of a number of factors, one of which will probably be of a constitutional nature. This is also supported by findings that indicate that only half of those who try smoking end up as smokers.

The review produced by Dunn, although dated, is a very good example of the variety of approaches researchers can use when studying the medical causal factors of a health threat. It also illustrates the fact that most of the outcomes of such studies provide only an indication of the approaches to be used when planning a health promotion and health education intervention.

Since Dunn's review, a number of new approaches to the study of the medical problem have been introduced. In particular, recent developments in genetics, gene mapping and genetic engineering are having a profound effect on the new realisation of the contribution of genetic factors to the causes and possible cures of certain diseases. The number of associations between diseases and the genetic makeup of a person is constantly increasing and is providing an insight into the contribution of 'assumed' constitutional factors to the occurrence of a disease.

The existing knowledge about the aetiology of the most common diseases of concern for health promotion and health education can be described as falling into three general categories:

- medical factors: these include causal factors and risk factors;
- social/environmental factors: these include certain conditions related to the physical and social environment;
- personal factors: these include the genetic and personality makeup of an individual, the individual's lifestyle, habits and routines as well as actions.

As we have seen, when using existing aetiological knowledge for health promotion and health education it is necessary to bear in mind whether the knowledge is based on established causality or only on probability. This should influence the way health promotion and health education is applied to individuals and a population.

Epidemiology

The study of the distribution of a disease or a health threat in a population (epidemiology) has made some important contributions to our understanding of causality, as well as to our insight into the concentration of these disease entities in a population. This has been of great importance for health promotion and health education since it has provided information about the potential target population for interventions.

Epidemiological studies are becoming increasingly important in dealing with complex causality or with probabilities concerning precursors or risk factors. These studies are based on a methodology characterised by scientific rigour related to the collection and interpretation of information.

According to McKeown and Lowe (1977) the main contribution of epidemiology has been in the investigation of the distribution and causes of infectious diseases. During the past few decades, epidemiological methods such as nutritional and toxicological studies have been used to study the distribution of non-infectious diseases. A good example is the establishment of the relationship between smoking and lung cancer as an outcome of extensive epidemiological studies. Another area of importance is human biology, which looks, for instance, at the distribution of intelligence among school children and the reproduction and the distribution of arterial pressure in a population. A further area of investigation has been the examination of medical and surgical procedures, which could be evaluated only through population studies using a random assignment of patients to study and control groups. This was very successfully applied in the clinical trial of vaccines used in the prevention of diseases such as poliomyelitis and measles. It also produced the awareness of potential harm in the form of side effects from such medical procedures. Most recently, epidemiology has contributed to the assessment of the validity of observations and the measurement of the range of errors associated with common laboratory and clinical procedures; for example, observer variation differences have been established in the interpretation of X-rays and ECGs owing to observer error or observer variation.

The use of population methods by epidemiologists has also been extended to the study of the health services, as well as to the assessment of health problems and population needs.

The methods used by epidemiologists are mainly concerned with the assessment of the distribution of morbidity and mortality rates in a population group and in comparison with a similar population group in an attempt to find the reasons for any observed differences in these rates. Since there is less information about morbidity in a population, the main source of epidemiological studies lies in mortality rates. The basis for assessing mortality rates is provided by the records of births and deaths in a population, which have been recorded in the UK since 1838. One of the outcomes of such studies has been the awareness of the rapid increase in world population numbers - the 'population explosion', so-called because of the exponential growth of populations. These methods apply to populations as a whole, to various types of population samples or as a means of comparison between experimental and control groups of populations. They use a variety of statistical methods to analyse information and draw specific inferences about the meaning of the data collected. This rigorous application of statistical methods to population studies has increased the credibility of epidemiology.

One of the results of widely accepted epidemiological studies has been increased awareness of certain factors and the risks from certain diseases. Some recent examples have been the sexual behaviour of humans and the risk from AIDS, risks related to diet attributed to eating eggs, milk and milk products, chicken, beef, shell fish, sugar, fat, margarine, artificial sweeteners, etc. The outcome of risk perception from such studies has been directly associated with the increase in preventive tests and examinations. These at present include health check-ups, cancer screening, screening for risk from coronary heart disease, screening for genetic abnormalities, etc.

Health promotion and health education has been influenced by epidemiological studies in two main areas:

- risk factors: the establishment of associations between certain environmental, socio-economic and/or behavioural factors and the risk from certain diseases has enabled the appropriate planning of health promotion interventions;

- behavioural factors: the relationship between certain forms of individual behaviour and the risk from certain diseases enabled the appropriate planning of health educational interventions on an individual level, especially in the areas of orientation to health care, utilisation of health services and the individual perception of specific health threats.

Epidemiological studies have made an important contribution both to health promotion and health education programmes by providing information about the distribution of certain diseases and risk factors in a population.

Health promotional variables

The main justification for the introduction of health promotion and health education into the health care system is the assumption that health is the function of environmental and personal factors. Health promotion deals with environmental factors and health education with personal factors.

The health promotion intervention will, therefore, be dependent on information about the environment and the choice of appropriate methods for solving the existing problems. This information includes the environmental variables, which will define the physical and social environment an individual lives in, and the personal variables describing the individual's adjustment to that environment. These two types of information are of great importance since they will, to a large extent, define the kind of threats an individual or a family is exposed to and the resources at their disposal in dealing with such threats.

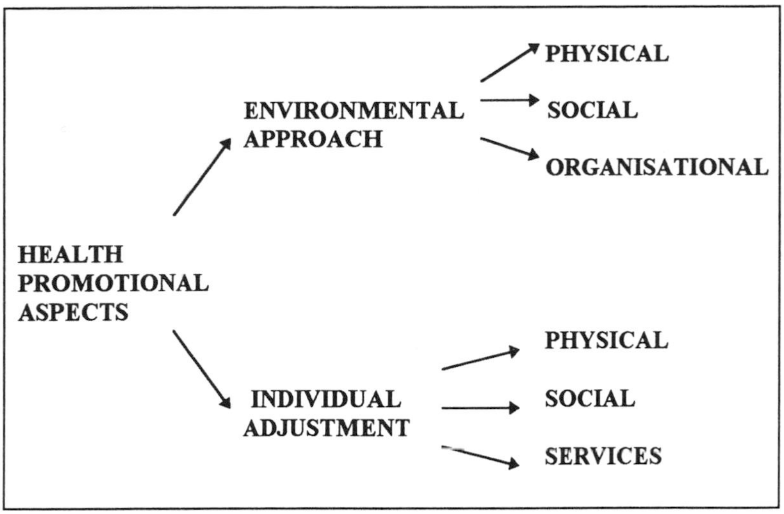

It is possible to discover the general subjects for health promotion, which should indicate the areas of measurement of health promotion activities, from the report of the Working Group on Concepts and Principles of Health Promotion (WHO, 1984):

- access to health with special reference to reducing inequalities, changing public policies, reorienting health services;
- development of an environment conducive to health, with special reference to the home and the work place;
- strengthening of social networks and social support for positive health actions and positive health behaviour;

- promoting positive health behaviour and appropriate coping strategies resulting in lifestyles conducive to health.

The method of achieving these aims includes advocacy, mediation and enabling intervention based on information and empowerment.

The environmental variables

The environmental variables can be differentiated according to the type of environment they describe:

- *physical environment,* the location of the individuals or families in geographical terms, including climatic conditions, which can have a direct influence on existing health threats and determine the requirements for management and prevention;

- *social environment,* the existing social organisation within which the individuals or families live and provide for themselves and their dependants, expressed in terms of individual participation in decision-making on a national, regional and community level, as well as in the degree of openness of the system and the type of social stratification of the population; the type of economy of the society the individuals or families live in and within which they must provide their livelihood; the existing value system to which an individual or a family belong, expressed in the dominant religious beliefs, existing norms and priorities related to health; the state of health of the population in general, expressed in mortality and morbidity rate, and indicating the most prevalent health problems associated with lifestyle, risk-taking behaviour and the availability of social support;

- *organisational environment,* which reflects the existing services and includes: the communication and transportation system available to the residents of a particular area within which an individual or a family live and which can be used by them; the existing educational system which is utilised by individuals or the members of a family; the existing health care system in that specific area and region where the individual or a family live, including the professional as well as the indigenous (local) system, expressed in terms of diagnosing the problem, providing treatment and ensuring the utilisation of services.

The information about the external conditions influencing individuals or families should be collected. This is an opportunity to use the historical research methods mentioned earlier. The sources will be varied, from official statistics to general impressions; all will help in producing a clearer picture of the physical, social as well as the organisational environment in which individuals or families live.

The individual adjustment variables

These variables should provide information about the ability of individuals to adjust and cope with their environment and will include:

- *physical environment,* in which various factors affect the way individuals adjust to the physical environment: the awareness of potential or existing risk factors in the environment; the location of each specific family in geographical terms within the general area, expressed in urban/rural terms; spatial mobility indicating whether the family is native-born or immigrant; the housing circumstances in which the family lives and raises the children;

- *social environmenst,* including the economic conditions expressed in the way the family earns its living, which will influence the state of health and the treatment of disease; the type of family in which an individual lives; the cycle of family development, which will indicate whether the numbers of children are expanding or contracting and the structure of the household; the type of conjugal roles within the family, defining the sharing of responsibilities by the spouses; the type of kin network, describing the closeness of relationships between the family and its relations; the nature of social networks, describing the relationships the family has with others in the community in addition to its relatives; the educational level of the members of the family; social position relative to others in the community; the religion of the family together with the description of the strictness of adherence and the implication for health behaviour; the perception of norms in terms of their accurate interpretation, the existing legitimisation and the existing sanctions related to health and illness; the state of health of the family members;

- *services,* the patterns of utilisation of health services including preventive services (screening and ante-natal clinics, etc.), management services (certain type of hospitals, self-help groups, etc.) and treatment services (GPs, hospitals, outlets for alternative medicine, etc.).

Health educational variables

The health education intervention deals with individuals and/or groups (families), with the aim of improving their competence in dealing with diseases and health threats. This will depend on the information about their knowledge, attitudes and skills related to the expected actions created as a result of a health education intervention.

Since health education mainly deals with individuals and groups, such as a family, the measurements involved will include variables dealing with these characteristics. The activity can be conducted on a formal (HE agents) or an informal (family, friends, etc.) basis. The formal approach may be direct or indirect, depending on the professional status of the agents. The methods include enabling, mediating and advocating.

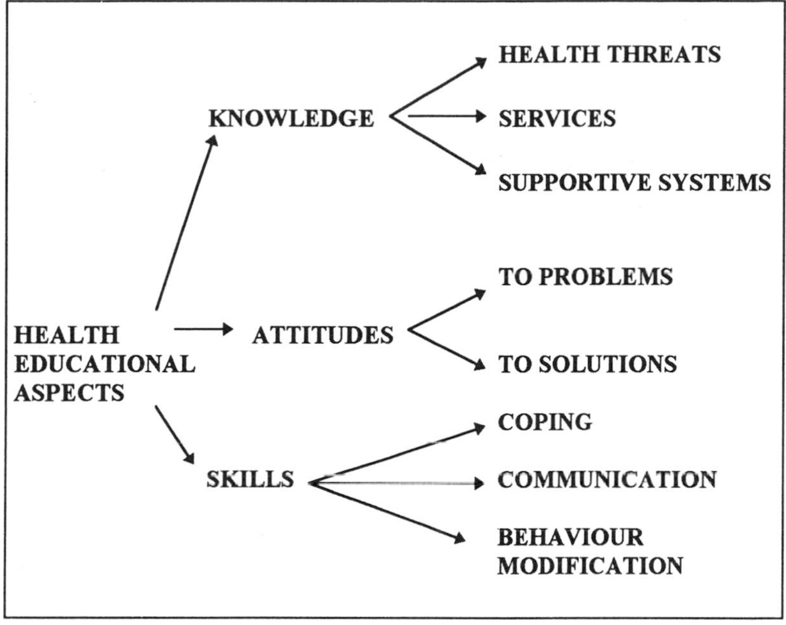

There are three main areas which can be used as a framework for measurement of health education activities: knowledge, attitudes and skills.

Knowledge

The basic assumption for any effective health education is the need of individuals to have knowledge or awareness about the health problems that could or do affect them. Depending on the type of health behaviour required, this knowledge can be differentiated as follows:

- *normative behaviour*: this implies the awareness of the existing social expectations or norms related to the behaviour;

- *decision-making about behaviour*: this will require the knowledge about the available choices, decision making process and coping with cognitive dissonance following a commitment.

The knowledge will include the following areas:

- *health threats*: this includes the awareness of increased risk from certain health threats owing to environmental influences, personality traits, genetic factors or types of risky behaviour;

- *services:* this includes awareness of available health services, with special reference to preventive services as well as detailed knowledge about the location, access and appropriateness of the services;

- *supportive systems*: this includes awareness of the existing supportive systems, including with the family and colleagues at work; professional counsellors will be required for behaviour modification if and when it is deemed necessary.

Attitudes

It is a well known fact that knowledge alone is not sufficient for the adoption of positive health behaviour, and that the attitudes towards such behaviour are a powerful motivational force for desired or planned change. Attitudes, which are considered to be internalised social norms, reflect the orientation of an individual towards the required behaviour and the support systems, and are of great importance for the increased probability of success of a health education intervention in that they provide a practical background for the measurement of its success or failure. One can differentiate the following attitudes:

- *to problems*, which can differ according to the 'image' of the problem: some health risks have the image of a killer disease (cancer), some carry a social stigma (sexually transmitted diseases including AIDS) and some are associated with a particular lifestyle (coronary heart disease);

- *to solutions*, which are different from attitudes towards a problem and can influence the acceptance of the desired solution: even when the attitude towards a problem is positive (e.g. prevention of lung cancer) the attitude to a solution may be negative (giving up smoking) and may act as an inhibitor for the success of a health education intervention.

Skills

A successful health education intervention will have to instil skills in addition to providing knowledge and creating positive attitudes. These skills will have to include:

- *coping skills,* which are needed when the awareness of an existing health threat and the increased personal risk from it result in a number of emotional reactions on the part of an individual: the individual will have to cope with the increased level of fear, which should be kept on an optimal level, since if excessive may act as an inhibitor; the individual will also need to cope with changes in the lifestyle and manage the implications of accepting an 'at-risk role';

- *communication skills,* which may need to be extended: the acquisition of awareness, the interpretation of the meaning of the newly acquired knowledge and the translation of such knowledge into action will require communication skills which can be different according to the type of threat, source of information and the orientation towards the health services in accepting a solution;

- *behaviour modification skills*, which may need to be acquired: once a commitment has been taken towards behaviour modification, an individual will require skills in implementing the required changes and maintaining them, without reverting back to the original risk-generating behaviour.

SUMMARY

The definition of areas of inquiry for any measurements related to health promotion and health education interventions is essential, since this definition circumscribes the various aspects of the intervention which will have to be taken into account when designing a measurement, whether it be for the purpose of evaluation, quality management or auditing.

There is a crucial difference in the type of indicators which will be appropriate for such measurements:

- health promotion, which affects the environmental factors will have to use environmental variables; these may include changes in physical environment or changes in the social environment;

- health education, which affects individuals and groups will have to use individual and/or group indicators for the measurement of changes.

It is, however, possible to group certain individual indicators into composite indicators such as 'good, indifferent or bad social environment', for environmental indications and 'levels of competence' when describing knowledge, attitudes and skills, to provide indicators on an individual or family level. The concept of competence is a theoretical construct and can only be measured if one develops indicators which will define what this concept entails. The indicators serve to translate abstract concepts into operational terms and thus allow us to use them for research purposes.

Keep in mind that for any health promotion/education study, the measurement of competence is always the main aim of the study, and the external conditions and family or individual characteristics should be treated only as a framework within which competence will be measured and assessed.

PLANNING AN INTERVENTION

Introduction
Definition of Aims
Objectives/Methods
Indicators
Data Collection
Instruments
Data Analysis
Summary

INTRODUCTION

The measurement of any health promotion or health education activity will only be possible if certain requirements are met, which allow measurement and a subsequent assessment or evaluation of the activity to take place. These preconditions will include the general description of the intervention, its aims and objectives, indicators and criteria, as well as the monitoring system for collecting data and drawing inferences.

The intervention

Health promotion and health education interventions are carried out in different ways, for different purposes and by different agents. To understand and assess an intervention it is necessary to distinguish between those interventions based on implicit planning processes and those based on explicit planning processes.

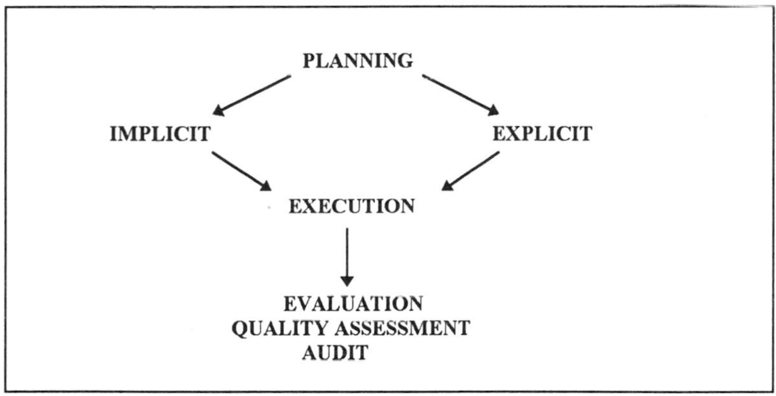

Within the organisational model, the agents carrying out health promotion and health education can either be members of a setting or health promotion and health education specialists. In the case of an integrated approach within a setting, the agents will not be engaged in a specific planning process but will integrate health promotion and health education into their daily activities. This could be described as 'implicit' planning, since they will still have to think and decide what should be done. Calling a specialist into a setting will result in the process of 'explicit' planning, which will include all the steps involved in such a process. The organisational model, based on the shift of emphasis from problems to settings with problems, includes the following range of settings in the UK:

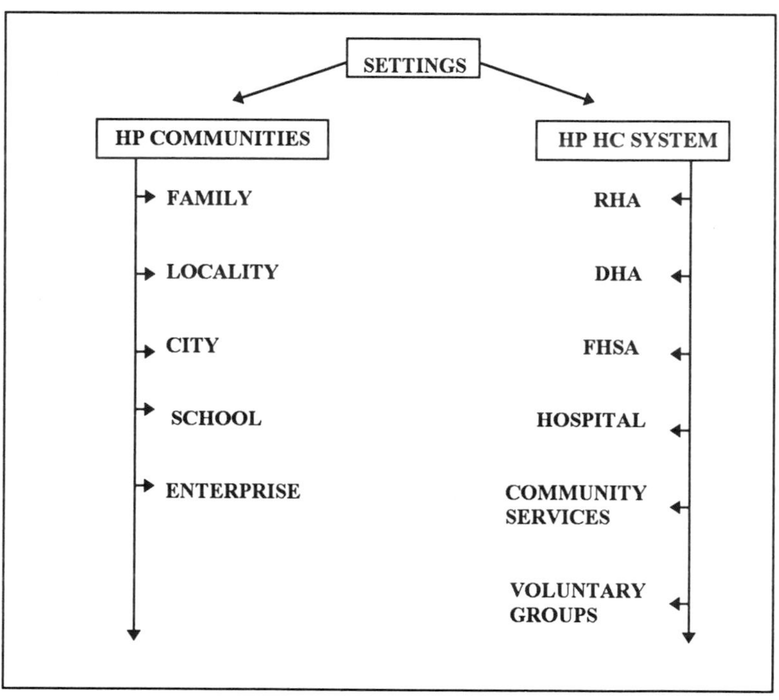

It can be assumed that health promotion and health education in a family setting will be subject to an 'implicit' planning process and that parents will 'do what is normal' in bringing up their children. The interpretation of 'normal' will be reflected in adults' normative behaviour according to social norms or expectations related to bringing up a child. The family household as a setting can, however, be exposed to a health promotion and health education intervention from outside, which will be subject to 'explicit' planning. Such a planned intervention usually starts with a number of questions that need to be answered before any planning can take place.

Health promotion : choice of topics

Under topic can be understood the content of an assessment of a health promotion intervention which may include:

- *a disease* entity or a disease complex, or even health as a content of a measurement; this can be measured in terms of its incidence and prevalence, distribution, causation, prevention, treatment, management and outcome;

- *a process*, which can include the stages of becoming ill; awareness of the problem; competence of dealing with it; communication with the social environment; coping, decision-making, learning, etc;

- *a structure*, which will include the organisation of the external, as well as the internal system within which the intervention is taking place; power structure; role distribution; networks, etc;

- *a model*, which will include the development of a new model of the system within which the intervention is taking place or testing the existing one; the theories linking the parts of the model; the instruments applied for measurement, etc;

- *a population group*, which could represent the whole or a part of the general population; population of a community or an institution; it could also include specific target populations defined by age, sex, occupation, people with specific lifestyles and/or behavioural patterns, educational level, competence and their potential to participate in the change process;

- *a relationship*, which could include the existing relationship frameworks such as doctor-patient, mother-child, manager-worker, teacher-pupil, etc;

- *an institution*, which could also be defined as a setting, such as hospital, school, family, workplace, etc;

- *a discrete action*, which could be an immunisation or a screening programme, improvement of physical environment, a behaviour modification clinic, etc;

- *a network analysis*, which could include the study of the existing professional, social, administrative, kin and other types of network.

Any of the above mentioned topics or a combination of several of them can be the subject matter of a health promotion and health education intervention. In each case, the planner should be able to answer the following questions:

- Why this specific topic?

- What is already known or has been done about that topic?

- What does the intervention hope and plan to achieve (aims) ?

- How can it be evaluated?

These questions require consideration to be given to a number of issues, such as the existing expertise, the opportunity of acquiring expert support, the time and money available and the expectations of the stakeholders. Some topics lend themselves to a specific description of the intervention in terms of aims and objectives, which will allow for the use of sophisticated analysis of data and an objective statement of inferences. There are, however, some topics that are relatively vague and where only descriptive inferences will be justified. Depending on the topic of the intervention, the intervention can be defined in terms of its feasibility and expected outcomes.

One of the usual aspects of choosing a topic is to identify a baseline. This serves a double purpose: it provides a background from which the effects of an intervention can be measured, and it indicates the most relevant problem areas which should be tackled by an intervention.

Very often the selected topic is related to the needs of the target population. This requires the examination and definition of such needs and the establishment of the difference between the needs and the wishes of the target population. In some cases, the health needs may be latent or of secondary importance, compared to the more generally felt needs such as poverty, bereavement, an imminent wedding or an unwanted pregnancy. If health promotion and health education need to deal with such crises, this will have to be taken into account in the planning process, since it will not be easy to concentrate the attention of the target population on some health needs which may be considered unimportant or irrelevant. The establishing of needs can be carried out objectively (externally) by using professional judgement or subjectively, by using the opinions of the target population.

Health education : differential diagnosis

Once the base-line information has been collected, the problem is how to translate it into a health education intervention. For this it will be necessary to work out a system for utilising each different kind of information collected. This process is known as 'differential diagnosis', which draws on the idea of a passage through the cause-effect system of the individual or group in question. By a process of elimination, it arrives at the factors which seem to be most promising for the achievement of the set aims. For this purpose, it is necessary to develop an indicator set, which will include the 'domains' relevant for the achievement of the set aims.

The information collected can only be operationalised for health education purposes if one looks at various domains separately and sees how they can contribute to planning an intervention. Each domain of information will provide a general picture of the factors contributing to the improvement of competence, if that is the aim of the study, while differential diagnosis will help in selecting those which can be affected by a health education intervention. It will be necessary to make a value judgement about the minimal and optimal needs affecting competence within the constraints of the social environment and influenced by the individual or group in question.

According to the kind of information collected, one can distinguish two main types of factors: enabling factors and contributing factors. From these, plans for intervention can be developed according to the established needs of the members of the population and the available opportunities and resources at their disposal.

The enabling factors

The enabling factors are considered to be those which contribute to the provision of an environment conducive to health within which individuals or groups live. This environment can be best described by a set of variables.

Location - There is no doubt that individual or family possibilities and needs will be different in different countries. The difference will lie in the type of settlement people live in, such as whether they live in an urban or a rural area. This may affect the availability of and access to the support systems, including the health services.

The health problems facing an individual or family will be strongly influenced by the prevailing climatic conditions, which have been found to be closely associated with various risk factors and mortality.

The importance of an existing water supply and appropriate sewage system will depend on the type of area the individual or family live in and the climatic conditions under which they live.

People live in different types of dwellings and utilise different energy sources for heating and cooking. The management of health and prevention of disease will be influenced by the availability of space and energy to meet family needs.

The information about the location of an individual or family will indicate the general problems which can be expected to affect their health. The separate factors included in the assessment of the location can be grouped into three main categories: inadequate, minimal and optimal. Individuals or families in each of these three categories will have different needs, most of which one cannot expect to meet by means of a health education intervention. It will, therefore, be necessary to treat this information as identifying the enabling factors that must be taken into account when planing a health education intervention.

Economy - The general economic state of a country will to a large extent be reflected in the economic conditions under which the majority of individuals or families live. In each country, however, different individuals or families will have different levels of prosperity within the existing general constraints.

The economy of the country can be assessed according to the income per capita, and according to the level of technological development or according to other indicators. The kind of source of income available to an individual or family, including the opportunities for employment or need for migration, is strongly influenced by technology.

The economic state of a country can also be boosted in the short-term by external aid, or incurring national debt, which is very often used to improve the health of the population. Although it can be assumed that within each country most individuals or families will have sufficient income to survive, some may be specially affected by poverty following a natural disaster or an uneven distribution of high levels of unemployment.

When planning a health education intervention, the main factors to be taken into account are those concerned with the general level of prosperity, as compared with occasional hardships some individuals or families may temporarily be exposed to, as a result of sudden unemployment or some other disaster.

Social organisation - The possibilities of leading a healthy life and bringing up children in an atmosphere which places a high value on health will be influenced by the political system which is predominant in that country. In general, one can differentiate, in this context, between political systems according to the degree of social responsibility that they include in their political programmes.

Another important factor will be the existing internal social stratification. In some countries there are clear demarcations between different religious groups, social classes, age groups and sex groups.

According to the type of political organisation, there will be a difference in the expected participation of the population in deciding about their own destiny and in solving existing national and local problems.

For health education purposes, one could differentiate between two types of social organisation: one enabling limited participation and the other enabling unlimited participation. The difference between the two types of systems indicates the level of expected participation of the population in improving their living conditions and solving their problems. This classification can be applied to the population as a whole or to certain groups within a country.

Communications - The existing system of communications in a country will be of great importance for any health education intervention. Communications include: the possibility of movement and travel which will enhance personal exchanges; the network of a media communication system, which would include film, radio, T.V., video, the press, etc; the organisational network, which would include meetings, gatherings and visits; personal communication systems which would include access by transportation systems to kin and social networks; and access to the existing means of communication, such as telephone and electronic communication.

Communication is vital for sharing information and knowledge, for finding answers to acute problems and for gaining support and help.

Any health education intervention must thus take into account existing communication facilities in a country or an area and make sure the methods are appropriate to the existing situation. For health education purposes, the following two communication systems can be identified: high technology and traditional/restricted systems of communication.

Value systems - Although one can generally say that health is considered a desirable condition in most countries and among most population groups, different value systems can influence the way this desirable state is achieved.

Prevalent religious beliefs reflect one aspect of the existing value system and can have an important influence on a number of health issues. Examples are treatment of illness, pregnancy and childbirth; nutritional rules and customs; and existing legal norms, which can directly or indirectly affect the access to health care and the treatment of individuals. Health education is able appropriately to involve and use different agents, which may include political, religious and social leaders, according to the varying value systems.

On another level, health education should take into account the existing norms, which can be either supportive or adverse in their effects on health.

Education - Most countries have an official system of education that is accessible to at least some parts of the population. There is a direct relationship between the level of education and the health state of an individual or a family. For this reason, it is very important for health education to take into account the educational level of individuals or families when planning an intervention.

For health education purposes, one can differentiate between levels of education in a simple way, as functional illiteracy, basic (primary) and higher secondary and above education.

State of health - The risks an individual or a family will run from different diseases will depend on the prevalent morbidity and mortality patterns in that country. Existing disease patterns will strongly influence the priorities of any health education intervention and the existing health problems will form a background against which health problems on a local or family level need to be approached.

For health education purposes, a distinction can be drawn between countries with endemic and epidemic diseases. In the latter category, the possibility and frequency of epidemics should be taken into consideration.

Health care - The availability of professional support depends on the type and extent of the existing health care system. Some countries will have a general health service available to everyone, whereas other countries may have a system which is only partly accessible through private insurance or direct payment. In many countries the availability and the access to health care may vary according to type of disease. Some diseases may have a nationally provided health service, whereas for others the access is controlled through special regulations.

For health education purposes, a distinction can be drawn between generally accessible and partly accessible health care systems and for the latter, there may be different levels of accessibility for special groups, special diseases and private initiatives. This will have to be taken into account when planning a health education solution.

The contributing factors

Within a specific physical and social environment, different individuals and groups (such as the family) will develop different ways of adjusting to the environment and will manifest different patterns of utilisation of available resources. Therefore, it is possible to differentiate between individuals and groups in terms of their social characteristics, which can directly affect their state of health and their ability to cope with different health problems. Different individual and group characteristics, which in turn influence the state of health of members, are strongly influenced by external conditions. To explore individual and group characteristics, it will be necessary to include the information about these characteristics that corresponds to the information collected about the external environment. In this way it will be possible to establish which kinds of opportunities are offered by the society and how they are utilised by individuals and groups.

The most important contributing factors are:

Residence- The type of residence in which an individual or group lives will reflect geographical characteristics as well as the individual's and group's socio-cultural and economic position. It will also reflect the available means of communication, mobility and transportation.

The health of a individual and group will also be influenced by the type of water supply and sewage disposal they have in their house or home. The type of energy source available to each individual and group is associated with their socio-economic position and will reflect the possible restrictions and limitations in terms of the available lighting and heating of premises, cooking and washing facilities.

For health education purposes, the residence can be classified as urban or rural and as optimal/adequate/poor. This means that there may be urban families living in poor conditions or rural families living in optimal conditions. Each of the combinations of these two dimensions will have special implications for planning a health education intervention.

Mobility - It is possible to classify families according to the amount of time they have spent living in a certain community. This can have important consequences for the level of individual and group competence necessary to cope with daily health problems. It can be assumed that an immigrant individual or group, living a short-time in a community and with relatively limited access to social support, will need a higher level of competence to deal with health problems than an individual or group living a long time in a community and able to mobilise social support in a crisis situation.

For the purpose of health education families can be classified as being static or mobile and adapt the health education interventions as appropriate.

Housing - It is important to take into account the housing circumstances in which a individual or group lives and brings up children. Distinctions can be made here according to the number of rooms per person, the placement of amenities and the type of existing protection against the elements, pests, insects, vermin, dampness, etc. For health education purposes, housing conditions can be classified as optimal/adequate/poor.

Subsistence - Within the general economic situation, family households will find themselves in different positions in terms of wealth. This will depend on the source of income they have, the number of economically active members there are and the amount of property they possess.

For purposes of health education, individual and group income levels can be broadly classified as wealthy, adequate and poor.

Domestic group - The immediate environment into which a child is born can take many different forms and include a number of people with different relationships. It is because of this that it is better to describe a family in terms of a domestic group to avoid the different interpretations of the meaning of family in different societies.

A domestic group can be described in terms of the number of generations living together, the kin relationships of the members of the domestic group, the cycle of individual and group development and the type of conjugal roles within the domestic group.

The structure of the domestic group can be differentiated between two-generation and three-generation domestic groups. The former includes parents and children and the latter includes grandparents as well. In addition to different generations a domestic group can be composed of different members, relatives and unrelated, belonging to the same generation. Kin relationships can be differentiated in terms of nuclear and extended domestic groups. The classification of families should take into account the dynamic changes that occur in the course of time as children are born, grow up and leave the domestic group. These changes can be described in terms of the cycle of family development, which will include the phases of expansion, dispersion, independence and replacement. For practical purposes, one can group the families according to the cycle of development into younger families that are in the phase of expansion and families with older members that are in the phases of dispersion or replacement. In terms of individual and group competence we can assume that we will be dealing primarily with families in the phase of expansion.

It is not only important to establish the residents living in a domestic group but also the kinds of relationships that exist among them. These relationships can be classified according to the amount of segregation or participation the members demonstrate in performing certain tasks. A role relationship is also important in terms of roles where the activities and decisions are interchangeable between the spouses and divergent roles where the activities and decisions are clearly allocated to different spouses. One can also assume an intermediate "cooperative" constellation where certain tasks and decisions are shared and others are segregated.

For health education purposes, one can group these various characteristics of a domestic group on two levels: on the one level, one can differentiate between isolated groups and extended groups, and on the other, one can differentiate between divergent (segregated) and merged conjugal roles within a domestic group.

Networks - A domestic group need not only rely on internal resources, but may, in a situation of need, mobilise external resources through their kinship or friendship networks. The differentiation of networks can be made on two levels: the extent of individual and group and friendship networks and the quality of relationship within those networks.

For health education purposes, domestic groups can be classified into those with close-knit and those with loose-knit networks, where the former represent domestic groups with a strong social support and the latter a domestic group with very few possibilities of mobilising social support.

Education - In different countries the existing educational system will provide different opportunities. Furthermore, different families may utilise the existing educational system in different ways. It can be assumed that the members of a family will have different orientations towards health problems and their solutions according to their educational level.

Two types of orientation should be differentiated for health education purposes: cosmopolitan and parochial. The former will include families with a higher level of education and a more scientific approach to health problems, while the latter will include families with basic education whose interpretation of health problems will depend on opinions of relatives, friends and the popular local press.

Social position - Depending on the type of the social structure of a society, its members will occupy different social positions. Social stratification, in terms of social class, status, caste, etc., differentiates a person's position on a social scale, which for health education interventions can at least be divided into three levels (with a possible transitional category) : high, moderate and low.

The social position of a domestic group is usually closely associated with the level of education of its members and, therefore, for health educational purposes, it can also be classified in terms of cosmopolitan and parochial orientation to health.

In the UK, the social position of individuals has been traditionally measured by allocating them to different social classes. In 1911 the Chief Medical Statistical Officer in the General Register Office, T.C.H. Stevenson, used the concept of social class to arrange the British census data into five social classes (Susser and Watson, 1962, p.64). From that time on, this system of stratification was used by the General Register Office. The population was classified according to occupation, type of industry, employment status and economic position. For use in the 1961 census, the over-elaborate occupational classification was reduced to 200 unit groups. This satisfied the requirements of mortality, morbidity and fertility studies and also permitted the preservation of as much comparability as possible with the classification used in the 1951 census and earlier. This new classification (1960) was based on the International Standard Classification of Occupations. Groups were based on at least one common characteristic, i.e. the kind of work done. Where necessary the groups could be broken down further according to material worked on, degree of skill involved, the physical energy required, the environmental conditions, the social and economic status associated with the occupation, or any combination of these factors.

As an aid to certain kinds of statistical analysis, the large number of unit groups of the Occupational Classification were arranged into a smaller number of broad categories called social classes:

Social Class I (Professional Occupations)
Social Class II (Intermediate Occupations)
Social Class III (Skilled Occupations)
Social Class IV (Partly Skilled Occupations)
Social Class V (Unskilled Occupations)

This social class stratification is based on occupation and status. Classes II, III and IV were subdivided into manual, non-manual and agricultural occupations.

With the introduction of social class stratification, a very powerful epidemiological tool was made available, which has since been in constant use for the purpose of manifesting the association between the prevalence of certain diseases and the social class of the population.

Although the five social classes were very useful in expressing the crude differences between various groups of the population, many research workers found them not to be a precise enough analytical tool. This is obvious from the census data (1951), which shows the following distribution of the population of Great Britain according to their social class:

S.C. I	3.31%
S.C.II	14.54%
S.C.III	52.89%
S.C.IV	16.14%
S.C. V	13.12%

Since more than half of the working population of Great Britain was allocated to social class III in this distribution, the deeper analysis of status differences related to diseases is obscured.

It was this situation that prompted the Register General subsequently to introduce sixteen socio-economic groups (SEGs). These are also based on a person's employment status and occupation and aim to group together people with similar social, cultural, recreational standards and behaviour. They are:

1. Employers and managers in central and local government, industry and commerce (large establishments with 25 employees and over).

2. Employers and managers in industry, commerce etc., (small establishments with under 25 employees).

3. Professional workers - self-employed (university degree standard).

4. Professional workers - employees (university degree standard).

5. Intermediate non-manual workers (not with planning or supervisory powers, not university degree standards, artistic work).

6. Junior non-manual workers.

7. Personal service workers (employees in services catering for food and drink etc.).

8. Foremen and supervisors - manual (employees other than managers who directly supervise others in manual occupation, whether they themselves work or just supervise).

9. Skilled manual workers (considerable skill required).

10. Semi-skilled manual workers (slight but specific skill).

11. Unskilled manual workers.

12. Workers for own account (other than professionals) - self-employed persons in trade etc., not requiring a university

degree and without employees, except members of the individual and group.

13. Farmers, employers and managers (who own, rent or manage farms, employing people other than their individual and group).

14. Farmers - working for their own account (with no employees except members of their own individual and group).

15. Agricultural workers.

16. Members of the armed forces.

The stratification of the population into sixteen SEGs, although intended to provide a more specific tool for analysis, has not as yet been generally taken up in health promotion and health education, and most of the epidemiological studies still use the five social classes for the purpose of stratifying a population.

The allocation of a social position (either SC or SEG) is determined by occupation, type of work and status within the organisation, as well as on the sex and marital status of the individual. The information about occupation, type of work and status is the basis on which the Classification of Occupations, prepared by the Office of Populations Censuses and Surveys (HMSO 1970) allocates social class to individuals. The sex of the individual is important because of the difference in attributing social class to males and females. In general males belong to the social class defined by their own employment. The attribution of a social class to females, however, depends on several factors: if the female is single and employed, then the social class is determined by her occupation; if she is single and has never been employed, then she is allocated the social class of her father; if she is married, whether employed or not, she will be allocated the social class of her husband. In the case of a person being unemployed or retired, the last occupation is taken into account.

To obtain the necessary information required to cover all the possible permutations the following questions should be included:

- sex of the respondent;
- marital status;
- own occupation;
- type of work;
- status within the organisation;
- occupation of spouse;
- type of work of spouse;
- status of spouse within the organisation;
- occupation of father;
- type of work of father;
- status of father within the organisation.

The following case can be used as an example: a male, fully employed working as a carpenter and occupying the status of a foreman. The allocation of social class based on Classification of Occupations, under the section "Alphabetical Index for Classifying Occupations" lists on page 12 "carpenters" as having code number 055. This code number refers to appendix B1 in "Socio-economic Group and Social Class Allocations of Occupations and Employment Status Groups", where on page 96, under the section VIII, "wood workers" one can find that "carpenters and joiners" who are in employment and have the status of a foreman belong to social class III manual and socio-economic group 8.

Values and norms - Every society has its general value system, variously interpreted within different domestic groups. In addition to differences in their perception of values domestic groups may also be differentiated according to the level of adherence to social norms, reflecting the existing value system. For health education purposes, the level of adherence will be closely related to the perception of social values and norms and it is, therefore, possible to differentiate between conformist, variant and deviant domestic groups.

State of health - The type and frequency of health problems met by a domestic group depends on the general state of health of its members. The state of health will also influence the need for and means of utilisation of available health services. There are different implications for a child born into a domestic group where the prevalent state of health is poor and for one born into a domestic group where the members are relatively healthy and expect to be healthy.

For the purpose of health promotion and health education domestic groups with a poor general level of health and frequent utilisation of services can be distinguished from domestic groups with a relatively good level of health and only occasional utilisation of services.

Personal characteristics

The position of an individual in the society can be established by using the same questions as for group characteristics.

There are, however, a number of additional characteristics which are specific to the individual. These are concerned with the individual's personality, opinions, feelings, intentions etc.

Since most of these characteristics are represented by concepts which are theoretical constructs, their measurement will depend on the development of specific tests. Theoretical constructs refer to concepts such as intelligence, being stressed, aptitude etc. They are not taken to be self-evident as are, for example, characteristics such as height, weight, gender and age, and need to be carefully defined before they can be measured. The individual characteristics necessary for a differential diagnosis depend on the aims of the intervention and should be selected with a view to the overall framework of health promotion and health education methods.

The planning process

Once the topic has been chosen, based on the existing situation and the needs of the target population, the intervention will follow the normal steps of a planning process. These steps can be summarised as including the definition of aims, establishment of objectives or the ways these aims will be achieved, choice of indicators and criteria for the assessment of processes and outcomes:

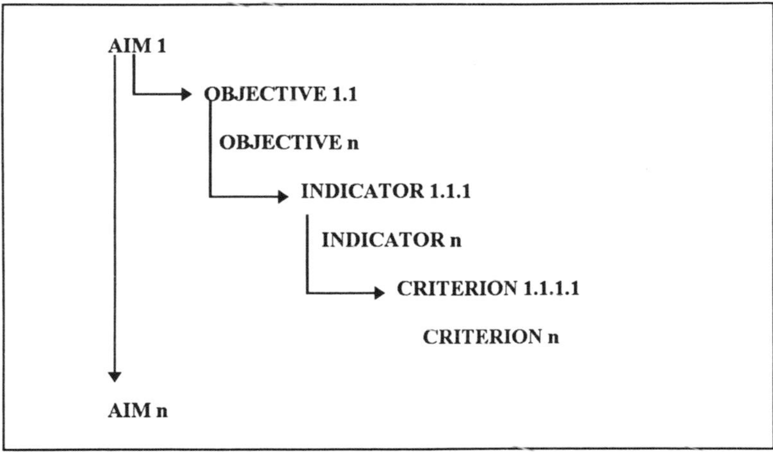

One can differentiate between a short-term and a long-term planning process. The short-term planning process will address an acute situation and will be expected to produce an immediate outcome. The long-term planning process is usually a part of a continuous effort of improving the health of a population and may include a number of short-term programmes. The outcome in this case will be cumulative and may be postponed for a number of years before it is clearly visible.

Depending on the problem, planning will have to differentiate between the health promotion and health education aspects of the intervention and will have to take into account the characteristics as well as potential of each aspect of the intervention.

DEFINITION OF AIMS

The precision with which the aims of an intervention can be defined will be decisive for the accuracy of the outcomes. Very often aims are vague and represent the wishful thinking of the agent or the optimistic expectation of the stakeholder. In such cases, it will be difficult to match the outcomes with the stated aims in any valid or reliable way.

There are various ways of defining the aims of a health promotion and health education intervention. They can be defined according to the needs and rights of clients or by some institution which is concerned with the rights and needs.

The needs and rights

The needs of the clients can be defined by carrying out a survey which will include exploring their objective and subjective needs.

The aims can also be based on the defined rights of the patients as in the "Patient's Charter" which defines seven well established rights and nine standards.

The Patient's Charter Rights

There are seven existing rights: you as a citizen have the following established National Health Service rights (see Baric, 1994, Appendix 5, pp. 573-579):

1. to receive health care on the basis of clinical need, regardless of ability to pay;

2. to be registered with a GP;

3. to receive emergency medical care at any time, through your GP or the emergency ambulance service and hospital accident and emergency departments;

4. to be referred to a consultant, acceptable to you, when your GP thinks it necessary, and to be referred for a second opinion if you and your GP agree this is desirable;

5. to be given a clear explanation of any treatment proposed, including any risks and any alternatives, before you decide whether you will agree to the treatment;

6. to have access to your health records, and to know that those working for the NHS are under a legal duty to keep their contents confidential;

7. to choose whether or not you wish to take part in medical research or medical student training.

Three new rights were established from 1st April 1992:

1. to be given detailed information on local health services, including quality standards and maximum waiting time.

2. to be guaranteed admission for treatment by a specific date no later than two years from the day when your consultant places you on a waiting list.

3. to have any complaint about NHS services - whoever provides them - investigated and to receive a full and prompt written reply from the chief executive or general manager.

National Charter Standards

1. *Respect for privacy, dignity and religious and cultural beliefs.* The Charter Standard is that all health services should make provision so that proper personal consideration is shown to the patient, for example by ensuring that the patient's privacy, dignity and religious and cultural beliefs are respected. Practical arrangements should include meals to suit all dietary requirements, and private rooms for confidential discussions with relatives.

2. *Arrangements to ensure everyone, including people with special needs, can use services.* The Charter Standard is that all health authorities should ensure that the services they arrange can be used by everyone, including children and people with special needs such as those with physical and mental disabilities, for example, by ensuring that buildings can be used by people in wheelchairs.

3. *Information to relatives and friends.* The Charter Standard is that health authorities should ensure that there are arrangements to inform the patient's relatives and friends about the progress of treatment subject, of course, to the patient's wishes.

4. *Waiting time for an ambulance service.* The Charter Standard is that when a person calls an emergency ambulance it should arrive within fourteen minutes if they live in an urban area, or nineteen minutes if they live in a rural area.

5. *Waiting time for initial assessment in accident and emergency departments.* The Charter Standard is that the

patient will bee seen immediately and their need for treatment assessed.

6. *Waiting time in outpatient clinics.* The Charter Standard is that the patient will be given a specific appointment time and be seen within thirty minutes of that time.

7. *Cancellation of operations.* The Charter Standard is that the patient's operation should not be cancelled on the day they are due to arrive in hospital. However, this could happen because of emergencies or staff sickness. If, exceptionally, the operation has to be postponed twice the patient will be admitted to hospital within one month of the date of the second cancelled operation.

8. *A named qualified nurse, midwife or health visitor responsible for each patient.* The Charter Standard is that the patient should have a name, qualified nurse, midwife or health visitor who will be responsible for their nursing or midwifery care.

9. *Discharge of patients from hospital.* The Charter Standard is that before the patient is discharged from hospital a decision should be made about any continuing health or social care needs they may have. The hospital will agree arrangements for meeting these needs with agencies such as community nursing services and local authority social services departments before the patient is discharged. With the patient's agreement, their carers will be consulted and informed at all stages.

WHO EURO targets for health promotion

Following the WHO EURO Regional Committee in 1985, a set of targets have been agreed upon in support of the European strategy for the achievement of Health for All by the Year 2000. (for a detailed description of the targets and their evaluation, see Appendix 1).

The DoH targets

The White Paper, "The Health of the Nation" (1994), published by the Department of Health, sets out a strategy for health for England. The strategy selects five Key Areas for action:

- coronary heart disease and stroke;
- cancers;
- mental illness;
- HIV/AIDS and sexual health;
- accidents.

Each Key Area has national targets and is supported by action required to secure progress.

Aims for "health promoting settings"

Some types of aims are derived from the type of health promotion and health education interventions appropriate to a specialised kind of setting. The issue here is the creation of "health promoting settings", which have to meet certain preconditions before achieving a recognised status. These are:

- creation of a healthy environment within a setting to enhance the living, working and leisure conditions of the members of that setting;

- integrating health promotion and health education into the daily activities of that setting (teaching programmes, dealing with patients, bringing up children, etc.);

- outreach into the community in the form of networks and alliances for the improvement of the outcomes in terms of a continuous process within the community.

Aims related to methods

Another way of defining aims is to link them with the health promotion and health education methods that are defined by WHO (see Ottawa Charter, Baric, 1994, Appendix 1, pp. 539-544) related to health promotion and health education interventions. These aims include taking action:

- *to enable* the recipients to be self-reliant in looking after their own health;

- *to mediate* between the recipients and the external system in achieving optimal health;

- *to advocate* for the rights of the recipients by ensuring that the existing rights are observed or by creating new rights if necessary;

The general aims of an intervention need to be subdivided into specific aims related to health promotion and those related to health education.

Health promotion aims

Specific health promotion aims should take into consideration the main aspects of such an intervention, which mainly deal with:

- *physical environment* - improvement in this context is usually the task of authorities or community forces and, in most cases, does not depend on the actions of the individual; it could include the reduction of air pollution, elimination of 'black spots' in the traffic system, appropriate working conditions, etc;

- *social environment* - may require changes in social norms or expectations concerning health behaviour and actions, as well as the developing and strengthening of social support systems; appropriate social norms are relevant for the decision-making aspects of individual behaviour, whereas social networks will influence individual decision-making and choices;

- *community services* - including health and social services, will be of importance for the health of the population and their ability to prevent, manage, treat and cope with health problems; the intervention could mobilise social services dealing with housing problems to improve the living conditions of certain population groups with specific problems (pregnant teenagers, AIDS patients, single elderly, etc.); health services could be motivated to undergo a transition to 'health promoting settings' and be fully active in helping people to cope with their health problems;

- *lay support systems* - play an important role in terms of community health; the existing systems may need to be activated or targeted to deal with specific problems; if and where such systems do not exist, health promotion intervention could help in their creation in the form of specific self-help groups etc.

Health education aims

The specific health education aims should take into consideration the main factors involved in such an intervention aimed at individuals or small groups which will be complementary to the health promotion and include:

- *level of knowledge* - this can include the creation of new knowledge or increasing, correcting and improving the existing knowledge; it should be related to the recognition of signs and symptoms of a health threat or a disease, ways of prevention, management and treatment; coping with the consequences on a personal and social level, utilising the services and activating the social support system;

- *attitudes* - if treated as internalised social norms, then they will be of importance for the behaviour and action of individuals; they will represent the personal perception of social norms; positive attitudes may enhance healthy choices and support behaviour modification processes;

- *skills* - will include the ability to learn and communicate with the social environment, cope with behaviour modification techniques, enhance social relationships; special skills will be required to cope with crisis situations or new problems such as child birth, bereavement, unemployment, divorce, etc;

- *competence* - represents a combination of factors mentioned above (knowledge, attitudes, skills), and defines the ability of a person or a group to cope with existing problems as well as to transmit such acquired competence to others through the process of socialisation.

OBJECTIVES/METHODS

Once the aims of a health promotion and health education intervention have been set, the next step will be to select the appropriate objectives. *Objectives define the ways the set aims are to be achieved and can be expressed in terms of methods used for the achievement of each specific aim.*

It can be assumed that the health promotion and health education aims in general will cover the areas of influencing normative behaviour, individual habits and practices, as well as encouraging the appropriate and timely utilisation of available health services. These aims should be considered in relation to the available health promotion and health education methods of enabling, mediating and advocating in the form of the following matrix:

AIM (n)	**METHODS**		
OBJECTIVE (N)	ENABLING	MEDIATING	ADVOCATING
NORMS ATTITUDES			
HABITS PRACTICES			
SERVICES UTILISATION			

In this matrix an imaginary aim (AIMn) has been used to illustrate the relationship between the objectives and the methods. The objectives are changes in norms/attitudes, habits/practices and the utilisation of services. These objectives should be achieved by using the health promotion and health education methods of enabling, mediating and advocating. In this way the aim (AIMn) should be achieved by the stated objectives and by using the stated methods.

This matrix can be a useful tool for planners as well as for those who want subsequently to assess the effectiveness of the planned activities. It provides a systematic representation of the relationships between the aims, objectives, and methods and will provide a useful framework for the selection of indicators necessary for measurement of specific outcomes related to this aim.

This approach obviously needs to be related to the subject matter. This can be seen in the example of a health education intervention, set out in the following matrix:

	AIMS		
OBJECTIVES	**A1 ENABLE**	**A2 MEDIATE**	**A3 ADVOCATE**
01 KNOWLEDGE	A1/01	A2/01	A3/01
02 SKILLS	A1/02	A2/02	A3/02
03 ASSESSMENT	A1/03	A2/03	A3/03

The table shows the relationship of each aim and each objective which needs to be specifically defined in terms of indicators and criteria. In this case the aim (A1), for instance, to enable the recipients to be able to look after their own health, can be achieved by objectives directed towards the provision of knowledge (01), transmission of skills (02), and the assessment of the effects (03). The same considerations will apply to the aims related to the role of a mediator (A2) and an advocate (A3) in carrying out the health promotion and health education intervention.

Each aim will have a number of particular sub-aims, which need to be related to the individual objectives, as shown in the matrix.

The matrix gives an example of the aim (A1), which is 'to enable' the client to be able to cope with his/her problems. The interventions in the areas of medical, organisational and consumer activities are sub-aims. The achievement of these sub-aims will depend on the specific objectives for each sub-aim which include transmission of knowledge and skills and the ability to assess the dangers and risks. The topics covered by these objectives are based on a complexity of knowledge and skills which are indicated in the following matrix:

AIM 1 **SUB AIMS**	**01** **KNOWLEDGE**	**02** **SKILLS**	**03** **ASSESSMENT**
A1.1 **MEDICAL**	EPIDEMIOLOGY AETIOLOGY TARGETS	STATISTICS PREVENTION SPECIAL NEEDS	DISTRIBUTION SOC. CHANGE PERS. CHANGE
A1.2 **ORGANISATION**	STRUCTURE MANAGEMENT WORKFORCE	PLANNING EXECUTION QUALITY	PERSONNEL QUALITY OUTCOMES
A1.3 **CONSUMERS**	NEEDS ACCESS UTILISATION	CHOICE EXPECTATIONS OUTCOMES	NEEDS EXPECTATIONS HEALTH GAIN

Health behaviour

A health promotion and health education intervention should take into account the type of behaviour that it aims to influence. One can, in general, differentiate two types of behaviour:

- *normative behaviour*: also known as 'normal' behaviour because it is defined by the norms or social expectations within a social group and is related to the specific status/role of an individual within that system;

- *decision-making*: relates to choices an individual will have to make in the absence of any social expectations of norms that could serve as guidance for the relevant behaviour based on selection among alternatives.

Normative behaviour

Within a social system, norms define the expected behaviour of individuals according to their status/role in that system. The characteristics of such a role are:

- exemption of social responsibilities;
- dependency on the health care system;
- motivation to collaborate with the system; compliance with the advice and prescriptions received from the medical system.

In health terms three roles can be differentiated: 'healthy role', 'at-risk role' and 'sick-role'. Each of these roles can be differentiated according to the processes of acquisition, maintenance and relinquishment of such a role:

- *the 'healthy role'* - this role is rarely mentioned because it is related to the state of health of an individual that in theory is the predominant state during a person's lifetime; because of this, there are no specific processes associated with its acquisition and maintenance; there are, however, situations where such a role needs to be confirmed by a socially recognised legitimising agent, as for example in applying for insurance, loans, driving licences and some specialised jobs;

- *the 'at-risk role'* - this role is associated with the status of an individual in a society who is recognised as being at higher than average risk from a certain health threat or disease; the role is acquired by an individual, in the course of becoming aware of the increased risk, validating this knowledge through the social as well as professional health care system; and having the role formalised in the light of a recognised legitimising activity or status, as in the case of a pregnant woman smoking, a driver drinking alcohol, or a worker not wearing the necessary protective clothing;

- *the 'sick-role'* - when a person translates awareness of a symptom into an action by seeking medical advice, he/she will acquire a sick-role; the role is acquired by awareness of a symptom, exploration of the social environment and seeking medical help; the acquisition as well as relinquishment of such a role will be confirmed by a legitimising agent who is a member of the medical profession; such a role is associated with any of a number of diseases and is characterised by the fact that the patient is not held responsible for the acquisition of such a role as long as he/she complies with the medical treatment and co-operates with the medical profession.

Normative behaviour will be influenced by two factors: the existence of a relevant norm and the type of individual behaviour. There are situations in which medical knowledge raises the issue of a new health threat or disease and society has not as yet had time to formalise relevant norms. A good example of such a case was the discovery of the association of smoking during pregnancy with negative effects on the unborn child. There was quite a time gap between the discovery of this association and the emergence of the social norm for pregnant women not to smoke, supported by appropriate medical and social sanctions. From an individual point of view, normative health behaviour can be classified as 'conformist' or 'deviant' with a middle category of 'variant', where the behaviour does not break the rules set by the norm but varies within socially acceptable margins.

Decision-making

A wide range of behaviour is not strongly regulated by norms and depends on individual decisions and choices. The decision-making process can be described by the following steps:

- *choice among alternatives* - a person can be aware of a number of possible alternatives related to a certain behaviour or action and will evaluate them; the evaluation can be based on efforts to maximise gain or minimise loss, attractiveness, symbolic value, etc;

- *taking action* - once a choice has been made it can either be to undertake or not to undertake an action;

- *commitment* - in the case of a positive decision a commitment to an action will follow; this commitment is characterised by cognitive dissonance which has to be resolved;

- *confirmation* - once the dissonance is resolved continuous action will follow.

In health terms, this process can be affected by existing attitudes towards the disease or the treatment. It may also be dependent on the level of fear which may influence the choices made.

Methods of intervention

The definition of objectives will be closely related to and conditioned by the available methods of intervention (see Baric, 1990, Module 1, pp.123-250). In general terms these can be classified as:

- *the personal approach*, which includes the learning and communication processes, socialisation, interviews and counselling;

- *the group approach*, which includes working with existing groups or creating new groups; and can be differentiated according to size into small or large groups, and according to type into family-, adolescent-, peer-, and work-groups, committees, problem-solving and creative groups, T-groups, therapy groups and self-help groups; behaviour modification clinics also represent a specific type of small groups;

- *the community approach*, which includes community organisation and community development processes; one form of this approach is represented by the 'healthy city' movement, which is based on community participation and is also relevant to work in different settings such as 'health promoting' schools, hospitals, general practices, enterprises, families, etc.

- *the mass-media approach*, which includes the transmission of information and advertising; it provides the background to the decision-making process and perpetuates or influences the change of social norms.

Linking objectives and methods

As we have seen, a health promotion and health education intervention will usually have a number of aims and each of these aims will have a number of objectives, which will define in general terms how each particular aim is to be achieved. Each objective may employ one or more of available methods.

The task of any assessment of health promotion and health education interventions is first to establish the links between the aims and their related objectives, as well as finding justification for employing specific methods as a part of these objectives. The usual way of establishing these links will be to examine the theoretical background associated with each objective and method and to draw on empirical evidence related to the existing use of such methods in relation to the defined objectives.

Each of the described general methodological approaches given below will have some advantages and some disadvantages:

- *the individual approach* - the advantage is that this is based on differential diagnosis (see p.114) and will, therefore, be specific to the needs of the individuals in question; the disadvantage is that it readily lends itself to an assessment of individual needs carried out by amateurs or non-professionals, with implicit danger for the recipient;

- *group work* - the advantages of such an approach lies in providing the possibility for members of a group to transform their attitudes towards a problem or a procedure; the disadvantages lie in the danger of creating dependency and group feeling in situations where this would not be appropriate;

- *community participation* - the advantage of this approach is that it requires the active participation of the community members, who are expected to take over the responsibility for their activities; the disadvantage lies in the attempt to apply this approach in situations where there is no 'community', with the result that the agents attempt to create an artificial 'community' so that they can apply this approach;

- *mass media* - the advantage in using mass media is that it is possible to reach simultaneously a large proportion of a population, which is the main precondition for the change of norms; the disadvantage is the danger that the type of information promoted will not be appropriate for all those exposed to the information.

In this section, we have looked at aims, objectives and methods and their interrelationships. They are the basis for health promotion and health education action. It is clear also that any evaluation of health promotion and health education activities will have as a first step to take into account the suitability of selected objectives for the achievement of set aims, and the appropriateness of the chosen methods for the achievement of the set objectives.

INDICATORS

Few topics or concepts in health promotion and health education are directly observable. To work with them, the practitioner needs identifiable and measurable correlates, in the form of indicators. To design indicators, relevant concepts should be clearly defined in terms of their constituent parts. They should then be translated into indicators, enabling the collection and the analysis of appropriate data. When a concept, such as competence, is a complex one, it is not possible to rely on a single indicator, so that a set of indicators is necessary. This indicator set will cover a number of relevant domains of investigation, each of which will include the criteria used for measurement and the instruments designed for the collection of data. This can be illustrated by the following diagram:

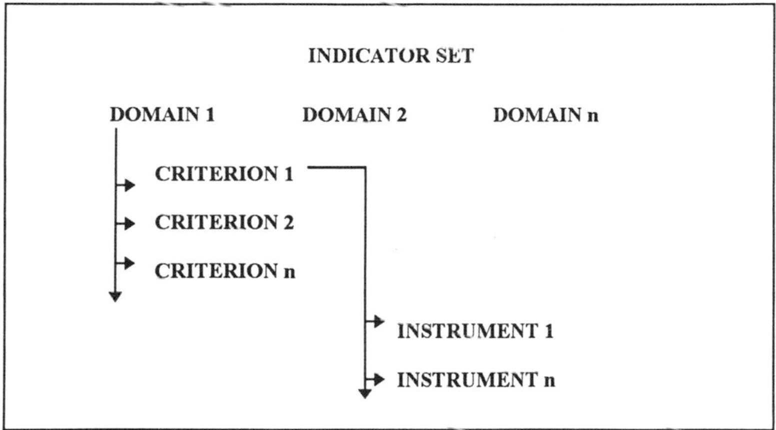

The domains of such an indicator set include problem areas derived from the conceptual framework used in designing a study. The criteria applied for each domain relate to the items used in defining the desired attributes which form the basis of the study.

Choosing indicators

What are indicators?

One can loosely describe indicators as variables, which can be used to design or to measure the success or failure of a programme. They should be linked to objectives, which in turn are linked to the aims; they should be measurable and should represent a valid and reliable way of assessing the various aspects of a programme.

'Validity' of an indicator refers to the fact that the indicator should measure what is intended to be measured; 'reliability' of an indicator implies that the repeated use of the indicator will produce the same results and not be influenced by the person who administers it.

Some indicators are in the form of 'hard data', such as the height of a person, which can be measured in metres. A metre as an indicator is universally standardised and has a prototype deposited in Paris, which is used to assess the accuracy of any metric tape measure. When using such a measure it is not necessary to test for validity and reliability, since it corresponds to an accepted prototype.

On the other hand, there are indicators that represent theoretical constructs, which are only measurable by 'soft data'. They need to be defined and tested for validity and reliability. For example, the indicator used for the measurement of 'competence' will require to be defined in terms of what the researcher means by competence and will have to be tested for validity and reliability.

Such indicators may take on different forms, one of which could be an 'opinion poll', if it is assumed that finding out about opinions will 'indicate' the success or failure of an objective in achieving a set aim (goal).

Indices and scales

Noack and Abelin (1987) describe the conceptual and methodological aspects of the measurement of health, which could be used for any assessment of health promotion and health education activities. The range of phenomena that may be measured is very wide and may include both subjective and objective factors and processes as well as continuous and discrete variables.

In this context, it is important to differentiate between the various types of scales available which include the following:

- *nominal scale* - arranges items (objects, persons, attributes, responses, etc.) into a set of unordered and mutually exclusive categories; these may include nationality, region, place of birth or method of intervention; an arbitrary value is assigned to each category;

- *ordinal scale* - classifies items into ordered qualitative categories; it can include social class, which may then be sub-divided; it can also include psychological variables such as subjectively perceived health gain, or clinical variables such as a medically defined severity of a disease; values are generally assigned to express an increase in quality of an attribute; the differences are in qualitative order and do not represent distances between the assigned levels;

- *interval scale* - orders attributes or variables with a defined distance between each category; this distance is standardised; an example is the measurement of temperature in degrees;

- *ratio scale* - is an interval scale with a specific starting point; this allows for comparative measurement because it enables a decision to be made about the relative increase of one category as compared with another; an example of this is the measurement of height, weight, blood count, etc.

The different character of scales is important if they are used for evaluating a health promotion and health education intervention, which may include a number of activities, both psychological and medical. The psychological variables will use nominal or ordinal scales, whereas the medical variables will probably be interval or ratio scales. The different kind of information obtained will have to be taken into consideration when analysing the outcomes of such an enquiry.

When designing scales it is necessary to take into account their validity, accuracy, precision, reliability, economy and acceptability:

- *validity* - is a measure of how far an instrument actually measures what is intended;

- *accuracy* - is the degree to which a measurement reflects a true value;

- *precision* - may not always be required and some events may be recorded in composite categories (an age category as compared with an exact age);

- *reliability* - represents the degree to which a measurement is constant, which implies that it will give the same result if repeated;

- *economy* - represents the cost effectiveness of a measure, which implies that the type of measurement applied should be within the available resources;

- *acceptability* - implies that the indicators used will be acceptable to the respondents and will in no way infringe their rights or integrity; they should also meet the requirements of the planned research, i.e. be acceptable in scientific terms.

As discussed earlier, it is important to realise that the measurement of any health promotion and health education intervention usually deals with theoretical constructs that represent complex categories of variables. In terms of the complexity, it is possible to differentiate between:

- *health statistics* - which are discrete measurements of certain specific attributes such as height, weight, etc.;

- *health indicators* - which are composed of a number of health statistics and provide approximate measurements of an event, such as a survival rate, which is composed of infant and maternal mortality rates, or 'healthfulness' which is composed of a number of most commonly reported diseases in a population;

- *health indices* - which represent an even more complex multi-dimensional measurement or scale and are often composed of several health indicators, such the 'disparity reduction rate', which is composed of infant mortality rate, life expectancy at one year old and the illiteracy rate of a given country or population group.

A distinction may be drawn between scales and indices (Babbie, 1989). According to Babbie, an index is constructed through the simple accumulation of scores assigned to individual attributes; a scale on the other hand is constructed through the assignment of scores to patterns of attributes and thus reflects a structure of interconnectedness or intensity that may exist among attributes. Thus, an index for example could be composed of a number of activities related to health and a person is allocated a score according to the number of activities he/she participates in. The scale would rank these activities in an order of intensity and a person would be scored according to whether he/she participates in the most or least heavily weighted activities.

Babbie gives a very good description of the process involved in constructing an index and deals with item selection, the relationships between items, the difference between cause and effect indicators, multi-variate relationships among items, as well as index scoring and validation.

There are a number of available indices and scales, which provide examples of the measurement principles and can be adjusted to specific projects.

One example is the *Likert-type scale*. It is a composite measure and defines the intensity structure among the items. It consists of statements to which the respondent replies choosing a point on the scale from "strongly agree - agree - undecided - disagree - strongly disagree". It is mainly used as a means of measuring attitudes and requires considerable preparation in the choice of statements used.

The semantic differential format is a variation of the Likert scale. Whereas the latter asks respondents to agree or disagree with a certain statement, the former asks them to choose between two opposite statements. Semantic differential exploration requires a careful selection of dimensions according to which a judgement should be made by the respondents. Once the dimension has been chosen it will be necessary to select two opposite statements which represent the extreme differences within the chosen dimension. Such opposite statements are 'good - bad', 'simple - complex', etc. The respondent is given an opportunity to record the intensity of feelings about each of the two opposite statements in terms of, for example, 'very much - somewhat - neither - somewhat - very much'.

A *Bogardus Social Distance Scale* uses a 'funnel' technique and provides the respondents with a selection of statements which differ in intensity from mild to extreme. The respondent is supposed to agree or disagree with each statement and is scored accordingly.

The *Thurstone-type scale* attempts to develop a format for generating groups of indicators with some shared empirical structure. It consists of a range of statements ordered in a specific way and the respondent is required to choose the appropriate statement. For example, a scale could include the following statements: "I like teaching so much I'd pay to do it", I don't mind teaching but it is only a job", "Teaching is pretty boring", "I dislike teaching so much that I have to force myself to go to work". The choice of the statements to be included in such a scale is validated by 'judges' who are required to sort them according to relevance and this ordering is then used to interpret the outcomes of applying such a scale to a population.

The *Guttman scale* draws a distinction between the significance of items within the scale in terms of their acceptability to the respondent. For example, this scale can be used for measuring the scientific orientation of students by asking them to answer questions in three domains: reading preference, ultimate interest and teaching role. The first one could be judged as the easiest to answer, whereas the latter two would require a certain degree of commitment expressed by the choice.

Such scales and indicators represent a format within which an enquiry can be carried out. Using standard scales or indices is one option, but it is also necessary to design appropriate instruments for each specific study. There are copyright scales and indicators, which have been produced and tested commercially and are now available for use by experts who have been specially trained in their use. These include ready-made tests for intelligence (IQ tests) or other psychological attributes.

Research indicators

Strauss and Corbin (1990, p.253) provide a set of criteria (indicators) for assessing a research project which could be useful for anyone involved in the assessment and measurement of health promotion and health education activities, using standard research methodology:

- How was the original sample selected? On what grounds?

- What major categories emerged?

- What were some of the events, incidents, actions and so on (as indicators) that pointed to some of these major categories?

- On the basis of what categories did theoretical sampling proceed? How did theoretical formulations guide some of the data collection? After the theoretical sampling was done, how representative did these categories prove to be?

- What were some of the hypotheses pertaining to conceptual relations among categories, and on what grounds were they formulated and tested?

- Were there instances when hypotheses did not hold up against what was actually seen? How were these discrepancies counted for? How did they affect the hypotheses?

- How and why was the core category selected? Was this collection sudden or gradual, difficult or easy? On what grounds were the final analytic decisions made?

These indicators could provide useful guidelines for anyone who wants to learn more about how a research or evaluation project was conducted. They are applicable to quantitative as well as qualitative research and are basically concerned with judging the coherence of the theories on which a study is based. Do the theoretical findings seem significant and to what extent?

In addition to these suggestions, any assessment of a health promotion and health education project will need to use other indicators related to the aims and objectives of a specific study and to the agreed criteria for the assessment of success or failure.

Needs indicators

Every intervention begins with a consideration of the client's needs. Doyal and Gough (1991) discuss the theoretical issues of defining and measuring 'needs', and describe the philosophical aspects of differentiating 'needs' from 'wants' and using 'satisfiers' as ways of measuring them. Satisfiers represent the factors which contribute to the satisfaction of needs or wants.

There is a long history of attempts to measure needs and need satisfaction. In the past, this has been closely associated with the determination of the Gross Domestic Product (GDP). This measure has two problems, one of which is that it leaves out large groups of population (agricultural workers and women in domestic occupations) and the other is that the amount of income does not accurately describe the level of need satisfaction, and does not differentiate between satisfiers and luxuries or welfare needs between groups and within families.

Consequently, efforts have been made to find more appropriate measures such as 'level of living', which is associated with need satisfaction in various areas of life. Other measures have differentiated between objective welfare and subjective happiness and a distinction has been drawn between three fundamental dimensions of objective wellbeing: having, loving and being (Galtung, 1982).

The measurement of needs has had to face the problem of developing social indicators concerned with different standards of living in different countries, in particular the Third World. The existence of relative and even absolute poverty in some of these countries has produced a very specific 'basic needs approach' which is not reflected in the changes in the GDP. This has contributed to attempts to develop a 'basic needs' approach, involving further development of social indicators, which were an important issue until the 1980s, when comprehensive planning lost its dominance in policy. Galtung (1980) accepts that there are basic human needs, although 'perverted' and 'contaminated' by Western conceptions. He suggests the development of alternative non-western indicators.

Basic individual needs for physical health and autonomy can be accepted as universal, although the various satisfiers will be culturally defined. Sen (1984) has developed a concept of wellbeing that distinguishes between a commodity and its set of characteristics or desirable properties, which is based on the work of Lancaster (1966). Sen quotes an example of a meal which can have a number of functions including satisfying hunger, creating an opportunity for social contact and providing a centre for family life. On the other hand, there are various commodities which can share a common function, as in the case of many types of foods which can satisfy hunger. He also distinguishes between the commodities and individual freedom of choice (functioning) in what to do with such commodities, and includes the state of mind of a person, such as happiness and desire fulfilment.

Doyal and Gough (1991) differentiate between universal and specific satisfiers and identify universal satisfiers with intermediate needs. The authors recommend that the measurement of need satisfaction should be carried out on the level of basic needs, intermediate needs, and the measurement of the consumption of specific satisfiers.

The measurement of basic need-satisfaction draws a distinction between physical health and autonomy. Physical health includes components and indicators for survival chances (life expectancy at various ages, age specific mortality rates), and for the existence of physical ill health (prevalence of disability, children's developmental deficiencies, suffering from serious pain and morbidity rates for various diseases). Under autonomy, are included mental disorder (prevalence of severe psychotic, depressive and other mental illnesses), cognitive deprivation (lack of culturally relevant knowledge, illiteracy, lack of attainment in mathematics, science and other near universal basic skills, absence of skill in world language), and opportunities for economic activity (unemployment, lack of free time).

The measurement of intermediate needs includes: "nutritious food and clean water; protective housing; non-hazardous work environment; non-hazardous physical environment; appropriate health care; security in childhood; significant primary relationships; physical and economic security; appropriate education; safe birth control and child bearing" (page 157-158). These intermediate needs represent a general contribution to physical health and autonomy. They should, however, be interpreted according to human differences, for example, women will have some additional needs such as safe birth control and support in child bearing.

The measurement of the consumption of specific satisfiers in a particular social context is used to establish which satisfiers represent necessities in a particular place and time. This kind of measurement is being used by researchers into poverty and also for the purpose of social auditing.

There have been numerous indicators of needs developed by different individuals and institutions, some of which are still in use, as for example, the work done by the UN Research Institute of Social Development, those used in the British Government's publication "Social Trends", OECD, International Labour Organisation, the World Bank and others.

The Department of Health Document "On the State of the Public Health" (HMSO, 1992) is more relevant to the development of indicators related to needs, as a basis for health promotion and health education activities. It devotes a chapter to the assessment of needs, effectiveness and outcomes and quotes a number of projects initiated by the Department of Health.

During 1991, the NHS Management Executive developed a number of initiatives to assist DHAs with the assessment of health care needs. It published "Assessing Health Care Needs", in which the needs were defined as "the population's ability to benefit from health care" and identifies the approaches which DHAs could use to measure health care needs in their own areas. It recommended three areas of enquiry: the epidemiological, the comparative and the corporate. The epidemiological approach involves the measurement of the distribution of diseases and the effectiveness of care, as well as the available care settings; the comparative approach looks at the quality and uptake of services between districts; the corporate approach synthesises the views of DHAs, GPs, provider units, local people, national agencies, national and regional guidance and others.

This was followed by the DHAs' commissioning a series of epidemiological studies of needs in their own areas. This pioneered the epidemiological method used for the need assessment which was followed by other DHAs. The first two studies covered diabetes mellitus and hip and knee replacement surgery.

The DHA project also commissioned a networking centre to enable DHA Public Health Departments to share their experiences in this field. The centre is based at the University of Birmingham, Institute of Public and Environmental Health. It is collecting information from DHAs and serves as a source of information about these activities.

In 1991, the Clinical Standards Advisory Group (CSAG) was established, composed of the members of the medical, nursing and dental royal colleges and faculties. Its aim was to advise on standards of clinical care, access to and availability of services.

In the same year, the DoH commissioned nine bulletins on the effectiveness of various health care interventions from a consortium of the Leeds School of Public Health, The Centre for Health Economics at York University and the Royal College of

Physician's Research Unit. They provide a critical assessment of existing literature on health care interventions.

In 1992, the Faculty of Public Health Medicine, was commissioned by the DoH to undertake a feasibility study of a number of proposed outcome indicators, which have subsequently been published by the DoH.

Within the DoH a joint Policy Group-Management Executive has been established to work on the development and application of health outcome assessments.

A joint DoH/NHS/Professional Expert Advisory Group has also been established to review progress on the work on health outcomes assessment and to advise on the funding of relevant research projects.

Overall, the work on measuring needs has been more extensive than satisfying because of the difficulty in defining the needs, their social and cultural characteristics, not to mention the problems in objective measurement even in cases where there is an agreement as to what the needs are. It should, however, be noted that the DoH has been investing considerable resources in developing indicators and in supporting studies related to need assessment in the UK.

Quality of life indicators

The use of the concept of 'quality of life' as a measure of change in many different fields has existed for a number of years. It has met with considerable criticism because of the subjective and objective differences in defining optimal as compared to minimal and inadequate quality of life.

So far there has been no use of 'quality of life' as an indicator for the measurement of success or failure of a health promotion and health education programme, although it would seem desirable. Hunt and McKenna (1992) give a number of reasons for the lack of success in using 'quality of life' as a practical indicator for any introduced changes:

- there is no agreed definition of quality of life; and there are no agreed indicators for measuring it;

- there is no conceptual basis for theoretical models which link quality of life to health interventions;

- the existing instruments have not been specifically designed to measure this variable;

- the existing descriptions do not include the social dimension;

- there is a tendency to use interchangeably 'quality of life' and 'quality of care'.

There have, however, been various attempts to use the concept of quality of life for the measurement of the provision of health care. A special variant of this approach is the measurement of 'quality-adjusted life years' (QALY). This has been used in the UK mainly in the field of disability and distress, using a matrix of features developed by Rosser (1972, 1978).

Hunt and McKenna have described the way this concept has been operationalised in the form of a QALY Toolkit (1988) and Euroqol (1990).

The concept of quality of life has not so far been used as an indicator in measuring health promotion and health education interventions. From the existing literature it is possible to conclude that this concept, although very attractive, cannot be successfully used in practice without further research and testing.

Social indicators

The measurement related to the health promotional aspects of an intervention dealing with populations needs to use social indicators. Carley (1981) examines the nature and problems of social measurement and social indicators, which need to be understood in applying them to any social or health policy.

The 'social indicators movement' developed as a consequence of the perceived success of the economic indicators used by economic policy makers. These indicators, such as the gross national product (GNP) were, however, criticised for not reflecting the social aspects of economic policies, which resulted in the need for the development of social indicators. This interest in the development of social indicators was shared by many countries and many institutions. A number of publications reported on the progress and the outcomes of this work, which was undertaken by a number of governmental bodies and research foundations

The pioneers of the movement associated with the development of social indicators had high hopes of the contribution they would make to decisions of policy makers. At present this enthusiasm has waned, since increasing information about social problems did not in fact provide the political decision-makers with ready-made solutions to these problems, so the social indicators to measure success were less relevant than anticipated.

The current lack of interest in social indicators, owing to expectation not being matched by grounding in social theory, means that pressure is put on researchers to provide, ad hoc, appropriate social indicators. The seriousness of decisions supposed to be based on social indicators is not in general matched by the quality of such indicators. Social indicators are nevertheless very important for health promotion and health education, so the extent of their usefulness needs to be explored.

According to Carlisle (1972), social indicators can be defined as "the operational definition or part of the operational definition of any one of the concepts central to the generation of an information system descriptive of the social system".

Carlisle differentiates the following types of indicators according to their policy use:

- *informative indicators* - which are intended to describe the social system and the changes taking place within it;

- *predictive indicators* - which are informative indicators fitting into explicit formal models of sub-systems of a social system;

- *problem-oriented indicators* - which point towards policy situations and actions on specific social problems;

- *programme evaluation indicators* - which are operationalised policy goals used to monitor the progress and effectiveness of particular policies.

One of the main problems encountered by those who were trying to develop social indicators was to attempt to find new ways to measure important but hard to quantify information in an accurate numerical way. A special case in point is the measurement of quality of life already discussed which became a fashionable political concept and prompted a number of definitions and measurements. After many attempts and disappointments, it became obvious that to quantify quality of life researchers must go beyond objective outputs and measure the reality in which people live, which will depend on objective conditions, as well as on subjective evaluation of those conditions.

More recently, research has been concerned with the development of systems of social indicators. The intention has been to bring together a number of indicators into a system, such as in the measurement of health status and welfare. For example, the Organisation for Economic Cooperation and Development (OECD, 1988) used the social goal approach in its programme to achieve standardised definitions of the social goal areas for which systematic indicators are needed by their member governments. The OECD developed eight goal areas based on twenty four fundamental social concerns. One such goal area is 'health'. It includes the measurement of the following concerns:

- the probability of a healthy life through all stages of the life cycle;
- healthfulness of life;
- the impact of health impairments on individuals;
- the quality of health care in terms of reducing pain and restoring capabilities;
- the extent of universal distribution in the delivery of health care.

The main effect of social indicators has been to supplement existing national data with socially oriented information. This has resulted in national social reports, one of which is 'Social Trends', published in the UK by the government statistical service. It includes information on the following topics:

- population
- households and families
- social groups
- education
- employment
- income and wealth
- resource and expenditure
- health and public safety
- housing
- environment and transport communications
- leisure
- participation
- law enforcement.

Other countries produce similar documentation, although with some differences in the categories for which the data are collected.

Although the hopes of the social indicators movement were not achieved, they are still useful tools. Nevertheless, it is necessary to beware of a number of political and bureaucratic constraints on the use of social indicators in policy making, including those associated with non-use, misuse, false quantification, value judgements and 'value weighting', which is an attempt to attach social values to quantitative data in policy analysis as an expression of preferences by politicians, experts or some population group.

Health indicators

In 1981, WHO Regional Office for the Eastern Mediterranean (EMRO) published a report on the basic health indicators used in assessing the existing health services in a number of countries in that Region.

The indicators included the following data:

- name of the country;
- total population;
- total area;
- overall population density;
- average annual rate of increase;
- general and total fertility rates;
- crude birth rates;
- percentage of population below 5 and below 15 years of age;
- dependency ratio;
- crude death rate;
- percentage mortality below 5 years;
- death rate below 5 years;
- infant mortality rate;
- child mortality rate (1-4 years);
- proportional mortality for infectious and parasitic diseases;
- maternal mortality rate;
- life expectancy at birth;
- per capita calorie supply;
- percentage fully immunised by the age of 12 months;
- number of schools of medicine;
- rate of physicians per 10,000 population;
- rate of nurses and midwives per 10,000 population;
- total nursing/midwifery personnel;
- total number of hospital beds;
- health expenditure as a percentage of the total government expenditure;
- per capita expenditure on health;
- percentage of urban population;
- percentage of urban and rural population with access to safe water;
- percentage illiteracy rate (6 years and over);
- school enrolment ratio (first and second level);

- GDP : percentage from agriculture and fishing; mining and quarrying; manufacturing industry;
- per capita GNP (in dollars);
- per capita national income (in dollars).

The general fertility rate was calculated as the number of all live births in a given year, per thousand women, aged 15-49 years.

The total fertility rate was calculated for a given year as the average number of children that would be born alive to a woman during her life time if she were to pass through all her childbearing years experiencing the age-specific fertility rates in that year.

The dependency ratio was calculated as the population in ages "below 15 years" and "65 years plus" per thousand population aged 15-64 years.

The school enrolment ratio was calculated as the ratio of the total enrolled at each school level of the population in a specific age group corresponding to that school level.

Measurement using health indicators is useful for obtaining a general picture of the available health and educational services in a country. It, does not, however, appear to be of use for the measurement of health promotion and health education activities unless a more detailed and direct measurement of the contribution of health promotion and health education services to the state of health in that country of that population can be achieved.

A different approach to measuring health is represented by the Nottingham Health Profile - NHP (Hunt, 1988), which is mainly concerned with the subjective perception of health as compared with the traditional medical model of the 'objective' assessment of a person's health state. The concept of health is difficult to define in a measurable way and most indicators used to measure it treat health as absence of illness. The NHP has been constructed with the aim of being applicable to people presenting a wide range of conditions, age groups and socio-economic levels so that it can be administered to a wide population through a postal enquiry.

The NHP is based on the assumption that the following 6 areas of inquiry will be acceptable indicators for the subjective perception of health:

- energy
- emotional reactions
- pain
- physical mobility
- sleep social isolation

The construction of the questionnaire included collecting over 2000 statements from people about their feelings concerning their health. The statements were sorted and classified to meet the preconditions for designing the instrument. Because the answers referred to problems of differing severity, a weighting system was developed and applied to the answers received. Reliability, which means that similar answers will be received by different investigators asking the same question, showed a higher level for answers to questions about severe experiences as compared with less severe experiences. The questionnaire was also tested for validity and was shown to be sensitive enough to differentiate between elderly people who do not consult the general practitioner, those who are physiologically fit and those with chronic disease. In general, however, the authors of the NHP came to the conclusion that the items included in the questionnaire did not measure the health status but rather felt distress which may be a consequence of health problems but may equally be the result of adverse living conditions.

The NHP using subjective indicators is the only instrument of that form developed so far in Europe and has attracted the interest of a number of other countries. The possibility of translating it into other languages for use in other cultures has been raised. This approach to measurement could be of special interest for health promotion and health education for a number of reasons:

- it allows people to express themselves in familiar concepts and language;
- they can articulate their own needs instead of having them defined by professionals;
- the expression of subjective experiences includes mental, physical as well as social factors;
- they elucidate the relationship between the way people feel, their health-related behaviour and the social and physical environment in which they live; this implies the necessity for a much wider approach in health promotion and health education;
- these indicators show how people feel and should, therefore, be closely related to people's behaviour.

The conclusion based on the existing experience of applying subjective indicators is, that such approaches can make an important contribution to the evaluation of health promotion and health education .

HFA 2000 indicators

The concept of Health For All by the Year 2000 introduced by WHO in 1978 has attracted a lot of attention and criticism, but it is still surviving and governments are still committed to its achievement. The consequence of this has been the responsibility of WHO (1980) to develop indicators for monitoring progress towards the achievement of HFA 2000 (see Appendix 1 for a copy of the document). The purpose of these indicators has been to enable the Member States to establish the background information about the health of their populations, to develop strategies for attainment of health and to monitor the progress towards the achievement of this aim.

In summary, the indicators suggested by WHO include the following categories:

- health policy indicators
  - political indicators
  - resource allocation
  - degree of equity of distribution
  - community involvement
  - organisational framework and managerial process
  - international political commitment

- social and economic indicators
  - rate of population increase
  - gross national product or gross domestic product
  - income distribution
  - work conditions
  - adult literacy rate
  - housing
  - food availability

- indicators of the provision of health care
  - availability
  - physical accessibility
  - economic and cultural accessibility
  - utilisation of services
  - quality of care

- coverage by primary health care
    - information and education concerning health
    - promotion of food availability and proper nutrition
    - water and sanitation
    - maternal and child health
    - immunisation
    - prevention and control of endemic diseases
    - treatment of common diseases and injuries
    - provision of essential drugs
    - coverage by the referral system
    - manpower

- basic health status indicators
    - nutritional status and psycho-social development
    - infant mortality rate
    - child mortality rate
    - under-five mortality rate
    - life expectancy at a given age
    - maternal mortality rate
    - disease specific mortality
    - morbidity
    - disability
    - social and mental wellbeing.

The WHO document lists the sources of health indicator data as follows:

- vital events registers
- population and housing censuses
- routine health service records
- epidemiological surveillance
- sample surveys
- disease registers
- nutritional indicators
- indicators based on births and deaths

- disease-specific indicators based on lay reporting
- estimation of demographic indicators based on incomplete data.

The governments have undertaken the commitment to monitor and evaluate the progression towards the achievement of HFA 2000 goals and assess the outcomes. They are expected to publish regular reports and exchange information with other countries.

DATA COLLECTION

The team

In the collection of data for evaluation a number of people are usually involved and they should work as a team. One can envisage the following composition of such a team according to the role each member of the team will play.

The director of the study, should have sufficient background in health promotion and health education, and knowledge and awareness of research methods, to be able to instruct and help other members of the team. His/her tasks should include:

- liaison with those commissioning the research;
- detailed study or design of the project document, possibly after exploratory study;
- briefing of other members of the team;
- design of instruments for questionnaire;
- choice of the pilot area, the subjects and the timing of the investigation;
- supervision of the field work;
- setting up and supervision of the coding of questionnaires and supervising the transfer of the coding on to the coding sheet or computer program;

- supervising the analysing of data;
- using statistical tests;
- writing the report;
- repeating the process for the full study;
- presentation of results.

Investigator(s), researchers carry out the field work. There may be one investigator or a number may be necessary, chosen according to their background. At least one investigator should have local knowledge of the topic which is being evaluated. Depending on the scope, it is possible that one capable investigator could carry out the whole exercise of data collection.

Coders who should be able to code the answers on each questionnaire and transfer them onto coding sheets. These entries are then transferred onto a computer for further analysis.

The method

There are various ways to go about collecting data for a study. They include:

Survey

A survey represents any method of data collection based on asking a set of questions, classifying and coding the answers, analysing them and drawing inferences. There are a number of types of survey:

- *exploratory survey*, which is aimed at exploring the characteristics of the problem without any expectations of finding solutions at this stage; this exploration can be concerned with finding out the scope of the problem, its characteristics, its distribution, or some difficulties and barriers which could endanger such a study;

- *pilot survey*, which is based on the main assumptions of the main study, but aims at finding out whether such a study will be feasible and what resources will be needed; it is mainly concerned with the exploration of suitable methods and approaches for the main study; its findings are fed back into the design of the main survey;

- *main survey*, which is based on the conceptualisation of the study, and uses pre-tested instruments, established indicators, chosen criteria and pre-tested instruments.

As was stated earlier, the survey is the most common approach to be used if one wants to find out specific and identifiable information from a population. The main reasons for carrying out a survey are:

- establishing differences, based on the assumption in health promotion and health education that different outcomes could be due to differences in the characteristics of the subjects, in their behaviour/actions, in the state of their health or in their exposure to risk factors;

- confirming causality, which tries to establish the cause-effect relationship between certain factors;

- drawing inferences on the basis of the data collected; this will include results from experiments, generalisation of findings, and/or predictability of outcomes.

Comparative survey

Where there is a need to compare two populations, two approaches, two methods or two kinds of instruments, a comparative survey can be conducted on two comparable population samples; the analysis of findings may indicate the advantages of one over the other in different ways and may indicate the best way of approaching the solution of a problem.

Double-blind trial

To be sure that unconscious bias does not affect the study design it is usual to conduct a double-blind trial; this includes two comparable populations between which two approaches or interventions are randomly distributed, without knowledge on the part of the investigators; objectivity is thus assured and either intentional or unconscious bias are eliminated.

Experiment

Whereas social research is usually conducted in a situation where the investigators cannot control the external factors, an experiment is conducted in a 'laboratory' situation where all the external factors are eliminated; this ensures that the intervention results are caused by the intervention agent and are not a result of some contaminating variable.

Case study

The case study approach is used in situations where there is no need for generalisation to a whole population and an issue needs to be explored holistically in one instance; it can include an institution (hospital), a group (family) or an individual; an in-depth method of collecting information is used and the findings are usually presented in a descriptive way.

Intervention study

There are occasions when the study is not so much concerned with finding out what exists, but is more concerned with what will happen if an intervention takes place; this implies that an intervention is planned and executed and the outcome evaluated.

Evaluative studies

In addition to identifying the outcomes of an intervention which includes an evaluation, there may be evaluative studies to find out what happened as a result of some other interventions perhaps carried out without a proper study design. Such evaluation of other people's interventions may look at the intervention as a whole, or may be limited to evaluating a part of it (conceptual model, methods, instruments etc.); it is also possible to explore the evaluation approaches included in a number of studies; this is an evaluation of evaluations, known as 'meta evaluation'.

Participant observation studies

There are situations where a researcher enters into a new situation or location and wants to discover the main elements, without having a specific research design or hypothesis on which to base the study; the observer becomes immersed in the situation and tries not to disturb the situation too markedly, or at least to observe what happens when he/she does. This is likely to lead to a descriptive qualitative report, and is particularly useful in the early stages of a systems analysis. It is also characteristic of ethnographic field work.

The study population

The term 'population' in research language can mean a group of people, but also a group of institutions, events, books in a library, etc. The term is used in different ways: the reference population is the general population within which the event under study can take place; from this population the experimental population is chosen, and this forms the basis for choosing the sample population. It is usual to use a sample since it is not practical to carry out a study using the whole population which could be affected by the intervention.

The idea of choosing a sample is to reduce the number of questionnaires to be administered while not losing the representativeness of the answers and ensuring that the findings can be generalised to the whole population. For this reason care should be taken to make sure that the sample is an accurate reflection of the whole population from which it is taken.

There are a number of available sampling procedures, both non-random and random. The former must be used with particular caution in generalising.

Non-random sampling procedures

Non-random procedures include:

- *accidental (haphazard) sampling* - which will include the population immediately available to the researcher (a school class, one's own family or friends, etc.); it can be useful for pre-testing certain assumptions or some instrument and it will not be representative of any larger population group;

- *accidental quota sampling* - will improve the relevance of the observations related to the study topic, since the researcher will chose people according to some pre-selected set of criteria (e.g. in case of cervical cancer, it will be women,);

- *purposive sampling* - is the result of a researchers 'intuition' that some population will produce the best results; they will chose a 'typical' population to represent similar groups or institutions (a 'typical' rural general practice, a 'typical' school in a deprived area, etc.);

- *systematic matching sampling* - is useful if the researcher wants to match two populations or groups (male and female head teachers); although this type of sampling can be useful for certain studies, its results must be used with care.

Random sampling procedures

These methods include:

- *simple random sampling* - is the ideal way to achieve representativeness, although it is not always easy or even possible; it guarantees that each element (person, group, class, school, general practice, etc.) in the population will have an equal chance of being selected and that every possible combination of the specified number of elements has an equal chance of selection; since the mathematics of such a procedure are highly complicated and often not within the scope of a practical researcher, simpler methods, such as using random numbers, have been devised; this implies that each subject in a population is allocated a number, and by using a 'random number table', a set of relevant subjects are selected according to their numbers; this 'lottery' type of approach gives each subject theoretically an equal chance of being selected, thus doing away with introduced bias in the selection;

- *systematic sampling* - involves the selection of subjects from a population according to a predetermined interval (choosing every 10th person on a list, etc.); the interval is calculated by taking the total number in the population and dividing it by the desirable size of the sample (population of 1000 divided by the desirable sample size of 100 subjects will give an interval of 10); the critical step in this kind of sampling is to select the first subject, which in our example should be one of the first 10 subjects; this method provides a broadly acceptable approximation of the ideals of a simple random sampling method;

- *stratified random sampling* - a randomised version of quota sampling, which involves the selection of categories of a population; within each category the subjects are selected by a random method (for example, we select three types of schools, but then randomly select pupils from each school);

- *cluster sampling* - is useful when we are dealing with a very large and complex population; it includes random sampling in a number of stages; rather than enumerating the whole population, it can be divided into segments or clusters, and then a certain number of segments are chosen at random; the elements within each segment are enumerated and randomly selected to be included in the sample (national samples are drawn on a multi-stage cluster sample procedure).

The most common question related to sampling is how large should a sample be? This question is difficult to answer because the size of the sample will determine how accurately it represents the whole population from which it was chosen. If the population characteristics are fairly evenly distributed then a relatively small sample will be sufficient. If the population characteristics are very variable then a much larger sample will be necessary to ensure that all of them will be represented in the sample. There are a number of other factors which will determine the size of the sample, such as:

- if statistics are used in data analysis then the sample should be sufficiently large to allow for certain statistical processes to be carried out;

- the accuracy of the findings required will determine the sample size since no sample is identical with the population from which it was chosen and each sample, therefore, includes a certain degree of error; the acceptable level of error will determine the size of the sample;

- the number of questions and the complexity of the analysis will determine the size of the sample; if an evaluation includes a large number of variables then a larger number of subjects will be needed.

This handbook can only offer an appreciation of what is involved in survey sampling. There are many good text books that cover the issues and procedures in detail, or a researcher can take specific advice from a specialist.

The briefing procedure

If one uses investigators to carry out the survey it will be necessary to brief them about a number of issues:

Familiarity with the instruments

The investigators should be familiar with the instruments that they are expected to use in a survey, in terms of the way they should be completed, how far they should enter into discussion with respondents, and which comments they are allowed to make without prejudicing responses.

Gaining entrance

Once a population of, for example, households, has been chosen and the addresses distributed among the investigators the actual survey will start by visiting the respondents. Before actually knocking on the door of a family or an individual it will be useful to find out certain things about a community, such as: what the working hours are, i.e. when the husband can be expected to return from work and when the meal will take place; what the general pattern of work in a household is; when mothers spend most time with their babies; when they do their housework, go shopping, visit friends etc.

It should not be forgotten that an interview of this kind represents a relationship, the conditions of which should be negotiated. This implies that the respondent should know what the interview will be about and should have a possibility to decline to participate in it. It is important to bear in mind that the privacy of the respondent will be to a certain degree violated and that the respondent should have a feeling of some gain if and when allowing such an intrusion.

It helps if the investigator is recognised as an expert in the field of investigation and can provide certain help and advice in addition to gaining information. The respondent should also be reassured if necessary, about the confidentiality of the enquiry, anonymity of the respondent and the valid purpose of the study.

In short, the respondent must be reassured about the right to refuse certain information and the value the investigator will give to the answers provided, respecting the integrity of the respondent's person and family.

In some cases the gender of the investigator will be of importance. This can be relevant to gaining entrance into a home where the female respondent may be alone, when this is not culturally acceptable, or because of the topic of investigation, which may be offensive if presented by a male investigator to a woman or vice versa. In such cases, the appropriate gender of the investigator can be chosen or the investigator should be accompanied by a person of the appropriate gender.

The success of the interview will depend on the ability of the investigator to speak the language or use the terminology which the respondent understands. Sometimes the respondents are embarrassed by the poor conditions in which they live, in which case the interview should take place on neutral ground that ensures sufficient privacy.

Conducting interviews

Once acceptance has been achieved, the interview can take place. An important thing is the requirement is to maintain the continued interest of the respondent. Once this interest is lost, one should either try to rekindle it or, if this does not work, one should stop and arrange for another meeting.

The best guarantee of the maintenance of interest will be the feeling of reciprocity on the part of the respondent. It may, therefore, be important to encourage as many questions on the part of the respondent as there are answers expected from him/her. If there are no questions raised, this can be remedied by interrupting the interview from time to time and prompting for questions by the respondent, provided these do not invalidate the responses through prompting inappropriately.

There can be certain areas of enquiry (Baric, 1994) which can be taboo or too sensitive for the respondent to discuss. The general areas of enquiry can be negotiated at the beginning of the interview. It should not, however, be taken for granted that a general agreement at the start will ensure full participation to the end of the interview. The respondent may not understand what is involved, may change his/her mind halfway through the interview or simply become bored and lose interest. This may be awkward, since it may involve several visits and one should be able to judge the sincerity of excuses given for pulling out on the part of the respondent. If the excuse is not serious one can discuss the continuation, but if it is serious, too great a pressure may create a feeling of guilt or intimidation with the respondent, thus creating more damage than the exercise is worth.

It can be envisaged that during the study of an individual respondent or a family a certain degree of dependence is being created, especially if the respondent is made to feel inadequate due to ignorance, poor conditions or lack of available resources. It will be of the greatest importance to introduce each topic tactfully and limit it to the level of the respondent without indiscriminately asking questions for which the answers are obvious.

In the case of mothers with children, it could easily happen that a child will be present at the interview. The child should not be disregarded and the interviewer should not show impatience with any possible interruption, nor make the respondent feel that the interview is more important than the wellbeing of the child. If other members of the household are present, their contribution should be taken into account as well as the answers of the respondent, because they will influence those answers. In that case such additional contributions should be noted on the questionnaire.

If a return visit is planned, the interview should be conducted in such a way that it does not endanger the willingness of the respondent to be visited again.

Conclusion of interviews

It is as important to be as careful about the way an interview is concluded as about the way it is started and carried out. The visit of the interviewer could represent an exciting event, which will be discussed among friends and relatives. The impression made and the conduct of the investigator will be critically assessed and success of one interview will possibly affect other interviews, if a survey is being carried out in a close-knit community.

In addition to influencing the chances of success of the study as whole the conclusion of an interview will be of importance for each family or individual and great care should be taken that the respondent is not left with a feeling of inadequacy, guilt, shame, resentment or feeling that they have wasted time due to the way the interview is conducted or the behaviour of the interviewer. The respondent should be left with a feeling of satisfaction and sense of gain, stimulated sufficiently to be willing to participate in any future health education or health promotion programme.

At the end of the interview the respondent should again be reassured about the privacy and confidentiality of the information. No doubt should exist about the possibility of the information given being misused or discussed with unauthorised persons. There is sometimes doubt that the information could end in the wrong hands since most studies are sponsored or carried out by some official organisation or institution. The respondent should be reassured that no one will have access to the answers of any individual case and that only the aggregated answers will be published, which excludes the possibility of identifying the respondent. This promise should of course be kept.

INSTRUMENTS

There are two basic forms for collecting data for a study: the aide mémoire (qualitative data) and the questionnaire (quantitative data). The former is used for case studies and participant observation approach and includes a set of reminders which are used to record and classify the information; the latter is composed of a set of questions and coded answers administered to every subject in the study. For the purpose of a quantitative survey the questionnaire is the instrument of choice.

Aide mémoire

Case studies are limited to individuals or small groups and include the method of participant observation and in-depth interviews with individuals. To achieve a systematic and comparable set of information collected in this way the researcher can use an aide mémoire (basically a list), which highlights the topics for observation or enquiry and thus helps in the analysis of the data and making inferences. The aide mémoire, however, does not limit in any way this kind of collection of information and allows for recording any additional information observed or collected within a case study approach.

The questionnaire

As has been pointed out, the study of a population usually includes a survey of the whole population or, more likely a sample, and uses a standardised set of questions in the form of a questionnaire. The design of a questionnaire involves selecting questions that are relevant for the achievement of set aims and objectives, the formulation of the chosen questions in terms of the form and the order in which the questions are presented, and the type of answers the respondents are expected to provide.

Help in designing a questionnaire can be obtained from a ready-made computer program (Epi Info, see Appendix 2), which offers the less experienced researcher a guide to how to go about designing a questionnaire.

The kinds of questions

The first step in designing a questionnaire is to decide on the questions which will be included. The process usually starts with reviewing the aims of the study and deciding on the groups of questions intended to provide answers relevant to the aims. The choice of questions will depend on the decision about what one needs to know (not what one would like to know) and which questions will provide that information. The questions will then be grouped into the main areas of information required and the questions within each group balanced so that no area of inquiry is under-represented. The grouping of questions will help in the analysis of findings.

Examples of groupings are set out below:

- *Factual information* - in social research, this usually includes the characteristics of the respondents such as name, address, age, sex, occupation and status (social class), number of children, marital status, educational level, etc.

- *Behaviour* - includes questions about some behavioural pattern (smoking, diet, etc.) or action (when did you see your GP?, have you had a smear test? etc.).

- *Opinions, attitudes, knowledge* - respondents may be asked their views about the relation between smoking and health, does he/she know about passive smoking, etc.; the measurement of attitudes is more complex and requires the administration of an attitude scale which is composed of a battery of statements, which are analysed in such a way to provide a measure of a general attitude towards an object or event; standardised attitude tests are documented in the literature.

- *Prognosis* - it is possible to ask whether the respondent intends to take an action, what opinion he/she has about their own chances of becoming ill (perception of susceptibility), etc.

- *Test questions* - it will often be necessary to test the given answers by including some test questions which ask the same thing in a different way (how long ago did you last see a doctor? when did you have a smear test?) etc.

- *Filler questions* - when the topic is sensitive or the aims are so obvious that there is a danger that the respondent will answer in a certain way to satisfy the interviewer, one can add some questions which need not have any relation to the study topic.

Types of questions

It is possible to differentiate between the questions according to how they are presented to the respondent, such as:

- *Open questions* - these allow for an answer formulated by the respondent (Why do you smoke?).

- *Closed questions* - these offer the respondent a limited choice of answers (Q: Do you smoke because you like it? -A: yes, no, don't know, no opinion, n/a).

- *Multiple choice questions* - these offer the respondent the opportunity to make a choice from a set of answers provided (Q: What in your opinion is the aim of a check-up? -A: Early discovery of disease; to relieve the patient's mind; to warn the GP of possible risk; any other reason; no opinion; don't know).

- *Evaluative questions* - these ask the respondent's opinion about an issue (In your opinion is the cervical smear test?: very good; good; average; bad; very bad; no opinion, don't know); another way of providing answers is to include a continuum with marked points from "agree ....disagree", asking the respondent to place him/herself on the continuum according to their opinion.

The order of questions

The order in which the questions are put to the respondent may influence the answer. An example from an American study before the Second World War has shown this very clearly (Stouffer, S.A. et al. 1949). The questions were put in two different ways and the answers were significantly different. The questions were: Do you think that American citizens should be allowed to join the German army? followed by the same question about joining the British army. When the order was reversed the number of "yes" answers was greatly increased (from 22% to 40%). One should, therefore, avoid putting together questions which could contaminate the answers. Such questions should be dispersed throughout the questionnaire. One way of avoiding such contamination is to use different order on different groups during pre-testing of the questionnaire to eliminate contamination.

The funnel technique - it can be assumed that people think in a sequential way and that questioning them in such a way will improve their ability to answer truthfully. It is helpful, therefore, to start with more general questions and move towards more specific questions. For example, one could start by asking: What do you think about cancer? Can cancer be prevented? How can it be prevented?...Did you have a smear test? Will you have one? This technique may, however, work in an opposite way, and by funnelling the questions too precisely from general to specific, one can "trap" the respondent in giving an answer, which he/she would not otherwise think of giving. The dispersion technique is therefore usually preferable and will avoid any positive or negative contamination.

The problem of non-cooperation

There may be sensitive questions which the respondent does not wish to answer. They may include some personal questions (What is your income? Are you married? etc.) or questions about certain practices (What contraceptive do you use? etc.). Some people may resent certain questions about a disease because of the effect of "negative magic", which implies that if one does not talk about a bad event it will not happen ("tempting providence"). A pre-test should show which questions could be 'sensitive' and the researcher should decide whether these questions are really necessary. There are situations where people do not wish to answer some question as a part of a general survey, but are willing to discuss the topic in a more "in-depth" interview conducted in a way that will include confidentiality and reassurance. One should be aware that there is usually no need to include 'sensitive' questions and embarrass the respondent, since these questions may not yield the desired answers anyway.

Number of questions

It is often the case that the researchers get carried away by the number of questions they include in a questionnaire without considering the consequences. It will be necessary to consider in the first place the total number of questions since that will influence the time an interview will take to be carried out. If the interview is too long the chances increase of the respondent's becoming bored and interrupting the interview. If the questionnaire is to be filled in without an interviewer (e.g. postal questionnaire), the form may just be discarded.

The other problem to be considered when designing a questionnaire is the number of questions about each topic. As was stated earlier, the questions may be grouped followed by a decision about the number of questions in each group. The number of questions will depend on the depth of the analysis required. It will also influence the amount of confusion and possibility of errors which could occur, as well as the possibility of cross checking the answers.

The decisive element, however, will be the type of analysis one wishes to carry out. The number of two-dimensional tables to cross-tabulate all the variables with each other (e.g. level of education with marital status, etc.) can be calculated by using the formula T x (T-1) and dividing it by N (where T is the number of variables and N is the total number of variables in the table). The analysis of answers to a questionnaire with 30 questions will thus have 435 tables, if all the questions are cross-tabulated in 2 x 2 tables.

To achieve a questionnaire of manageable size a critical selection of the questions should be made and cross-tabulation should be made of only those questions that follow the research hypothesis.

There are certain situations where many questions are necessary to find out about a composite characteristic such as an attitude. In this case a battery of questions is used and analysed separately to establish the attitude, which is then included into the main study.

Formulating the questions

The formulation of questions will to a certain degree influence the answers. Use simple text and familiar language, and aim it at the level of comprehension of the presumed least 'intelligent' respondent in the sample. Personalised questions are in general more likely to get true answers.

As we have seen, questions may offer the respondent a choice among a number of possibilities or they may require a simple yes /no answer. There is also a possibility that the respondent has to rank choices in order of importance or preference. The questions may also be formulated in such a way that they require a descriptive answer (open ended questions).

Validity

A questionnaire should be valid, which means that the questions should tap the information required, through being understood by the respondent in the way intended. Internal validity ensures that the questionnaire measures what was targeted whereas external validity has to do with assessing how far the results of research are specific to a particular measure, group of people or setting.

Reliability

A questionnaire is said to be reliable if it will produce the same results when administered at different points in time to the same subjects.

Possible biases

There are a number of ways to avoid possible biases when designing a questionnaire. Some of the most common biases are described below, adjusted from the observations made by Stouffer et al., in their study of 'The American Soldier' (1949):

- *The conservative deformation* - this is a common bias which depends on two aspects of formulating a question: the attraction of replying 'yes' and the fear of 'implied change'. In the former case one could ask 'do you want to prevent cancer?' as compared to 'do you want to contract cancer?'. In the latter case one could ask 'do you want to improve your health by stopping smoking?' as compared with 'do you want to change your habit of smoking?'.

- *The fear of words* - there are certain words that people are reluctant to talk about or mention some words, such as the names of certain diseases or certain actions. Some people are reluctant to answer questions which mention cancer, operations, or isolation. There are also certain actions to which people are reluctant to commit themselves, as for example 'do you want to defend your country?' as compared with 'do you want to kill the enemy?'

- *Influence of personality* - respondents are more likely to agree with statements if they are attributed to a specific person as for example when asking 'do you agree with the statement of Doctor X that smoking can cause cancer?' as compared with 'do you agree that smoking can cause cancer?'. The influence of certain personalities can act positively as well as negatively.

- *Sympathy and antipathy* - the question can be formulated in such a way as to arouse the sympathy or antipathy of the respondent. For example 'Do you think that we should do more for AIDS sufferers?' as compared with 'do you think that we should do more for AIDS sufferers to help them in dealing with their affliction and enable them to lead a fulfilling life?'.

- *The interviewer* - a number of characteristics of the interviewer may influence the type of answers from the respondent, including educational level, race, religion, social class, sex, age, appearance and attractiveness. The opinions of the interviewer about the topic of the study may unintentionally influence the responses (for example expressed through body language, or intonation or some other way of expressing what the expected answer should be).

Administering the questionnaire

The questionnaire can be administered by post or by an interviewer who either asks questions as above and writes down answers, or present the questionnaire to the respondent expecting him/her to write down the answers himself/herself. A combination of these two approaches is an interview conducted by telephone where the questionnaire is delivered by post, but the interviewer uses a telephone. A telephone interview where only the interviewer uses the questionnaire is also possible.

Although postal questionnaires require less effort and can simultaneously reach a large number of respondents, one should take into account the fact that they are more likely to be refused. Some people do not like to answer written questionnaires and may find it easier not to reply than to refuse when facing an interviewer.

Tests and testing

A distinctive type of standardised questionnaire, a test, may be used to discover more about those affected by an health promotion and health education intervention. There are a number of personality traits that can be useful in understanding and predicting people's chances of staying healthy or becoming ill. These 'personality traits' have been associated with certain diseases either in a positive or in a negative way.

Tests using a battery of questions, formal or informal observation and recording, as well as projective tests, measure such personality traits. A person is exposed to such a test and has to react in a given time. The reactions are scored in a way that is specific for that test. On the basis of such a score the presence or absence of a trait, its direction and the strength, or any other characteristic that has been built into the test can be established.

Validity of tests

To be valid, a test must meet certain standards (Phillips, 1976). There are four main types of validity:

- *Content validity* - a test has content validity to the extent that the items in the test are judged to constitute a representative sample of some clearly specified universe of knowledge or skills. This judgement is usually based on the consensus of experts in the field of knowledge or skills that the test items are expected to sample. This type of validity is most relevant to achievement tests, job-knowledge tests and work-sample tests. For example, a test of general musical knowledge will include items that musical experts think are relevant for such testing, and will include a broad and varied selection of factual information about music. Any musician seeing the test would be likely to agree that it is a test of musical knowledge.

Work-sample tests are performance tests consisting of a representative sample of the kinds of skills that analysis of a job reveals a person must actually posses to perform adequately on the job (typist, computer programmer, etc.). Specific aptitude tests (clerical, mechanical, musical, etc.) often aim for content validity, although the test must depend on other types of validation. One could have aptitude for music without having the necessary musical knowledge.

- *Criterion validity* - this is the ability of test scores to predict performance in some endeavour that is external to the test itself, called the criterion. A test's validity coefficient is simply the correlation between the test scores and measurement of the criterion performance. For example, a college aptitude test would be said to have a good criterion validity (also called predictive validity) to the extent that the test scores are correlated with grades in college (the criterion). The criterion performance can be measured by other tests such as scholastic-achievement test and job-knowledge tests, using as the criterion grades in courses, supervisor's ratings of performance on the job, or direct indices of work proficiency and productivity. Criterion validity is probably the most important, defensible and convincing type of validation in the practical use of psychological tests. Its objectivity is derived from the fact that the results depend on the correlation of a performance with clearly defined and measurable criteria. Sensitive decisions such as assessment of employment skills should, however, be made by using as the validity coefficient scores from multiple correlations.

- *Concurrent validity* - this is used in two ways: it can mean that the correlation between a test and a criterion are measured at practically the same point in time (scholastic aptitude test and scholastic achievement test administered on the same day); the other meaning relates to correlation between a new, not yet validated test and some other test that is already established. There are instances when a new shorter or simpler test has been developed in a specific area where a more cumbersome test has been validated. The correlation between the new and the old test may serve to give confidence in the new test, avoiding the long process of validating it, although this is a risky strategy.

- *Construct validity* - this is most important from a scientific standpoint since it attempts to define in scientific terms what the test measures. The validity of the test will depend on the accuracy of the definition of the 'construct' that it tests. Constructs include, for example, intelligence, satisfaction etc. Most recognised personality traits are constructs of this kind. Construct validity will depend on the soundness of theories explaining the construct. In that sense, questions associated with the test should be relevant to the construct that they are supposed to measure. They should also seem reasonable to respondents, since this will affect respondent's attitudes, motivation and performance.

IQ test - an example

Scientist are still trying to find a definitive meaning for the concept of intelligence. In common use are three explanations of intelligence:

- the capacity of organisms to learn by experience and make adaptive responses to new situations as contrasted with instinctive or reflex responses;

- the faculty of understanding, which is the cognitive aspect of mental functioning and in particular the higher thought processes and conceptual activities, and the grasping of relationships;

- a measurement of the common element or factor underlying successful performance at varied mental tasks such as those included in intelligence tests or intelligence quotients (IQ).

These definitions represent three different approaches (biological, psychological and statistical). Piaget (1926) an early researcher on the subject, has tried to bring them together by explaining the development of associative mechanisms in the brain in terms of the product of genetic potentialities for the formation of schemata (neurone assemblies in the association areas of the brain), and of experience or stimulation by the environment. From the point of view of the mental tester, intelligence is a fluid collection of overlapping abilities, rather than any single identifiable faculty.

The construct 'intelligence' has a widespread use in scientific circles as well as in common language. There is no wonder that it has attracted a great number of scientists engaged in developing and refining the test to measure this construct. A great number of tests which have been developed for the measurement of intelligence. Although different in a number of ways, most of them produce results which are reasonably correlated with each other.

A critical review of intelligence tests has been given by Honzik (1979) whereas McCall (1979) explores the misconception of interpreting 'intelligence' as an unitary concept which has misled researchers in the past, and explores the hereditary aspects of intelligence. Whatever the opinion about testing 'intelligence' the way it is usually done, the IQ score has been found to be correlated with a great many abilities, aptitudes and various other achievements, such as scholastic, associated with learning and problem solving, occupational performance, income, etc. In recent years the notion of 'creativity' has become popular. The implication is that there is an inverse correlation between creativity and intelligence, i.e. people with 'low' intelligence can be highly creative. This notion is questionable since there is no acceptable definition of 'creativity' as such.

Attempts have also been made to link IQ with non-intellectual activities such as personality adjustment, social responsibility, delinquency, crime, etc. These have not been greatly successful in establishing a causal relationship between IQ and such traits, although statistical associations may be found.

Ability tests

In addition to the IQ test, the most popular and most used tests are those of a person's ability. These tests have been divided into achievement and aptitude tests.

- *Achievement tests* - These are concerned with determining what a person has learned to do after being exposed to a specific kind of instructions. They are mostly used in education and training programmes. In the construction of an achievement test, efforts are made to determine the knowledge and skills that are commonly taught at different grade levels and the test items are constructed to appraise these. Students' achievement can be measured by using 'teacher-made tests' as compared to other standardised achievement tests. Standardised achievement tests include a wide range of items representing the aims of a teaching programme such as testing reading ability, comprehension, retention and recall. Many standardised achievement tests exist, some specific for different educational levels.

- *Aptitude tests* - These are concerned with measuring specialised aptitudes, with the aim of establishing existing aptitudes as well as providing a prognosis and predictions. These tests are designed for vocational guidance and vocational selection. The main areas included in aptitude tests are concerned with specific verbal, numerical, reasoning, and mechanical aptitudes. They are intended to give an indication of whether a person is more appropriate for a particular occupation, since each occupation will require specialised abilities as well as different levels of general mental ability. For example, a mechanic requires a good deal of mechanical knowledge but little verbal fluency while a lawyer needs verbal comprehension but not mechanical skills.

Self-appraisal methods

One of the important personal characteristics related to health is the personality of the individual. Five relevant aspects of personality are sometimes identified as: temperament, character, adjustment, interests and attitudes.

The methods of studying personality (Allport, 1969) can be divided into what the individual says about himself/herself, appraisal through the opinion of others, using measures of behaviour and by means of exploring the individual's world of imagination.

The methods of measuring personality can include interviews, where a person is asked to answer a battery of questions making up a personality inventory. Various personality inventories are available and they categorise respondents in different ways. An example is the MMPI (Minnesota Multiphasic Personality Inventory), which was originally developed as a tool for studying individuals suspected of exhibiting some degree of psychopathology. It develops nine clinical scales, which, when correlated and analysed, give an indication of the type of personality of an individual.

The individual can also be asked to complete interest inventories which will reveal the domains of interests and likings.

Another way in which an individual's personality shows itself is through the impression he or she makes upon others. It is, therefore, common to use the opinions of others to assess someone's personality. The most common form is the reference, where the referee is supposed to make a statement about a person. A more objective way of looking at certain personality traits concerning a person's position in a group is to use the method of developing a sociogram which traces the network of interactions within a group and the position a specific individual occupies in that group.

Since personality shapes behaviour, any appraisal of personality should include behavioural outcomes. There are many tests available which measure people's behaviour. To provide an insight into an individual's 'standard' behaviour as opposed to that arising in exceptional circumstances, a test must be an indirect one. This is especially true for tests aimed at finding out about behaviour that runs against accepted norms.

Other tests

Miller (1991) provides a good review of a number of available tests and measurements in the following areas:

- *sociometric scales and indexes for social status* - Duncan's socio-economic index; Siegel's (NORC) prestige scores; occupational classification system of the US Bureau of the census; Alba M. Edwards' socio-economic groupings of occupations, and others;

- *sociometric scales and indexes for group structure and dynamics* - Hemphill's index of group dimensions; Bales' interaction process analysis; Bogardus' social distance scale; Seashore's group cohesiveness index; Hagoel's friendship value scales and others;

- *social indicators* - National social indicators 1980; National economic indicators; Social indicators at a national level; Social indicators at a community level; it also includes a selected bibliography;

- *measures of organisational structure* - Index of job related tensions in organisations; and others;

- *community measures* - Community attitude scale; Community solidarity scale; Community rating schedule; Scorecard for community services activity; Hunter's community leadership index and a bibliography of related publications;

- *social participation* - Chapin's social participation scale; leisure participation and enjoyment; Wallin's scale for measuring women's neighbourliness; citizen political action scale;

- *leadership in the work organisation* - Leadership opinion questionnaire; Supervisory behaviour description; Work patterns profile;

- *morale and job satisfaction* - Schuessler's social life feeling scale; Morse index of employee satisfaction; Brayfield and Rothe's index of job satisfaction; and others;

- *scales of attitudes, values, norms* - Neal and Seeman's powerlessness scale; Kahl's achievement orientation scale; Miller's scale battery of international patterns and norms;

- *family and marriage* - The dyadic adjustment scale; Burgess's marriage adjustment schedule; The PREPARE and ENRICH inventories;

- *personality measurements* - Minnesota multiphasic personality inventory, Authoritarian personality scale;

Miller's excellent summary includes an extensive bibliography related to the various scales and measurements as well as guidance on how to design one's own scales.

The design of tests

The researcher will often be faced with the decision whether to use ready-made tests or to create them.

To make use of existing tests it is sometimes necessary to pay a fee to use them and to find someone who has the recognised professional status to be able to administer them. Sometimes it will be necessary to adapt the tests to the existing needs of the project in question. The researcher should, however, be aware that any adjustment of an existing test or if using part of that test will require new assessments of validity and reliability since it will not be the original assessed test.

Where there are no appropriate tests available or easily obtained, or even where the tests exist and are available but the researcher considers them as being of poor design and not valid or reliable, the researcher may decide to design appropriate tests or scales. A good scale or test can be used by others. For this it will be necessary to meet certain preconditions such as defining the theoretical construct and meeting a number of evaluative criteria:

- *item construction criteria* - selected items should accurately reflect the universe of items encompassed by the variable to be measured; items should be simply worded and easily understood by the respondents; item analysis should demonstrate that each item is closely related to the selected variables by using item-intercorrelation matrix, factor analysis, complex multi-dimensional analysis, item-correlation with external criteria; items should be pre-tested and the undesirable ones eliminated;

- *response set criteria* - avoidance of response sets which are prone to attract agreement by discarding items that are leading questions, switching occasional response alternatives between positive and negative ones, and using forced choice items which include two or more replies where the respondent is asked to choose only one; avoiding sets leading to responses influenced by social desirability ratings, by analysing and eliminating efforts of respondents to fake responses, and by analysing and eliminating spurious replies due to the respondent's wish to appear consistent in the image he/she is presenting;

- *scale matrix criteria* - include representative sampling; adequate normative information; reliability; homogeneity; and validity.

The process of creating new scales or tests also requires high level expertise in statistical methods since meeting a number of the mentioned criteria will depend on the application of statistical methods. This area of expertise is not covered by The Epi Info software (see Appendix 2) and the researcher, if not a statistician, will require professional help and advice.

The researcher will also be faced with the need to assess the pay-off from the tests and scales to be used in a research project. This could include the cost-benefit analysis of either using an existing test or developing a new one, since the latter might not justify the investment in expertise and resources for development. This kind of cost-benefit analysis will have to use realistic indicators and consider the results within the framework of budgeting for health promotion and health education activities.

DATA ANALYSIS

The analysis of data will depend on the type of data collected and on the aims and objectives of the study or research programme. In this section a description of the analysis of two types of data from two kinds of studies are given: qualitative data obtained from case studies and quantitative data obtained from population studies. The outcome of a case study should provide the researcher with information about the *possibility* of an event or a relationship occurring, whereas the population study will provide information about the *probability* of such events or relationships occurring in a population. The description of the methods appropriate for the analysis of these two kinds of data is here limited to offering an appreciation of the requirements as well as approaches available for data analysis. Although it is not intended to provide detailed knowledge and skills for handling and analysing data, the reader should become aware of the various possibilities on offer, in order to be able to make an educated choice. The technical knowledge for data collection and analysis can be obtained from specialist literature, or by employing experts, while Epi Info (Appendix 2) again provides some guidance.

Qualitative research in health

Qualitative data analysis by doctors and patients

Exposure to qualitative data gathering in a doctor - patient interaction is the basis of medical practice and is treated as a normal procedure by those involved without generating any discussions or conflicts. The examination (study approach) is carried out by the doctor and is limited to a single subject. Based on the outcome of the examination, the patient receives information about his or her state of health (qualitative data) and the analysis carried out by both the doctor and the patient follows the processes involved in the qualitative data analysis approach. This method is known as the *differential diagnosis* approach, already discussed earlier, and the outcome is applicable to the patient in question.

Before seeing a doctor, the patient will undergo a decision-making process which involves several stages. The patient will become *aware* of a health related problem and will carry out *self-diagnosis* which will be followed by a *decision.* The decision could be to *do nothing*, to carry out *self-care* or to seek *outside help*.

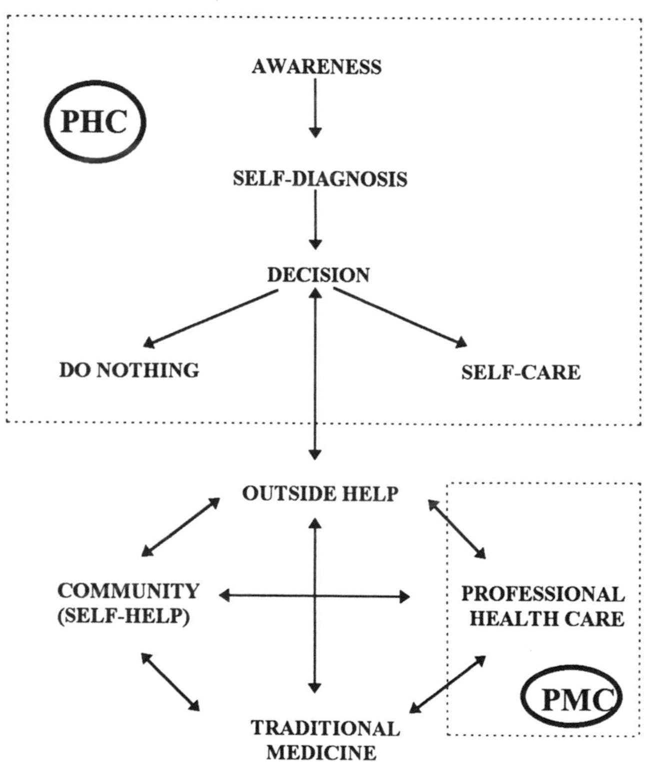

The outside help can be in the form of a *self-help group*, some aspect of *traditional or alternative* medication, or a visit to a doctor to ask for *professional help*. The patient moves from primary health care system (PHC) into the primary medical care system (PMC).

The outcome of a differential diagnosis will depend on the communication and interaction processes between the two actors, on the problem(s) presented by the patient and the choice of solutions made by the doctor. This will be reflected in the social roles allocated by the doctor to the patient and will define the interaction according to the role acquired by the patient.

PATIENT'S ROLES

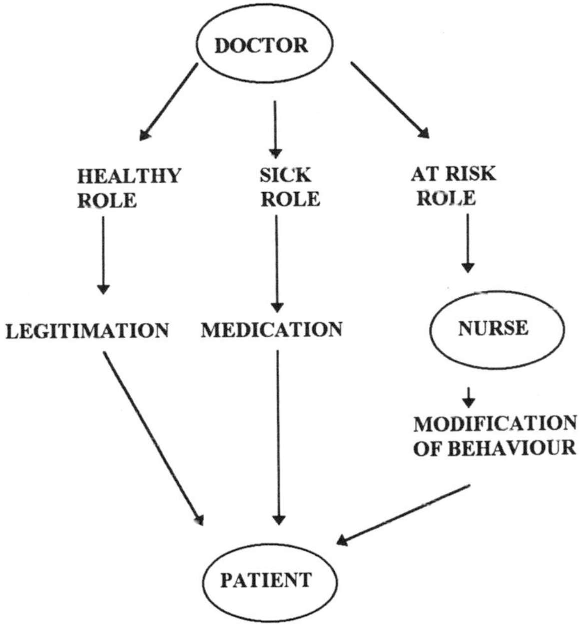

To carry out the monitoring and analysis of data it will be necessary to trace the processes through which both the doctor and the patient are involved during such an interaction.

The doctor, after *meeting the patient*, will activate the standard procedure for a differential diagnosis, which includes: *interview, observation, examination and tests resulting in a diagnosis followed by the prescription of a treatment.*

The process will be monitored and the information collected will form the basis for predicting the outcome. In the case of a break-down in the process, analysis of information (data) can indicate its location and character. The indicators of a possible break-down on the patient's side are failure of understanding or retention, coping with information, resolving anxieties associated with the diagnosis and the cost-effectiveness of the prescribed treatment. On the doctor's side, it will be failure of existing knowledge about the disease, personal competence in diagnosing and treating the disease, communication skills, available technology for diagnosis and treatment, available medication and time for repeat visits by the patient and follow-up of the prescribed treatment.

PRIMARY MEDICAL CARE

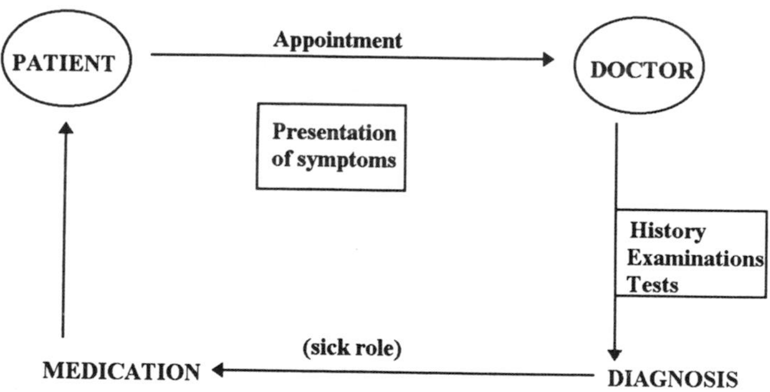

The qualitative data analysis by the doctor includes: observation, interpretation of information about symptoms, examination and testing of the patient. The differential diagnosis adopts a funnel type analysis by exclusion of irrelevant diseases and interpretation of aggregated data to match the fit for a specific disease. This will be followed by monitoring the effects of prescribed treatment, with a built in feed-back and modification of the treatment until the patient recovers. The patient's handling of information (qualitative data analysis) includes testing the doctor's expectations about the information the patient should provide, interpretation of the doctor's expectations concerning collaboration in examinations and tests and the understanding and acceptance of the prescribed treatment, which in turn is translated into compliance by the patient.

Doctor - patient case studies

Another aspect of the use of qualitative data has been by researchers in the study of doctor - patient interactions, which has been a popular topic in medical sociology. In most instances these studies used a case study approach and depended on the collection of qualitative data. The studies have been reported in a number of publications in the field of medical sociology (for example Freidson, 1961; Wilson, 1963; Cartwright, 1967; Francis et.al., 1969; etc.).

Most studies depend on reported events, since the doctor - patient interaction is a privileged situation and the researchers can only be present with the approval of both the doctor and the patient. Even if the approval can be obtained, the use and publication of findings would represent a breach of the confidentiality of medical records.

Because of these limitations, most of the studies could not use participant observation but have relied on interview techniques.

Patients are interviewed before and after seeing a doctor, and the doctor is interviewed after seeing a patient.

Typically, the patient would be asked about:

- the feeling of satisfaction in being able to explain the problem to the doctor;
- the feeling of satisfaction that the consultation took sufficient time and the doctor was able to understand the information provided;
- the feelings about the competence of the doctor;
- the trust in the diagnosis; the acceptance of examination and tests by the patient;
- the question of accessibility of the practice in terms of location and the waiting time and the assessment of the waiting room and the surgery;
- the interest and support from the receptionist;
- the follow-up service and the referral system;
- the acceptability and effectiveness of the treatment.

The doctor would be asked:

- satisfaction with the communication process;
- the main points of advice given;
- the opinion about the patient's acceptance of advice and treatment;
- need for follow-up;
- past experiences with this patient;
- prognosis of the problem.

This is only a general outline of the domains of inquiry concerning the doctor-patient interaction. Such qualitative data are usually analysed according to some generally acceptable standard, which in some cases can be formalised, as in the case of The Patient's Charter (Baric, 1994, Appendix 5). They are usually presented descriptively; point to some problems; such studies cannot be generalised to general practices as a whole.

Health promotion and health education

The case study approach is especially relevant for research and evaluation of the new 'health promoting settings' in their initial pilot stage. The use of qualitative data is important because it provides the researcher with an insight into the important aspects of this process and allows for feed-back and the 'learning - by - doing' approach as well as providing an opportunity to understand a situation holistically, using a systems approach.

The European Health Promoting Pilot Hospitals Network provides an example. It consists of 20 pilot hospitals throughout Europe. The testing of the concept of a 'health promoting hospital' includes the monitoring of a number of intervention studies, which the hospitals have to carry out. The aims of these intervention studies is to enable the researchers within each hospital to develop their own programmes, choose their own appropriate indicators and criteria, and assess the processes as well as outcomes of this kind of approach. The method used in these intervention studies is the case study approach and the findings are expressed in the form of qualitative data. The ultimate analysis of such data will be presented in a descriptive form and should serve as a test of acceptability of the approach by the staff and the patients, of effectiveness of such an approach, and efficiency as compared with the traditional integrated approach.

The collection of data and the subsequent analysis is carried out on two levels, the organisational and the patient level:

- *The organisational level* - Here data will be analysed according to: the changes in the structure of the setting; the changes in the management style; level of participation of the staff; inclusion of health promotion and health education into the evaluation or quality assessment process; the existence and operation of the newly created networks; outreach into the community (through measuring and describing the relationships within the new alliances formed as a part of the outreach).

- *The patient level* - These data will be analysed according to: the patients' noticing a change in the quality of services and the expected outcomes; the particular instances of improvement; signs of continuous care as a part of the networking; and newly created alliances in the community.

The pilot study approach, using case studies and relying on qualitative data, increases the insight into the processes and outcomes of this new approach. The final conclusion of such an analysis can only be expressed in terms of the 'possibility' of the introduction of the new approach, with its advantages and disadvantages. Other similar settings may learn from these examples and find out for themselves whether and to what extent such changes are necessary and desirable.

Qualitative research in the social sciences

The importance of qualitative research in the social sciences has been recognised only relatively recently in health promotion and health education programme research and evaluation, although it has been the preferred method in anthropological and ethnographic research for a long time. It has gained respectability by becoming the subject of theoretical and practical studies.

Denzin & Lincoln (eds.1994) provide a good historical overview of the movement towards the acceptance of qualitative data as a meaningful and credible means of describing social events. They also provide an overview of the various theoretical frameworks that are available to researchers, as well as a selection of methods for data collection.

Their summary of the research process is divided into chronological phases (p.12):

- *Phase 1*: the researcher considers requirements for participation in 'other' cultures, is aware of history and research traditions, explores the concept of self in relation to the observed events, and makes judgements about the ethical issues involved in such a study approach;

- *Phase 2*: the choice is made about the most appropriate or preferred paradigm as the conceptual framework for the study (for example, positivist, post-positivist, constructivist, feminist, ethnic, Marxist or cultural studies model);

- *Phase 3*: a decision is made on the theoretical and methodological research strategies to be adopted (study design and case study approach, ethnography, participant observation, phenomenology, ethnomethodology, grounded theory, biographical method, historical method, action and applied research; clinical research);

- *Phase 4*: the researcher chooses the appropriate methods of collection and analysis of data (interviewing, observing, examining artefacts, documents, records, visual methods, personal experience methods, textual analysis, computer-assisted analysis);

- *Phase 5*: decisions are made about the way the findings will be interpreted and presented (criteria for judging adequacy, the art and politics of interpretation, policy analysis, evaluation traditions, applied research).

From the description of the process of planning and carrying out a qualitative research project a number of important issues emerge:

- the researcher, when using a case study approach, cannot completely detach him/herself from the setting, and this will have consequences for the choice of the informants, the questions asked and the interpretation of the findings;

- the personal choice of the researcher will decide on which theoretical approach from a set of those available to be used in the study;

- the researcher will make personal decisions about the appropriate methods for data collection; he/she will decide which of the frameworks will be used in the interpretation of "meaning" events, "process" events and behavioural events but the emergent material will shape the findings, often unanticipated;

- the descriptive format of presentation of findings, based on the choice of the analytical framework, will ultimately depend on the value system and ethics of the researcher.

It is important to note that this personal involvement also applies to some extent to quantitative research, but there it is much more hidden by the methodology, assumed to be 'objective'. The qualitative approach has become an important area of development in social sciences, which is reflected in the increasing numbers of researchers and publications. The main advantage of qualitative research is that it allows the researcher to penetrate more deeply into the complex relationships and meanings within a social or cultural system, and does not dictate from the outset the limits of the study or the selection of elements that are important. These emerge as the field work progresses. In a quantitative study, such as a survey, the researcher gets out of the study what is put into it, and to that extent it is predetermined. Qualitative methods are for open-minded, open-ended discovery. (There is, however, a use of the term 'qualitative' in statistics, which is not to be confused with its meaning in this context).

Quantitative research in health

Most health-related information has traditionally been quantitative. In the field of health, the collection of quantitative data has aimed to provide information in two main areas: epidemiology or the study of the occurrence and distribution of a disease in a population including the characteristics of that population; and the study of medical needs of a society or the study of health care. Both fields of study include surveys and use statistical methods in analysis.

Epidemiology

Epidemiology has a long history and forms the basis for preventive medicine, public health, community medicine, and, more recently, for health promotion as a part of public health.

Most data, derived through epidemiological methods are collected and recorded on a regular basis and form the background for the annual reports of the Chief Medical Officer of the Department of Health (1991). These reports provide information about the health of the nation and include vital statistics about, for example changes in population size, the age and sex structure of the population, fertility, mortality and morbidity rates, as well as trends in the development of most prevalent infectious and chronic disease.

In addition to the regularly collected data, an epidemiological method is also used in surveys dealing with special diseases and health problems. A classical example is the pioneering study of smoking and the distribution of lung cancer (Doll & Hill, 1950), based on the collection of data from hospitals about smoking and non-smoking patients dying of lung cancer. The outcome of the analysis of data showed a significant association between cigarette smoking and lung cancer. This study was followed by numerous other studies, which confirmed the initial findings and contributed certain refinements to the existing association by examining the number of cigarettes smoked, the type of cigarettes, what happens if a person stops smoking, effects of smoking during pregnancy, up to more recent studies of association of passive smoking with lung cancer, bronchitis and other diseases.

Another example of the application of the survey method to the study of the state of health is the 'Black Report' (Townsend & Davidson, 1982) which examined the distribution of a number of diseases according to social class, and subsequently also according to the location of the affected population. It was found that lower social classes, as defined in the Report, suffered more from most diseases and that the diseases were more prevalent in the north than in the south of England. These results are now well known and used in many arguments against inequalities in health care and in attempts to attract additional resources for health care.

Health care

The other main areas of study are the provision of health care and the distribution of health care personnel. The report 'On the State of Public Health' (1992) brought together material from these studies to describe the general area of the nation's health, the health of various minority groups and the special needs of some population groups, the distribution of the provision of health care, the medical and para-medical professions, as well as the control of medicines, medical equipment, environmental health and toxicology.

Medical statistics

The intention in this handbook is to provide information about what is available rather than to impart statistical skills. Nevertheless, in order to appreciate the importance of statistics in health promotion and health education it is necessary to understand what medical statistical concepts can offer in terms of analysing a problem or the relationship between two or more problems. Some of the most commonly encountered concepts (Bradford Hill, 1961; Smith, 1968; McKeown & Lowe, 1977; Polgar & Thomas, 1991) in medical statistics are, therefore, set out below:

- *incidence* - denotes the proportion of a population becoming ill from a disease in a certain period of time, usually a specific year; this is calculated by looking at the number of new cases in a population in a defined time as compared with the total number of the population during the same period, expressed as a rate per 1,000 or per 100,000 population, thus showing the number of new cases in each year; this measure is useful for short-term illnesses or when the onset of disease is important, as in the case of studies of causation;

- *prevalence* - denotes the proportion of the population suffering from an illness at a defined point in time; it is calculated by dividing the numbers of people who are ill by the total population; it shows the total number of people ill in a population; it is useful in the study of chronic diseases, where a measure over a limited period, as in incidence rates, is not useful;

- *disease duration* - denotes the average duration of a specific disease; it is calculated as the arithmetical product of incidence and average duration expressed in appropriate time units; it shows the number of people currently suffering from a disease and is useful for studying the hospital utilisation;

- *hospital admission rates* - this denotes the average stay of people in hospitals; it is calculated from the number of admissions to a hospital in a year divided by the number of the population served by that hospital; if the admission and residence rates are known, average duration of hospital stay can be calculated; if the catchment area population is not known, the average duration of hospital stay can be calculated by comparing the number of admissions during the year, the numbers of beds in the hospital and the average proportion of beds that are occupied at any time; this measure is useful for the comparison of average stay rates for a specific disease in different hospitals;

- *mortality rates* - these are the number of deaths during a year and are calculated by dividing the number of deaths during a year by the number in the population at risk during the year;

- *crude death rates* - these denote the deaths in a complete population such as in a country, and are obtained by dividing that population with the number of deaths at the mid-year; they are expressed as rates per 1,000 in a population; these rates can be contaminated by the age structure of the population and thus produce some anomalies as compared with the expected outcomes;

- *age-specific death rates* - these denote the death rates for specific age groups; they are calculated by dividing the number of dying at a specific age by the total number of the population at that age; ages can be grouped into five or ten year intervals; these rates are usually calculated separately for males and females;

- *standardised mortality ratio (SMR)* - this denotes the relative mortality of the real population with that in a 'standardised' population and corrects for differences in age between the two populations; it is used for comparing populations and is calculated for each of the populations under study by using the number of deaths that would occur in the population, if at each age it experienced the age-specific death rates of a suitably chosen standard population; the actual number of deaths is expressed as a percentage of the calculated number; the measure is used for comparing mortality in populations with dissimilar age composition; the problem is to find a suitable standard rate for comparison, for example, the measure for workers in industry can be derived by using as a comparison the death rates of all employed in that country, all males in that country, or some similar measure;

- *infant mortality rate* - this denotes the death rate of infants and is calculated from the number of live births in the country during the year and the number of deaths during the year of children under one year of age; it is expressed as a rate per 1,000 live births; the picture provided by this rate can, however, be distorted if the number of births in a year increases unexpectedly, which may result in an artificial apparent lowering of infant mortality;

- *neonatal mortality rate* - this denotes deaths that occur in the first month of life; it is calculated by dividing the number of deaths of infants less than 28 days old in a specific year by the number of living births in that year; it is expressed as a rate per 1,000 live births;

- *post-neonatal mortality rate* - this denotes the number of deaths in the first year of a child's life excluding the first month; it is calculated by dividing the number of deaths of children between 28 days and one year old by the number of live births during that year;

- *stillbirth rate* - this denotes mortality of the unborn child; it is calculated by dividing the number of stillbirths in a year by the sum of the number of live and still births in that year; it is expressed as a rate per 1,000 total births;

- *perinatal mortality* - this denotes the deaths from stillbirth as well as the death of infants under one week old; it is calculated by adding the number of stillbirths and the number of deaths within the first week of life and dividing the result by the sum of stillbirths and live births; it is usually expressed as the rate per 1,000 of total births;

- *expectation of life at birth* - this refers to years of life that would be lived by a hypothetical population if it experienced the age-specific mortality rates of the matching real population; as an index it is used in calculating life tables; it is calculated by taking a hypothetical population of newborn individuals whose numbers are reduced by applying the age-specific mortality of the real population; such life tables are mostly used by actuaries for the calculation of risk incurred by life insurance companies; a simpler way of calculating life expectancy, where no prediction is required, is carried out by summing up the total years of life lived by the hypothetical population and dividing it by the size of the population on which the study is based.

There are other statistical units that are used in assessing a population's health and the availability of health services. To calculate these indicators medical statistics have provided standardised methods which are used in many countries for the purpose of comparability.

For example, the WHO document on the development of indicators for monitoring progress towards health for all by the year 2000 (see p. 173) provides information about calculating some of the most common indicators, in addition to those already mentioned, such as:

- *population ratio to health personnel* - this is an important indicator for calculating the availability of health services for a given population; it is calculated by taking the size of the overall population divided by the number of health personnel of a certain type; this gives the average number of people served by a health worker; it is important for assessing the work load of various health workers such as doctors, nurses, etc.;

- *percentage of low birth weight* - this is an important indicator of the risk to the survival of a baby and the chances it has for healthy growth and development; low birth weight is defined as a baby weighing less than 2,500 grams which is preferably assessed within the first hours of the baby's life; it is calculated by dividing the number of live born babies with birth weight of less than 2,500 grams divided by the total number of live born babies; by multiplying this number by

100, the percentage of low birth weight babies in a population is obtained;

- *weight and height of children* - this is a measure of chances for survival of children in a population; it is calculated by working out the percentage of low weight for age babies (number of children with low weight for age divided by the total number of children and multiplied by 100), percentage of low height for age babies (number of children with low height for age divided by the total number of children and multiplied by 100) and the percentage of low weight for height of babies born in that population; the low weight for height (number of children with low weight for height divided by the total number of children and multiplied by 100) is defined as less than the value corresponding to two standard deviations below the median of the respective frequency distribution for healthy children; to help in the calculations necessary for this indicator there are international and national tables published which give the standard weight and height for children of different ages and different sex;

- *small upper arm circumference* -this is an indicator of the state of nourishment of children in a population; it is defined as an indicator for malnourishment if it falls into the range of less than the value corresponding to the fifth percentile of the frequency distribution for well nourished children; it is a less precise measure than the height for weight measure, although it is preferred in some situations because of the simplicity of obtaining the required data.

In addition to regularly producing the various measures of health of a population, descriptive medical statistics are also used for specific purposes such as looking at the distribution of a disease in a population, as well as the causes and consequences of certain diseases. Where statistical methods are used to draw conclusions about cause-effect relationships, they are referred to as 'inferential' (see p. 232). In this context, medicine and health promotion and health education use the same approaches as general research statistics, described in the following section.

Quantitative research in the social sciences

Quantitative methods of data analysis are used for studies which collect population data and use statistical methods. Guidance on collecting population data by means of questionnaires and analysing them by using statistical methods is given in Appendix 2, which deals with the Epi Info computer program.

Population studies in the social sciences are the basis for a number of official documents produced by the government and other institutions, such as the household survey, the survey of British attitudes, social trends, economic reports and many others. They all use statistics in their analysis and some provide an appendix where they explain how different statistical operations have been used, especially in designing some complex indicators.

There are, however, problem areas where health promotion and health education researchers have to plan and execute studies dealing with specific problems. They will have to master the process of conceptualising a problem, choosing the right methodology of collecting data, and deciding on the techniques of analysing the findings. In all of these aspects of a project the understanding of statistics plays an important part.

Sampling

The first problem that will face health promotion and health education researchers is the selection of the population under study. In most cases the total population is too large or the resources of the researcher are seriously limited. In either case the answer lies in selecting a sample of the population under study. The way the sample has been chosen will define the meaning of the findings based on that sample. We have already looked at some aspects of sampling (see p. 182). Here the statistical implications that are relevant for data analysis are highlighted. There are various ways to select a sample, each with certain implications for the analysis:

- *non-probability sampling* - this implies that the probability of each subject in the sample being chosen is not known; the consequence is that it is not possible to estimate the error due to sampling and it is not possible to determine the level of accuracy to generalise from the sample to the whole population;

- *probability sampling* - this implies that every member of the population (or sampling universe) has had an equal chance of being selected and the representativeness of the sample can be calculated by estimating the sampling error; the representativeness of the sample justifies the use of sophisticated statistical methods of analysis and allows for generalisation of the findings to the population from which the sample has been drawn.

The convenience of using samples instead of the whole population should be considered against the loss of accuracy. The fact that a sample is only a more or less accurate representation of the whole population, depending on the type chosen, requires that the accuracy be measured and stated. The researcher should be aware that there are techniques, such as the estimate of the sample error, which will be dependent on the size of the sample and composition of the population in terms of variability. This will allow the researcher to decide what size of error will be acceptable in relation to the aims of the research.

The choice of a sample of a population requires expert knowledge and the researcher may need outside advice.

Statistics

Population studies produce considerable amounts of quantitative data and require statistical methods for making some sense of what these data mean and how they can be justifiably interpreted. There are degrees in statistics, textbooks and handbooks for self-instruction and computer software which bypasses expert knowledge and produces statistical analysis at the press of a button, which is a risky procedure if the basis for it is not understood.

Those who are not experts in statistics could benefit from becoming sufficiently 'literate' in statistics to be able to ask for the appropriate support from experts or to use computer software.

It is important to bear in mind the fact that here are two main branches of statistics:

- *descriptive statistics*: this is used to describe the main characteristics of the collected data; this includes the presentation of the frequency distribution of the answers to each question in the questionnaire in terms of numbers of people who selected each of the available answers to each question; this can be presented in full numbers, in percentages, ratios or rates; it also includes the calculation of the central tendency and the dispersion of answers around the mean; it is also possible to compare the frequency distribution with the 'normal' distribution within a population; the data can be presented in tables, graphs, histograms or pie-diagrams;

- *inferential statistics:* this is used in analysing data for the purpose of drawing valid inferences; it is based on random sampling and allows for testing hypotheses, calculating associations between various characteristics or actions within a population, and for calculating regressions and correlations between variables; the results are presented in tables with the indication of the tests used.

The research design will ultimately determine how sophisticated a statistical analysis is needed. The validity and reliability of the data collection method should be considered when deciding on the methods of analysis. Because of this, it will be important to use expertise in research methods (either from outside or through developing the researcher's own statistical skills) when planning a study, when choosing the indicators and instruments, as well as when carrying out the analysis of the collected information.

SUMMARY

This section has dealt with planning an intervention and has covered the definition of aims, objectives, methods, indicators, data collection, instruments and data analysis. Although the planning process must meet certain preconditions to produce a good intervention, these can very often be integrated into the process and do not necessarily represent rigidly differentiated stages. Usually a health promotion and health education practitioner involved in research decides what should be done and how it should be done and then attempts to translate intentions into formalised aims and objectives. Once this has been done, the choice of indicators and criteria will decide how relevant the efforts to evaluate an intervention are to the stated aims and objectives. The success of an evaluation will depend on effective methods of collecting and analysing the information by using the appropriate instruments.

The intention of this section has been to inform those involved in health promotion and health education about the requirements and the preconditions for researching the topics or evaluating their efforts. It does not provide detailed knowledge of how to do this, since this topic is very large and there are many relevant texts from which this approach can be learned. The intention of this section has, therefore, been to encourage appreciation of what is involved in the processes of research, assessment and evaluation so that those involved in health promotion and health education would know what to demand and expect from experts whose help they may need to seek.

This expertise can be available in-house or can be contracted from outside. The experts can be assessed according to their experiences and knowledge so that the health promotion and health education intervention will be evaluated in an appropriate way.

The discussion of the aims of health promotion and health education interventions concentrates on aims arising from the two approaches, i.e. aims based on the needs of the clients or the predefined targets set by some stakeholder. The stakeholders mentioned are WHO and the Department of Health, as two main sources of policy and strategy concerning health promotion and health education. The WHO targets are only briefly mentioned in this section as they are described in detail in Appendix 1, which provides the report on the evaluation of achievements related to these targets.

The methods of health promotion and health education are based on the Ottawa Charter and have been placed within the framework of an organisation model. This model arises from the new WHO setting's approach, and replaces all previous models.

The methods discussed, including the collection of qualitative and quantitative data, have been set out in the light of the recent understanding of the methodology required by the new approaches to health promotion and health education.

EVALUATION

Introduction
A Guide to Evaluation
Health Promoting Settings
Meta-evaluation
Summary

INTRODUCTION

The present situation concerning the promotion and maintenance of health, as well as the prevention and management of disease, has created new demands and expectations from the health care delivery system and the consumers. These new expectations are also reflected in the new health promotion and health education activities, which are operating within an organisational model and depend on the full participation of the members of different settings. One of the main expectations is the accountability of the agents carrying out health promotion and health education activities, which will have consequences for their planning and evaluation.

Evaluation related to health promotion and health education activities can be defined as the assessment *of the achievement of the stated aims* of an intervention.

The need for evaluation and auditing has been felt for a long time and has been demanded by the agencies providing financial support as well as by the clients who have been on the receiving end. The situation at present is that most interventions have not been assessed, or if they have been assessed, then the methods used may not have been scientifically sound and acceptable.

Therefore, the aim of this section is to provide readers with knowledge necessary to ensure an appropriate evaluation of their work.

Any evaluation will depend on the findings based on the data collected about the intervention and its outcome. To achieve credibility, the evaluation should achieve standards which will meet the required level of scientific rigour in its methodology. It is, however, important to realise that the function and procedures of evaluation and research, although related, can differ in a number of respects. The consumers of pure research are other scientists and researchers; the findings are published in professional journals for open criticism and the aims of those concerned are to discover the 'truth' about phenomena. The consumers of evaluation, on the other hand, are the stakeholders; an effective evaluation does not receive recognition by being published in a professional journal, but by contributing to action; and the aims of an evaluation are to allow a judgement to be made, by those involved, about the success of an intervention.

The conceptualisation of the research aspects of an evaluation depends on the precision in defining the aims and objectives of the intervention. The assumptions or hypotheses to be tested will depend on the set aims, and the effects of the intervention will depend on the association between the set objectives and the achieved outcomes.

The research methods used in collecting data depend on the scope of the intervention as well as on its aims and objectives. If the intervention has been planned to affect a limited population group, then the population sample will be selected to represent that group. If, however, the intervention has been planned for the general population, then the population sample should be chosen for data collection. If the aims have been expressed in measurable terms, the collection of hard data will be required. If, however, the aims have been stated in terms of feelings, opinions and levels of satisfaction, which are all theoretical constructs, then the collection can be restricted to qualitative or 'soft' data, although this may be presented as tables or matrices. In the first case a survey will be necessary, whereas in the second case an in-depth study will be more appropriate. The kind of data involved will also define the most useful instruments. In the first instance a questionnaire will be needed, whereas in the second case an aide-mémoire may be necessary as a guide for an in-depth interview.

The type of data collected will determine the applicable mode of analysis. In the case of a survey, a statistical analysis may be necessary, whereas different methods of analysis will be required for a qualitative analysis. The discussion earlier, on analytical methods (see p. 60), is relevant here.

The inferences made depend on the aims of an intervention and should state whether the expected outcomes were achieved or not. The outcome should also indicate any possible and unexpected side-effects from the intervention.

Once the base line has been established, the development of indicators and criteria, the collection of data and the inferences will follow the pattern defined by the requirements of recognised research methods. In this way the credibility of the findings will be enhanced.

This section includes a summarised guide to evaluation and provides a practical example of its application to a health promoting setting.

A GUIDE TO EVALUATION

There are certain practical aspects which need to be taken into consideration when planning and carrying out an evaluation of health promotion and health education activities. The requirements will be different according to the responsibilities a person has in planning and carrying out an evaluation, which are summarised briefly in this section.

The evaluation of any health promotion and health education programme or project will have special requirements, which will differ according to whether a person is directly involved in carrying it out as a member of a project team or if he/she is a team leader (Guba and Lincoln, 1989, Posavac and Carey, 1985, Smith, 1981, Suchman, 1967). This section covers a number of issues in evaluation particularly relevant to a team leader's decision-making. They include:

- what should be evaluated;
- the relationship between the project's aims and objectives and the appropriate evaluation methods;
- choosing appropriate indicators and agreeing on the criteria for success;
- creating and collecting data;
- analysing data;
- drawing conclusions and writing up the report;
- utilising mechanisms for feedback;
- exploring the research aspects of evaluation.

It should be realised that evaluation of any project depends on a number of subjectively defined decisions and that an evaluation cannot be expected to be a purely objective assessment of a project. In addition to the subjective decisions of an evaluator, the whole process will depend on reaching some consensus about acceptance between the evaluator and the people involved in the project. It should be clear to anyone who wants to carry out an evaluation that the evaluation process can only be as good as the planning process of the programme being evaluated.

The reasons for evaluation may be clearly stated by those stakeholders who finance a project, or they may be implicit in the character of the project and related to the accountability of the agents carrying it out. With the introduction of the organisational model of health promotion and health education, the aspect of accountability cannot be avoided. It is for this reason that the evaluation is becoming an integral part of any project and cannot be set aside by using the convenient excuses of lack of time or resources.

Evaluation has developed from its early days, when it was often limited to personal opinions about the success of a project, or when it concentrated on evaluating the effort put into a project rather than outcomes. In health promotion and health education programmes, it was usual to measure success or failure by quoting the number of distributed leaflets or attendance at lectures. At present, evaluation is becoming recognised as a professional activity with professional organisations and dedicated journals

There are various ways in which an evaluation can be carried out depending on what should be evaluated and how it should be done:

- *evaluation* in its broadest sense covers all procedures which allow a judgement about the success in achieving the stated aims of a project;

- *programme evaluation* provides a framework which covers all the aspects of a complex programme, as in the case of a large scale activity in a hospital or a school;

- *project evaluation* deals with individual projects within a wider programme, as in the case of the required intervention studies within a health promoting hospital or school;

- *product evaluation* deals with the outcomes of programmes and projects, in terms of their products such as publications, materials or specific techniques, which can then be transferred to other similar settings and used in further interventions as well as for preparation of teaching material.

It will also be useful to differentiate evaluation according to the expectations which are associated with the outcome such as:

- *effectiveness,* which assesses the outcomes in terms of stated aims;

- *efficiency*, which aims to show that the objectives of the programme are the best in terms of cost effectiveness and probability of achieving the desired outcome;

- *effort,* which aims to show whether a project is capital - or labour-intensive and gives an indication about the required resources necessary for a successful conclusion of a project or programme.

This guide to evaluation should help those involved in planning a health promotion and health education intervention to consider and meet the necessary preconditions which will allow them to evaluate their work.

Linking evaluation to aims and objectives

Evaluation in general is mainly concerned with the achievement of the aims of a project and does not necessarily also include the evaluation of the aims as such (Anderson, 1975, Campbell and Stanley, 1966, Checkland and Scholes, 1990, Rossi and Freeman, 1985, Stecher and Davis, 1987). This issue forms a separate topic and its consideration would include a number of philosophical and ethical criteria by which the aims could be evaluated. The starting point in this guide is the acceptability of the stated aims and the efforts involved in assessing whether they have been achieved or not.

Since an evaluation will depend on the way the aims have been defined and the choice of appropriate objectives, it will be necessary to define these two concepts for the purposes of an evaluation programme:

- *aims* are defined as desired or planned outcomes of a programme or a project; they are usually stated in general terms and represent the basis for carrying out a project or a programme;

- *objectives* are defined as the means of achieving stated aims; an aim may have a number of different objectives which are related to the methods used as most appropriate for the achievement of the stated aims.

Sometimes planners understand quite different things when concepts are turned into actions. For evaluation, they need to state the aims precisely enough to be measured. They must also justify the choice of objectives for the achievement of each stated aim. This justification can be based on existing experience, empirical evidence or on tested theories. In some cases the objectives themselves may be the reason for evaluation. This can occur in situations where it is not clear which objectives can be linked to the achievement of aims and a set of alternative objectives may be tested as part of the evaluation project in order to discover those most appropriate. In this case, the evaluation process will be closely linked to the research processes related to the topic under study.

The decisions about aims and objectives can also be dependent on the interests of the stakeholders. Stakeholders are people who have a legitimate interest in the outcome of the project. If the evaluation does not take at least some of their needs into account, then it is hardly worth doing, since it will not make a contribution and is unlikely to be used. Usual stakeholders include: the staff carrying out a project, the consumers or clients of the project, the fund givers or the management of the institution which hosts the programme. In some cases evaluation is a part of a research project contracted from outside for the purpose of gaining information about the performance of the institution or the programme, or as a condition for the researchers gaining higher qualifications.

The aims and objectives will be decisive in choosing the most suitable type of evaluation, which can be:

- *monitoring* - this refers to keeping constant track of the progress of a project and can be a part of a more general evaluation;

- *assessment* - this is used to test the knowledge and skills of people involved in carrying out the objectives, as well as those considered to benefit from the outcomes;

- *appraisal* - this usually denotes a subjective assessment of a process which forms a part of the objectives; sometimes the term is applied to an evaluation of an individual's contribution as a whole;

- *formative evaluation* - this examines the process and the direction in which the programme or project is going with respect to the aims and objectives;

- *summative evaluation* - this examines the outcome and provides an insight into what has been done and whether it was worth doing in relation to the aims of the project or programme.

This differentiation of various kinds of evaluation is important, because it allows the evaluator to review the literature that deals with various aspects and provides detailed information about the methodology relevant to each type of evaluation.

A useful way of drawing up an initial plan for evaluation and what could and should be done is to try and visualise the whole system, which will include the relevant parts, as well as the relationship between those parts in terms of role definitions or expectations. This visualisation is a practical step in a systems approach (see p. 65) and can be helped by the use of certain cognitive tools which are available.

One such tool is the *diagram*. Diagrams can be used to sketch out the system with its boundaries, the hierarchical order of parts and the relationship between those parts in the form of 'boxes and arrows'. Another type of diagram is used to represent the actions and the consequences with decision points in the form of 'trunk and branches' diagrams. Different types of diagrams have special names such as *'cognitive maps'*, *'soft systems diagrams'* or *'relevance trees'*. The choice of diagrams used will depend on the personal preference of the evaluator since in this context it serves only to help in the conceptualisation of the whole field of activity.

Some evaluators may become confused by visual modelling and prefer to conceptualise an issue by using words and lists. For this purpose, they may find it useful to use a *matrix* in which they set out the system, with its parts and relationships, by using rows and columns. The cells in this type of a matrix contain words describing the items of interest instead of the numbers in a table, which are not appropriate for this purpose. Such a matrix can also be used to reveal whether the expectations of a project are realistic with respect to the time and resources to be devoted to parts of the whole. This approach is greatly enhanced by using a computer with a spreadsheet which will allow for manipulation of the entries. It is also much easier to work with a computerised database in keeping track of evaluation data.

In addition to helping the evaluator to conceptualise the problem, this kind of visualisation can be used to explain the project to other collaborators. There is a need for constant interaction and a flow of information about the project among those participating in it, the best way of doing this is by using visualisation methods at the regular meetings that should be a part of any evaluation process. The purpose of visualisation methods is to enable and support discussion among the team members and allow them to share the available knowledge and information and to reach agreement about the essentials of the process and the outcome.

Measuring success

The main methodological problem in evaluating a project is to choose the right *indicators* for the measurement of success or lack of it (Babbie, 1989, Baric, 1994, Fitz-Gibbon and Morris, 1987, OECD, 1988, King, Morris and Fitz-Gibbon, 1987,

Webb, 1971). The indicators will obviously be linked to aims but will also be relevant to the objectives chosen to achieve these aims. In a way it is a double measure: a sign of success or failure and a test of the links between aims and objectives. If the wrong objectives have been chosen for the achievement of an aim, then failure can be as much due to inappropriate objectives as to the wrong implementation of the right objectives.

The issue of indicators has been examined in detail elsewhere (see p.151). At this point, the evaluator should be reminded that an index may use variables or attributes, may distribute the findings on an ordinal or a cardinal scale, or may be expressed in a battery of questions which jointly will represent an index or a scale.

There are various ready-made indicators designed to measure the changes in the state of various attributes or variables. These must be used with caution and should relate directly to the aims of the study. It should also be realised that partial use of a ready-made instrument may require adjustments and consequently fresh testing.

Whether ready-made or newly created, the indicators for the purpose of evaluation must be tested for validity and reliability. Validity implies that the instrument is measuring what it is supposed to measure, whereas reliability implies that a similar result will be obtained when the measurement is repeated by other researchers.

Among available instruments are those using different methods of data collection: opinion surveys, tests of various kinds (achievement, ability, competence, etc.), different types of scales and finally simple straightforward questions.

Even when appropriate indicators have been chosen, the evaluator will be faced with the problem of deciding on the *criteria* that will indicate the success or failure of a project. The recognition of criteria relates to the acceptable levels expected to be achieved in a successful intervention and indicates the area of failure. In simple terms, 25% of positive replies in one study may be defined as success (for example in reduction of smoking), whereas in another study it may indicate a failure (as in an immunisation programme). To identify the accepted level as a criterion of success it will often be necessary to consult specialists in the field, such as for example, doctors, teachers and others.

The evaluation of the complex processes that are usually involved in a health promotion and health education intervention may require a multi-methodology approach, which will include a combination of a number of different instruments.

The evaluator should be aware that designing new instruments, as well as using some of the existing ones, requires expertise and in some cases, a recognised professional status, as is the case for example, with psychological tests.

Gathering information

The method of gathering information will define what kind of data will be collected and what kind of inferences can be made from such data (Burstein, Freeman and Rossi, 1985, Henerson, Morris and Fitz-Gibbon, 1987, King, Morris and Fitz-Gibbon, 1987, Miles and Huberman, 1984, Morris, Fitz-Gibbon and Lindheim, 1987, Patton, 1987). A case study approach using observational methods will produce qualitative data providing an insight into the relationship between the problem and solution, but will not allow for generalisation to other similar settings. A survey approach, on the other hand, whether it includes the whole population or a sample of it, is based on a structured instrument (questionnaire, test or scale), and will produce quantitative data, which can be statistically analysed and whose outcomes may be generalised for other similar settings.

The quality of the collected information will depend on the way it is produced. It is important to realise that data are generated: they are created as a result of an act by the researcher and reflect existing concepts and purposes. This applies also to even the most 'objective' measures. Inappropriate questions will produce inappropriate data, and no real information. The design of the instruments, collection and the analysis of data has been dealt with in detail earlier (see p. 191).

The evaluator should, however, be warned about some problems that might arise during the evaluation process:

- *respondents* - if they are selected for the purpose of convenience, some administrative reason or because they are willing to participate, this may seriously affect the accuracy and applicability of the outcome; this has to be taken into account, as well as the stability of the agents participating, with special reference to their geographic and occupational mobility;

- *methods* - different methods of intervention will have a different history of success or failure; past experience is likely to influence the approach the evaluator will take in selecting methods;

- *temporal changes* - this becomes an issue in projects which are of longer duration; respondents may change in terms of their age and maturity, their marital status or their occupation; some health promotion and health education outcomes can sometimes be the result of the maturation of respondents more than of the intervention;

- *experimental approach* - some interventions are more sophisticated than others; such sophisticated interventions may apply a research design which includes an experimental and a control group, where the outcomes are compared between these two groups; although this approach, using 'before and after' measurements, can produce very valuable insights into the changes due to the intervention as compared to other reasons, it has also been much criticised, since a problem lies in matching these two groups in terms of relevant parameters.

There are some general rules which apply to designing the instruments used for collecting data. The questions should be in a language that can be understood by the respondents; they should be precise, unambiguous and exclusive; they can be open or closed and leading questions should be avoided. The expected answers should be clearly defined; they should be ordered in a specific way (positive answers before negative ones), since the ordering of answers may influence their choice (see the extended discussion of these topics on page 191).

Finally, it should be borne in mind that the case study approach will provide an insight into the *possibility* of an event occurring, whereas a survey will also provide an insight into the *probability* of this event occurring in a given population.

What to do with the findings

The type of data collected will define how it can be most appropriately analysed and what kind of inferences it is justified to make from the findings (Cook and Campbell, 1979, Fitz-Gibbon and Morris, 1987, Hamilton et.al, 1977, Toh and Hu,

1991, Wurman, 1991). The details concerning the data analysis in general also apply to evaluation studies and have been dealt with earlier (see page 211).

The evaluator should, however, be aware that there are different rules for analysing qualitative, as compared to quantitative data. In many evaluation studies the data collected will fall into both of these categories and the evaluator will have to be competent in using both kinds of analysis, or seek expert help in doing so. The descriptive method is usually applied to analysing qualitative data, whereas it will be necessary to apply statistical methods for analysing quantitative data. The latter can be analysed by using descriptive or inferential statistics, discussed earlier.

The analysis of the data should be related to the intended purpose. In the case of evaluative studies, the purpose will be different from that of a general research project. In the former, it will be necessary to find out whether something works or not, whereas in the latter it will be necessary to find out *why* something works or not based on the accepted theory of the discipline involved. A combination of the two approaches, which evaluative research is expected to adopt, satisfies both needs.

The aims of a formative evaluation will be different from those of a summative evaluation. For a formative evaluation, the information needed will include evidence that the activity is reaching the consumer, that it is being conducted in the way intended, and that monitoring will enable the team to find out how far into a project they are or how far they are from the outcome; it is a judgement of whether the programme or project is on course. For a summative evaluation, where the final judgements are made, it is necessary to distinguish what was done from whether it came out exactly as intended and had the hoped-for consequences or whether in fact it had some unforeseen advantages or side-effects.

The analysis of the data will also have to meet the expectations and requirements of the stakeholders. If this is not taken into consideration, then the outcomes, even when they are positive, may not be accepted by the stakeholders.

The main aim of analysing data is to translate them into information. Data by themselves may mean nothing. They may have been created with a particular aim in mind, but still need to be put into context and have the meaning extracted. This is one role of the evaluator, who should take into account the wider context in which the programme or the project has been conducted. Awareness of the difference between data and information may also prevent evaluators from collecting meaningless data. The principle is to extract maximum information from a minimum of data. This principle is very important since a large number of questions will produce an enormous amount of data and threaten the practicability of the whole evaluation process. As has already been pointed out, if there are 50 questions in a questionnaire and they are subjected to the first level analysis by cross-tabulating them in 2 x 2 tables to find out which variables and attributes are significantly associated, then, applying the formula n (n-1)/2, where 'n' is the number of questions, the number of tables generated will be 1,225. To avoid a deluge of information it will be necessary to be selective as far as the number of questions is concerned and to use common sense in choosing the variables or attributes which need to be cross-tabulated.

Statistical data analysis has been made much easier by the development of ready-made computer programmes specifically dedicated to statistical analysis of data. (Epi Info, discussed in Appendix 2 gives some guidance on statistical analysis).

Writing the report

The main rule of report writing is that it should be kept simple (Morris and Fitz-Gibbon, 1987). There is a difference in writing a 'thesis' for a higher degree and writing a report for some stakeholder. The latter are interested in the outcomes and will trust the researcher to know the details of conceptualisation and methodology. Such details can be described in an appendix to the report.

There is a difference between formative and summative reports. Formative reports are a basis for decision-making within the ongoing context of the project itself. It is usually concerned with such issues as 'are we on the right course?' The function of a formative report is to report back to an external steering committee or the organisation providing the funds; to provide a record of actions taken, to check that actions are in line with what was agreed and that they justify the resource expenditure; and to provide a basis for internal decision-making about the direction in which the project is moving. The advantage of a formative report is to allow corrections and to provide a reflexive mechanism for making them.

The summative report is the interface between the evaluation team and the outside world. The main external message of a summative report in the framework of action is whether the reader could build on the work done in one project to apply it to another project. Some summative reports are, however, formalistic and have to meet the format required by the commissioning stakeholder, so they are less generally useful. Many potentially valuable reports are effectively shelved in this way.

It is helpful to bear in mind that in a sense 'a project never fails', whatever its outcome as revealed in the summative report. The judgement of success or failure of a project will depend on a number of intervening variables, and if an evaluation is conducted with sufficient rigour, both the 'success' and the 'failure' will have an important lesson to teach. It is in the interests of any programme to incorporate a thorough evaluation.

The contents of a typical summative report include:

- descriptive cover including the title of the project, dates, names of the evaluators and the body to which the report is addressed;
- executive summary;
- background and description of the project, including its origins, resources, aims and objectives, respondents and staff, financial and material resources and the description of the implementation;
- detailed description of the evaluation, including its purposes, its design and methodology, its data collection and analysis;
- cost-benefit analysis, which is required by some stakeholders, and should then be given in detail, documenting accurately the expenditure in terms of amount and timing;
- conclusions, including findings and recommendations.

Feedback

The summative report represents the main feedback for the needs of the stakeholders (Parlett and Dearden, 1977). Evaluators may be asked to participate in follow-up discussions and illuminate certain aspects which have not been fully covered in the report.

They may also be required to participate in training programmes based on the findings of the report.

The respondents who have provided the information on which the evaluation and the outcome have been based are very often forgotten or disregarded. There are few health promotion and health education intervention studies which incorporate a feedback mechanism that includes the respondents.

Another important group are other professionals active in this field. The best way of providing them with a feedback is to publish articles based on the report in professional journals. This moves evaluation towards research.

Policy makers in general should be interested in the study and the outcomes. If these are sufficiently general or indicate a radical change, they may be used for reform of existing or the creation of new policies.

The public may be interested, especially if the results are unexpected; they may not be so interested in the fact that a programme is being run successfully. Any indication of failure, mistakes or misdeeds as a result of evaluation will attract the attention of the press and the general public. This raises the issue of confidentiality and ownership of the research material and the reports, which is especially important where one or more of the researchers intend to use the project and its evaluation for a higher degree. For this a special agreement has to be written into the initial contract.

EVALUATION IN HEALTH PROMOTING SETTINGS

The aim of this section is to raise some important points for consideration when planning the evaluation of health promotion and health education activities within the context of the new approach of health promoting settings, expressed in terms of a number of questions:

Why health promotion in a setting?

We should be aware that the settings in general are a part of a larger system, such as for example the health care system, with specific tasks carried out within a defined structure by a defined set of professionals and auxiliary staff. This implies that the *emphasis should be on the setting* and that we should be able to explain to the management and staff of the setting in a language that they will understand how can health promotion and health education contribute to the improvement of the achievement of their task.

In this explanation it is necessary to *distinguish* between *health promotion in a setting* and the *health promoting setting.* Every setting involved with clients has certain aspects of health promotion as a part of normal care for clients. The "health promoting setting" represents a qualitative innovation, since health promotion becomes an integral part of the general cultural climate of the institution, of the way the setting is managed, and is an integral part of the extended care provided for clients, which includes their social and physical environment and mobilises other community and professional services as a part of this extended approach to care.

The setting as a system can be considered to have an *input* (clients), a production *process* (care and treatment) and an *output* (health gain of clients). The main variable in this equation is the difference in clients according to their readiness and competence related to coping and management of their health problems (input), whereas the health gain (output), and the process can be considered as being standardised (i.e. current best practice).

To explain the contribution of health promotion and health education to normal activities within a setting, it is possible to use an analogy from the field of education where the concept of *value added* has been introduced. It represents the gain from the educational process, which the students with poor entrance grades (input) achieve when they get high grades at the end of the educational process (output), in comparison to the expected high end grades of the students with high entrance grades. By analogy, one can say that health promotion and health education contribute to the *value added* of the clients with low levels of competence and readiness at the point of entering the setting, to enable them to achieve as high levels of health gain at the end of the process as any other clients who enter the setting with an already high level of competence and skills related to health.

What are we evaluating?

The answer to this question is not as obvious as it seems. We should be quite clear whether we are evaluating health promotion or a setting. Deciding on the starting point will have important consequences for procedures. Each of the two points of departure has its own characteristics, which will influence the evaluation process.

Health promotion and health education

Following the Alma Ata Declaration, the European developments arising from the initiative provided by WHO EURO have been mainly concerned with *health promotion,* which in general terms is concerned with influencing environmental factors conducive to health in the hope that they will positively influence the life style of the consumers. In USA, developments have been more concerned with *health education,* which is aimed at individuals and their knowledge, attitudes, motivation and decision-making about life style insofar as it is related to preservation of health and avoidance of risk and diseases. This is a broad differentiation, which does not imply that health promotion (in Europe) fails to take into account the health education of consumers, or that health education (in USA) fails to include environmental factors. The question is that of *emphasis* reflected in the resources devoted to research and interventions, and in the types of evaluation carried out.

A health promoting setting is appropriate for both types of intervention, and this should be taken into consideration when planning and evaluating interventions. For evaluation purposes it is important to keep in mind the differentiation between population-related and individual-related interventions. The *population-related* interventions will use *surveys* and statistical data interpretations, whereas *individual-related* interventions will use individual records, case studies and *qualitative* analysis of outcomes. Community-related interventions may also use qualitative analysis.

The health promoting setting

Although the introduction of health promotion and health education in a setting can produce *value added* to the outcome, in helping the clients, the concept of a *health promoting setting* represents a qualitative difference in the services provided.

A setting already has a clearly defined role in the community and within the health care system. The introduction of the concept of a *health promoting setting* can only mean that such a setting *should carry out its predefined tasks as well as enlarge its role within the community, on the assumption that this role could be made more effective by the introduction of health promotion and health education.* The three parameters in question are:

- creating a healthy working and living environment;
- integrating health promotion (and health education) into its daily activities;
- outreach into the community in the form of health promoting alliances.

Success in introducing a *health promoting setting* will depend on the changes which are required for such a transformation. These will include, in the first place, a change in the style of management of the setting. The management changes will be necessary in relation to the following key result areas (KRAs):

- Customer satisfaction
- Quality
- People growth
- Organisational climate
- Innovation
- Productivity
- Economics

The new style of management for success in these KRAs (known as *total management*) will require a basic change in the corporate climate, development of a horizontal instead of a vertical organisational structure, change from a *conveyor belt* to a *group* production approach, full participation of all employees (in *quality* and *health* circles), interchangeable roles within working groups, and the introduction of total quality management.

It should be realised that the creation of a health promoting setting is a *new venture* which has no precedent. Its novelty requires the support an advisor or consultant. This fact will affect the role of the *consultant* and the link with an academic institution, which is necessary to complement any lack of expertise within the staff of the setting in the field of health promotion and health education, as well as research and evaluation. The consultant cannot be expected nor should attempt to provide "ready made" prescriptions of what should be done and how it should be done and evaluated, but provide ways and means for the *staff of the setting* to mount intervention studies for the purpose of *exploring their role* in health promotion and health education and validating the experiences from these intervention studies for transmission to other settings where this is appropriate.

The novelty of the venture is also the reason for creating *pilot* settings, which are intended to provide empirically tested methods of producing health gain for the clients, including the documented contribution to this aim of health promotion and health education.

The consequence of such an approach will be that *evaluation* will not be concerned with health promotion as such, but with the *setting's activities and the role of health promotion and health education* in achieving the expected health outcomes within the given framework.

How should we evaluate settings?

Evaluation of a setting is particularly demanding, since there is little previous work on evaluating organisations to draw on. There is, however, a great deal of work on evaluation in general and on organisational behaviour which can be relevant. In addition to general principles derived from these sources, it will be necessary to consider the special requirements which an evaluation of a 'health promoting setting' may have.

In a health promoting setting, evaluation methods will have to take into account evaluation or assessment activities already taking place within a setting. This means that, for example, in a community care service setting evaluation will have to be included into the *existing quality management* of activities of the setting.

Since the role of a health care setting is defined by the health gain of the clients, any evaluation related to the health promotion and health education interventions will have to include the *health outcome evaluation*, in addition to programme impact evaluation.

Aims and objectives

In this section, a guide to an evaluation in a setting is outlined in some detail. It uses as an example an intervention study designed to test the feasibility of creating a health promoting setting, and from the stated aims and objectives, develops indicators, which can be used for the evaluation of this intervention. This is of great importance since there is so little existing experience in creating or evaluating a health promoting setting.

The example used is based on an intervention study designed to test the feasibility of creating a health promoting hospital. The aims and objectives of the intervention are given and followed by the definition of indicators, which can be used in evaluating this specific intervention. The aims are divided into those concerning the base-line information, the intervention and the post-intervention activities:

a) Base-line information:

Aim 1: to establish the needs of the patients in relation to their utilisation of setting services; to achieve this aim the study will have the following objectives:

Objective 1.1: to explore the ways and reasons for patients attending different setting units;

Indicators 1.1: records of admissions and referrals;

Objective 1.2: to explore the 'patient career' as a part of the treatment;

Indicators 1.2: records on duration of stay; types of treatment; access to specialists;

Objective 1.3: to explore patient satisfaction with the outcome of treatment;

Indicators 1.3: statements by patients about the satisfaction of expectations; objective and subjective expectations;

Aim 2: to describe the internal structure of the setting as a means of satisfying patients' needs; to achieve this aim the study will have the following objectives:

Objective 2.1: to define the organisational structure, power structure, role definition and role relationships, professional expertise within the setting;

Indicators 2.1: the management structure; role definitions; role relationships;

Objective 2.2: to explore potential conflict areas and possible resolutions within the staff of the setting, as well as between the staff and the patients;

Indicators 2.2: survey data on conflicts among the staff and between staff and patients;

Objective 2.3: to explore the available technology as well as accommodation for staff and patients within the setting premises as a means of satisfying patients needs;

Indicators 2.3: opinions of staff about technology and existing accommodation;

Aim 3: to describe the links of the setting with other institutions, the community and the environment; to achieve this aim the study will have the following objectives:

Objective 3.1: to explore the means and the level of financing of the setting and its activities;

Indicators 3.1: information about the available resources related to the needs for running the setting; potential shortcomings;

Objective 3.2: to explore the relationship between the setting and the DHA, FHSA, or other community and voluntary bodies;

Indicators 3.2: descriptive data about these relationships with an assessment in terms of expressed expectations;

Objective 3.3: to explore the interaction between the setting and the wider environment in terms of provision of services, source of employment, utilisation of transport and sources of waste disposal and other aspects of potential contamination;

Indicators 3.3: data on any negative assessments of the setting activities affecting the environment;

Aim 4: to describe, in addition to treatment, the preventive and promotive activities relevant to the successful treatment of patients; to achieve this aim the study will have the following objectives:

Objective 4.1: to explore the existing preventive services on offer;

Indicators 4.1: information on the existing preventive services;

Objective 4.2: to explore the existing health promotive activities;

Indicators 4.2: information on the existing health promotion activities concerning the behaviour of staff and patients;

Objective 4.3: to explore the links between the setting and other preventive and health promotive actions in the area;

Indicators 4.3: information about existing links;

Aim 5: to explore with the setting staff the possibility of undertaking a commitment to become a 'Health Promoting Setting' within the WHO conceptualisation of the requirements for such a commitment; to achieve this aim the study will have the following objectives:

Objective 5.1: to explore the felt needs of the staff and possibility of meeting their requirements;

Indicators 5.1: survey data on the needs of the staff; exploration of existing mechanisms for satisfaction of those needs;

Objective 5.2: to explore the necessary resources to meet the existing shortcomings within the provision of setting services;

Indicators 5.2: data on existing and required resources for provision of setting services;

Objective 5.3: to organise a workshop for members of the setting staff and other relevant institutions (DHA, FHSA) for the purpose of establishing a joint commitment for collaboration and support in this endeavour;

Indicators 5.3: curriculum for workshop for the setting staff;

b) The Intervention:

Aim 6: the creation of a "Health Promoting Setting" movement in the setting; to achieve this aim the study will have the following objectives:

Objective 6.1: the self-selection of members of staff who will undertake commitments and carry out role definition and task distribution among its members;

Indicators 6.1: list of members and their commitments;

Objective 6.2: the organisation of training ventures for staff concerning their commitments;

Indicators 6.2: timetable for training venture;

Objective 6.3: provision of skills for monitoring and evaluating the progress of the intervention as well as the changes within the setting;

Indicators 6.3: content analysis of training ventures concerning the skills necessary for evaluation and monitoring;

Aim 7: the planning and provision of health promotion and health education ventures as a part of the normal activities of a 'health promoting setting'; to achieve this aim the study will have the following objectives:

Objective 7.1: planning of tasks for each subgroup in the setting involved in health promotion and health education;

Indicators 7.1: list of subgroups; lists of tasks for each subgroup;

Objective 7.2: definition of indicators and criteria for the evaluation of each health promotion and health education venture;

Indicators 7.2: list of agreed indicators and criteria for evaluation;

Objective 7.3: carrying out the planned tasks;

Indicators 7.3: data on each health promotion/education activity carried out within the setting; assessment of each activity using the set indicators and criteria;

Aim 8: integration of setting health promotion and health education activities into the overall activities of the "health promoting health care system"; to achieve this aim the study will have the following objectives:

Objective 8.1: collaboration with the existing activities of the Health Promotion Unit of the DHA;

Indicators 8.1: data on collaborative activities;

Objective 8.2: collaboration with the existing activities of the FHSA;

Indicators 8.2: data on collaborative activities;

Objective 8.3: integration of all these activities into the health promotion and health education activities of the health care system in the district;

Indicators 8.3: District Health Authority programme on health promotion and health education; data on setting aspects of these activities;

c) Post-intervention activities:

Aim 9: to carry out the monitoring of the intervention study; to achieve this aim the study will have the following objectives:

Objective 9.1: developing computerised instruments for monitoring the ongoing activities within the intervention;

Objective 9.2: application of instruments for monitoring the activities;

Objective 9.3: analysis of data collected by means of the monitoring process;

Aim 10: to carry out the evaluation of the intervention; to achieve this aim the study will have the following objectives:

Objective 10.1: evaluation of the health promotion activities within the intervention study;

Objective 10.2: evaluation of the health education activities within the intervention study;

Objective 10.3: evaluation of the outcomes of the intervention study in terms of staff satisfaction and improvements in the health of the patients;

Aim 11: the auditing of the intervention in terms of staff and patient satisfaction of the expressed needs; to achieve this aim the study will have the following objectives:

Objective 11.1: establishment of existing professional and social norms related to the aims of the intervention;

Objective 11.2: measurement of intervention outcomes in terms of the established professional and social norms;

Objective 11.3: definition of areas where the existing professional and social norms need reinforcement or change.

This extended example of a process of creating a health promoting setting, in this case a health promoting hospital, provides an opportunity for the examination of the intervention aims and objectives and for the selection of appropriate indicators for their evaluation. From this exercise a number of general points emerge:

- it is necessary to realise that the *emphasis* is on evaluating the setting's activities and that health promotion and health education are only contributing factors;

- it is important to *differentiate* between health promotion and health education interventions and their contribution to 'value added' for the maximisation of the client's health gain, as well as for the influence of the setting on the improvement of the health in the community;

- the process of evaluation should be *adjusted* to the existing methods of assessment already existing in the setting; this includes the introduction of health promotion and health education indicators into the existing activities in terms of the quality assessment with special reference to "total management" and "total quality management" approaches;

- the pilot status of a setting can be a means of developing standards and specifications for the treatment of clients in terms of health promotion and health education; the pilot setting can provide a *"benchmark"* for other settings. There must also be 'realistic' expectations from the contribution of *consultants* and external institutions. Participants should be ready to find their own answers, by means of intervention studies, as a part of their new status.

META-EVALUATION

It can be maintained (Baric, 1989) that since evaluation is a recognised activity it can also itself be 'audited'. The concept of 'auditing' is interpreted as implying an assessment of an activity according to externally set rules or expectations. In this sense a process of evaluation can be assessed (or 'audited') according to the externally imposed standards which apply to a credible evaluation. This 'auditing' of evaluation is known as *meta-evaluation*. In the USA, evaluation has long been a required aspect of programmes or projects which attract external resources. A meta-evaluation of this kind was carried out in 1970 by Bernstein and Freeman (reported in Hudson and McRoberts, 1984, p.219-236). The study included 1,000 federally funded evaluation studies, and found that approximately half were deficient either in design, sampling or the validity of measures used.

There are different ways of carrying out meta-evaluation. Cook and Gruder (1978) mention seven models of metaevaluation and dismiss three as of little use since they were carried out simultaneously with the evaluation (consultant meta-evaluation, simultaneous secondary analysis of data and multiple independent replications). They state that auditors, unlike evaluation consultants, prefer to carry out auditing after the completion of a programme. The remaining four models that they consider useful include meta-evaluation in the form of an essay review of evaluation work, a review of literature about a particular programme, empirical re-evaluation of an evaluation study and an empirical re-evaluation of multiple data sets about the same programme.

A distinction should be made between 'multi-site evaluation' and 'meta-evaluation'. Multi-site evaluation is considered to be a set of comparable evaluations of a number of intervention programmes (of similar kind) in a number of settings (of similar kind) and carries out a comparison of the evaluation programmes and their outcomes. *Meta-evaluation on the other hand is the evaluation of the evaluation procedures in different programmes and involves a comparison of the standards of the evaluation procedures applied.*

There are a number of approaches which can be used in planning a meta-evaluation. They will depend on the character of the actual evaluation programmes which are being evaluated. These evaluation programmes can be differentiated according to the intentions and extent of the assessment such as:

- formative and summative evaluation: formative evaluation is concerned with the programme and processes, whereas summative evaluation is concerned with outcomes;

- evaluation of programme, processes and outcomes; these three aspects of an intervention need to be taken into consideration.

Rossi and Freeman (1985) consider meta-evaluation to be just one aspect of impact evaluations. It is suggested that meta-evaluation can put programme impact in perspective and provide summative findings about it; this can be achieved by systematically examining the results of individual evaluations as a single body of evidence.

The authors illustrate this point by an example concerning meta-evaluation of several hundred studies of the effectiveness of psychotherapy for increasing the functioning of patients, which was carried out in the early 1980s. Some of these studies could have been criticised for their methodology and the comparison was difficult because the studies were concerned with different types of therapies. Only some of the studies had adequate controls or relied on shadow controls. The outcomes of studies ranged from improvement in subsequent functioning to no improvement or even actual deterioration.

An attempt to make sense of this range of findings of various studies has been made by Smith et al. (1980), who decided to treat each of the studies as a case study and carry out a meta-evaluation of the study's evaluation processes. They used a multivariate analysis in which the various characteristics used in the research were health-constant. An examination of literature produced 475 evaluations based on groups of individuals undergoing psychotherapy, each compared with one or more control groups. Meta-evaluation measured the types of evaluations carried out in each study (e.g. randomised experiments etc.). Using as the dependent variable the estimates of the net effects of studies and the quality of evaluation as the independent variable, by means of a multivariate statistical analysis, the researchers estimated the true net effects of psychotherapy, which was derived from the results, taking into account the ways in which evaluations differed from each other. The outcome of the meta-evaluation supported the finding that there was a considerable improvement in experimental groups receiving psychotherapy, with the members of experimental groups being better off than 80% of the controls (.85 standard deviation). Another interesting finding was that there was no noticeable difference between the various types of therapies.

Similar meta-evaluations have been carried out in other fields. (Glass et.al, 1981; Light & Pillemer, 1984; Hunter et.al, 1982). The authors report on studies including prisoner rehabilitation, vocational training and surgical interventions.

Scriven (1991) defines meta-evaluation as the evaluation of evaluations, or indirectly the evaluation of evaluators. It is considered to be an ethical as well as a scientific obligation in cases where the welfare of others is involved. Meta-evaluation can use a specific checklist or a general checklist. An example of a general checklist is the 'key evaluation checklist (KEC)', as described by Stufflebeam (1981). This can be used for a 'repeated design approach'; involving planning and evaluation based on the checklist, which is then compared with the actual evaluation of the project; or as the basis for assessing the original evaluation using the checklist elements:

- description (design, staffing, time of the evaluation; sources of data, specifications and parameters);

- background and context (demand and opposition to evaluation, prior evaluations, credibility of the proposed evaluation approaches);

- consumer (client, audience, evaluators);

- resources (for evaluation, for design, for execution);

- values (criteria of merit, clients' needs, professional standards, timeliness, relevance, cost-effectiveness, justice, validity, evaluators' assumptions);

- process (general assessment of the evaluation design and execution, reporting, confidentiality, credibility, assessment of results, false positives and false negatives, consideration for those affected by evaluation);

- outcomes (reports and their good or bad effect, process of evaluation, its effects on productivity, morale, use of information in decision-making);

- costs (of evaluation, alternative costs);

- comparisons (with alternatives, such as no evaluation, using informed judgement, other evaluation models);

- generalisability (other applications for other programmes, sites, use at later date);

- significance (synthesis of above to achieve assessment of value and merit of evaluation);

- recommendations;

- report (of the metaevaluator).

Another available checklist (Stufflebeam, 1981) is that of the General Accounting Office (GAO), which involves ten criteria divided into three groups:

- need for the programme;
  problem magnitude,
  problem seriousness,
  duplication;
- implementation of the programme;
  interrelationships,
  fidelity (implementation of treatment),
  administrative efficiency;

- effects of the programme;
  targeting success,
  goal achievement,
  cost effectiveness,
  other effects.

A criticism of this checklist is that there is a duplication between "duplication" and "interrelationships"; there is no mention of ethics and legality; and there is little mention of comparison, resources and generalisability.

Three specific checklists quoted by Stufflebeam (1981) are :

The Meta-evaluation Checklist (MEC), which includes:

- conceptual clarity;
- comprehensiveness;
- cost-effectiveness;
- credibility;
- ethics;
- stated standards of merit used;
- feasibility;
- precision;
- political and psychological sensitivity;
- appropriate reporting (including clients' needs, security, timeliness and validity).

This list, it should be noted, does not mention implementation.

QUEMAC, by Bob Gowin, deals specifically with unquestioned assumptions in the design and includes: questions, unquestioned assumptions, evaluations, methods, answers, concept.

Evaluation Standards is the title of a set of principles applied to programme evaluation. It is based on discussions with many professional groups and associations and summarised by Stufflebeam (1980). A similar set of standards was also produced by the Evaluation Research Society. The criticism of both attempts is mainly that neither includes "needs assessment". The positive side is that they can help in standardising the evaluation approach, whereas the negative side is that they may produce too rigid an approach to evaluation. Their main use is as a reminder of various issues which should be taken into account when planning an evaluation.

Meta-evaluation thus includes a critical analysis of the research design, as well as the method of analysing the findings, comparing strategy against empirically validated standards.

Internal evaluation may be unreliable and it is suggested that an external independent evaluator should be used to carry out meta-evaluation. This approach involves the question of power distribution, as the researchers and evaluators are exposed to scrutiny from an external source. The effects can be expressed in increasing validity and performance and reducing costs.

Meta-evaluation is an important aspect of any evaluation since it draws attention to the accountability of the evaluators. It represents the answer to the question "who evaluates the evaluators?". This question could also be extended to include "who evaluates the meta-evaluator?" Common sense suggests that there is no point in an infinite regress.

The outcome of any meta-evaluation should be presented in a draft form to the evaluators involved before it is given to the client.

SUMMARY

Evaluation, as described in this section, is concerned with assessing the aims of the intervention or of a programme. There are a number of specific characteristics of evaluation that a researcher has to take into consideration. The main precondition for a successful evaluation is that its planning should be integrated into the initial planning of the intervention or the programme. Inclusion of evaluation into the planning process should ensure that the programme or intervention is based on clearly defined and measurable aims and that the objectives are directly linked to the achievement of these aims.

The actual aspects of measurement involved in evaluation are similar to those described in planning a research project. The need to conform to scientific standards and provide an acceptable level of objectivity result in the possibility of generalising the outcomes.

A specific case is the evaluation of health promoting settings, which have a character of their own and are required to meet some predefined conditions.

Evaluation programmes can also be evaluated; this is known as meta-evaluation, which is concerned with assessing the evaluation procedures in each programme under consideration.

It is important to recognise the complexity and rigour associated with evaluation procedures because of the importance an evaluation report could have on the setting, the staff within that setting and the justification for the resources invested. In a number of countries, evaluation is, therefore, considered to be a professional activity, which implies a professional relationship between the evaluators and the people involved in a programme. In this context, a professional relationship is interpreted as including the objectivity as well as the accountability of those who carry out evaluation.

QUALITY MANAGEMENT

Introduction
History of QMS and TQM
TQM in HP/HE
Standards
Implementation of QMS
Criticism of QMS
Summary

INTRODUCTION

The emphasis in health promotion and health education now placed on settings has resulted in the introduction of an organisational model and extended the possibilities of evaluation of health promotion and health education activities. There are some settings which already have a mechanism for the assessment and evaluation of processes and outcomes which can also be utilised for the assessment of health promotion and health education. Most of these mechanisms are concerned with quality assessment. The idea of introducing health promotion and health education into the existing quality assessment mechanisms represents an innovation which, has not as yet, been tested and empirically justified. This description of practical steps in introducing health promotion and health education into quality assessment represents an experiment for health promoting settings, which may explore this method of monitoring and evaluating their activities. Those concerned with health promotion and health education should try to find out whether it produces any noticeable improvement on the established ways of checking on what is going on in the field and what, if any, are the benefits for the consumers/patients/clients.

The role of the *purchasers* of the services to be provided for users in a setting is very important in supporting this development. Purchasers are expected, together with professionals in the field, to approve the *standards* and to set the *specifications* for health promotion and health education services in these settings. Within the setting, in turn, it should be able to introduce appropriate procedures and standard practices and observe a clear advantage, through increased benefits in terms of support and resources.

The main principles of introducing quality into evaluation of health promotion and health education activities, as well as introducing health promotion and health education activities into existing quality management systems has been described elsewhere (see Baric, 1994, pp. 304-316).

In recent years, the general idea of quality assessment has undergone a radical change through the introduction in industry of the concept of Total Quality Management.

Recently, however, there has been some criticism directed towards the way the quality assessment has been implemented. It has been accused of degenerating into bureaucratic form-filling, instead of concentrating on the contribution the systems make to the quality of people working within the settings as the important precondition for success.

HISTORY OF QMS AND TQM

The introduction of the processes of quality management systems (QMS) and especially the idea of a total quality management approach (TQM) into health promotion and health education is an innovation and requires the understanding of the underlying principles before it can be accepted as a part of the existing assessment procedures. This understanding can be enhanced by a historical overview of the developments in quality management with special reference to total quality management.

The measurement of the quality of the product as a part of the production process has a long history (Bendell, et.al, 1993). It was only more recently that a formal approach to quality management systems (QMS) has been implemented. This led to further developments, notably the total quality management (TQM) approach.

The concept of quality management has its origins in America in the period before the second world war, where a number of big industries became concerned with quality control with the aim of increasing customer confidence in their products. One of the pioneers in this field was Western Electric, where a system of quality control was introduced in 1920.

In 1924, Western Electric set up the Inspection Engineering Department at their Bell Laboratories in New York. The man in charge was **Dr Walter Shewhart,** who together with his colleagues designed the first control charts and developed other techniques using statistical methods for the measurement and control of quality. Shewhart is considered to be the inventor of the control chart and SPC or Statistical Process Control. SPC meant that the quality was measured during the process of manufacture and not only at the end of the line. A number of chart interpretation rules were developed, which allowed the process operator to see whether the process was still, in statistical terms, under control or not and whether it was likely to produce outputs conforming to standards. Shewhart differentiated between "common" and "special" causes of variation. The former are a part of the system and out of operator's control, whereas the latter are due to specific circumstances and can be modified.

In 1925, **Harold E. Dodge** (Shewhart's colleague) developed statistically based methods of acceptance sampling.

The use of statistical methods to analyse variation is based on the work carried out in Britain by **R.A. Fisher,** who in 1925 published a work detailing initial experiments at Rothamstead Agricultural Research Station, concerned with potato yields.

In 1931, Shewhart published "Economic Control of Quality of Manufactured Products", followed by a lecture tour at the University of London in 1932, which resulted in the setting up of the Industrial and Agricultural Section of the Royal Statistical Society.

In 1935, Fisher published "The Design of Experiments" . At the same time, **E.S. Pearson** developed the first British standard on quality control BS6000, entitled "Application of Statistical Methods to Industrial Standardisation and Quality Control".

After the second world war, one of Shewhart's colleagues, **Dr. W.E. Deming,** (Walton, 1989) who had been engaged with

Shewhart in developing statistical methods of quality control, was invited to Japan to assist Japanese industrial development. During his visits in 1951, Deming met with members of JUSE (Japanese Union of Scientists and Engineers), together with some other experts from the Bell Telephone Laboratories. The Japanese were taught how to use statistical methods for quality control based on BS6000 and also the Z-1 American standards. During his stay in Japan, Deming taught five hundred managers and engineers how to control production variations by the use of control charts. He also introduced a systematic approach to problem-solving and improvement by using a model (known as Shewhart's cycle, Deming cycle or PDCA cycle). The model includes four factors: *Plan, Do, Check, Action*, which includes a sequence of activities as well as a feed-back loop. Deming also stressed the need to work closely with suppliers to improve the uniformity and reliability of incoming materials, as well as the need for maintenance of equipment. He included the consumer into the equation, stating that *"the consumer is the most important part of the production line"*. The Deming approach became known as the Total Quality Management approach. It looks at the process of production as a system, including the raw material process and the end product. The principles and the 'fourteen points for management' developed by Deming (1986) were published in his book 'Out of the Crisis'.

The concept of 'total quality management' has been very influential. The basic idea promoted by Deming is very simple, although at the time highly original. Deming postulated that the economic success will depend on the quality of goods. At the time, immediately following the war, it was a sellers' market and one could sell anything that was available. Deming foresaw that this would change and that in a buyers' market the quality of goods would be decisive.

Stating *"quality sells the product"*, Deming examined the production process as a system into which he included the supplier and consumer as well as the production process. This was new and proved to be critical for the success of quality control. Following this approach, Deming maintained that one person's 'raw material' is somebody else's 'end product', and that one person's 'end product' is another's 'raw material'. In this way, a *production unit* is composed of suppliers' raw material, the process of production and the end product aimed at consumers. It is, therefore, logical that quality assessment should include the quality of the raw material, the quality of the production process and the quality of the end product.

A *production line* is a system which can include a number of production units. If one divides the production line into these units, then quality control will apply to all the stages within each unit as a part of the production line.

The indicators for quality assessment will be the needs of the production process and the needs of the consumer. Deming did not rely on asking consumers about their needs and emphasised that the producer should lead in the definition of consumers' needs by anticipating new developments and possibilities in a specific production process.

Deming developed this idea in the form of a training programme for managers, which he originally carried out in Japan. The success in Japan led to the approach being adopted in America and Europe.

The Deming training programme covers fourteen points, includes 'seven deadly diseases', and lists thirteen obstacles. The relevance of the aspects identified by Deming to health promotion and health education in settings is that the health promotion and health education can and should be built into the organisation's quality system.

The fourteen points of the Deming training programme are as follows:

1. create constancy of purpose for improvement of product and service;
2. adopt the new philosophy;
3. cease dependence on mass inspection;
4. end the practice of awarding business on price tag alone;
5. improve constantly and forever the system of production and service;
6. institute training and retraining;
7. institute leadership;
8. drive out fear;
9. break down barriers between staff areas;
10. eliminate slogans, exhortations, and targets for the workforce;
11. eliminate numerical quotas;
12. remove barriers to pride of workmanship;
13. institute a vigorous programme of education and training;
14. take action to accomplish the transformation.

Deming also listed "seven deadly diseases" which can thwart successful economic growth. These are:

1. lack of constancy of purpose;
2. emphasis on short-term profits;
3. evaluation of performance, merit rating or annual review;
4. mobility of top management;
5. running a company on visible figures alone ("counting the money")
6. excessive medical costs;

7. excessive costs of warranty fuelled by lawyers who work on contingency fees.

Deming also included some less important negative aspects which he called "obstacles", such as:

1. neglect of long-range planning and transformation;
2. the supposition that solving problems, automation, gadgets and new machinery will transform industry;
3. the search for examples;
4. "our problems are different";
5. obsolescence in schools;
6. reliance on quality control departments;
7. blaming the workforce for problems;
8. quality by inspection;
9. false starts;
10. the unmanned computer;
11. meeting specifications;
12. inadequate testing of prototypes;
13. "anyone that comes to try to help us must understand all about our business.

Acting as a consultant for a great number of years, Deming accumulated valuable experience on how to successfully carry out the required and often radical changes in an enterprise. He learned that the only way to achieve transformation is to *involve top management* and get them to learn about the elements of their commitment before they take it on. A radical transformation will only be possible if the top management is behind it. This was tested in a number of situations where Deming acted as a consultant and where his model produced direct profits for the enterprises.

The Deming theory of management control is of special interest to those involved in evaluation of health promotion within an organisational model, since it has been tested and proved successful. The application of a tested model in health promotion would represent an innovation, since most of the models and approaches in present use are justified only on the grounds of preference or common-sense, without any proof that they work.

Deming postulates that ensuring the highest possible level of quality of a product will require the selection of the best available "raw material", the most appropriate "method of production", and the detailed knowledge of the "needs" of the consumer. The inclusion of resources and the consumers into the model of production has been an innovation which has resulted in considerable gains in industry and commerce. It seems that the adjustment of this model to the needs of health promotion could represent an improvement of the existing method of evaluation in this field.

The Deming method was very successful in Japan and the interest in the West was created only in 1980 when the American broadcasting company NBC made a documentary entitled "If Japan Can, Why Can't We?" . This lead to the rediscovery of Deming by the West and the gradual introduction of TQM in many Western companies.

In 1954, **J.M.Juran** went also to Japan as an expert in management and quality. He emphasised that quality control should be an integral part of management control ('Quality Control Handbook', 1951). He used the measurement of cost attributable to quality problems within an organisation to capture the attention of managers in the West.

Dr Armand V. Feigenbaum was the third American quality expert to visit Japan in the 1950s. His main contributions were to the improvement of such Japanese companies as Toshiba and

Hitachi. Feigenbaum (1991) defined the concept of total quality control as all the functions within the quality process and not just the manufacturing area. It includes the administrative function and the measurement and control of quality at every stage from customer specification and sales, through design, engineering, assembly and shipment. He defined total quality system as:

"The agreed company-wide and plant-wide operating work structure, documented in effective, integrated, technical and managerial procedures, for guiding the coordinated actions of the people, the machines, and the information of the company and plant in the best and most practical ways to assure customer quality satisfaction and economical cost of quality".

Ishikawa, working with Deming wrote 'What is Total Quality Control? The Japanese Way' (1985). It was an effort to help the Japanese understand the statistical methods involved in quality control. He wrote:

"In management, Japan also lagged behind, using the so called Taylor method in certain quarters.......Quality control was totally dependent on inspection, and not every product was sufficiently inspected. In those days Japan was still competing with cost and price, but not with quality. It was literally still the age of 'cheap and poor products'."

Ishikawa (1985), a Japanese follower of Deming, was involved in teaching the application of statistical methods for quality control at university level. He also pioneered the Quality Circle Movement in Japan and was involved with the Japanese Industrial Standards Committee in their work. He developed the so called "Seven Tools of Quality Control":

1. Pareto charts - to prioritise action.
2. Cause & effect diagrams - to identify causes of variation.
3. Stratification - to divide data into subsets.
4. Check sheets - for data collection.
5. Histograms - to display variation graphically.
6. Scatter diagrams - to confirm relationships between two factors.
7. Shewhart's control charts and graphs - to monitor and control variation.

Ishikawa's book 'Guide to Quality Control' (1976) is a classic text and was translated from Japanese to English. He is most famous for the 'Ishikawa diagram' or 'fishbone diagram', which can be used to express the source of problems in achieving a result. Ishikawa has been a major contributor to the development of the Company Wide Quality Control movement in Japan which implies that everyone is involved in measuring quality and needs to know statistical methods; every function and all levels should participate in the improvement process; incoming raw materials, manufacturing processes, personnel issues and sales problems are measured and after sales services, quality of management, the company itself and the people working in it are also included.

An offshoot of the Company Wide Quality movement was the concept of Quality Control Circles. These will vary between companies but they share some common characteristics: small groups from five to ten people from the same work area meet voluntarily on a regular basis to discuss, investigate, measure and analyse work related problems. The Circle is led by a foreman or one of the workers, using Ishikawa's 'Seven Tools of Quality Control'. The outcome of the work of the Circle is transmitted to the management for implementation or authorisation of implementation by the workers. The aims of the Circle are:

- to contribute to the improvement and development of the enterprise;
- to respect human relations and build a happy workshop offering job satisfaction;
- to deploy human capabilities fully and draw out infinite potential.

The idea of the Quality Circles spread in Japan where there are an estimated ten million in operation. The idea has also spread in the West and a number of European industries have introduced Quality Circles (WHO, 1993).

Two other Japanese quality experts, Taguchi and Shingo, also contributed to the prosperity of the Japanese industry by evolving methods for the prevention of quality problems in manufacture and for the design of efficient processes. **Taguchi** had been associated with Toyota and was able to simplify complex statistical methods for the use of non-academics; especially applicable to the design of new production processes. **Shingo** has also had an enormous impact on the quality of Japanese products. He was also associated with the Toyota Motor Company and with Mitsubishi Heavy Industries. He is known for halving the time for the hull assembly of a 65,000 ton super tanker from four to two months. He is best known for developing the Poka-yoke system, which literally means "mistake proofing". By using devices which prevent defects from occurring, like physical contact, limit switches, photo-electric cells, pressure sensitive switches, thermostats, etc. which give a warning in the form of a flashing light or an alarm buzzer or by automatically taking control and shutting the machine down, the need for measurement is avoided. The outcome of this system is Zero Quality Control, which enables defect-free operations to run for several months. Shingo is also known for reducing the time of changeovers in equipment which practically guarantees a non-interrupted production. This together with Zero Quality Control enables the Just-In-Time approach to stock, which means that one can avoid large stocks of parts lying idle. All these methods were developed at Toyota and were later adopted by the West.

Claus Møller, a Danish business economist, contributed to quality improvement by developing training programmes and customer services, under the label of "Putting People First", which was applied by Japanese airlines with great success. Møller's Personal Quality Grids (1987) provide individuals with a series of grids and tables which allowed them to measure and monitor their personal quality performance. Møller sees personal quality as the basis for all other types of quality. Two standards for personal quality can be successfully measured, the IP-level or Ideal Performance Level which reflects a person's desires, expectations and demands concerning his/her performance; and the AP-level or Actual Performance Level which shows what a person is currently achieving. The difference between IP and AP reflects what one is capable of achieving and what one actually is achieving and is used as an indicator for personal development or improvement.

A relatively new tool in this field of activities is *Quality Function Deployment*, which is a process starting by mapping customer requirement to potential product or service features and ensures that the voice of the customer is heard throughout the business.

Another tool is *benchmarking* which enables the establishment of realistic improvement targets by looking at the best practice as performed by leaders in the field. This then represents the target for the quality improvement of an organisation.

TQM IN HP/HE

Total Quality Management (TQM) concentrates on the process. The process is sub-divided into the various points in the system and each of these points is differentiated in terms of 'raw material (RM) - end product (EP)'.

The first assumption of TQM is that any production process can be sub-divided into various points in terms of production units. For example, a doctor-patient interaction in a general practitioner's surgery could be sub-divided into the family context from which the patient comes, the receptionist as the first contact, seeing the doctor and then returning into the family and community. Each of these points in the system can be conceptualised as consisting of the patient being 'the end product' of the family and becoming the 'raw material' for the receptionist. The same idea can be taken forward through the whole system of interactions.

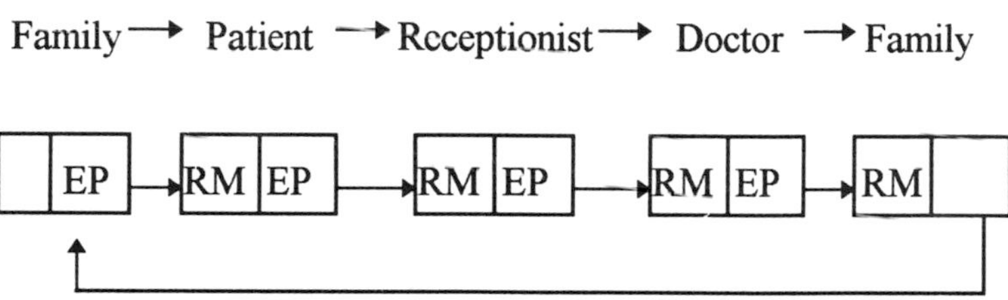

The diagram defines the points in the system in terms of functions, interactions and activities: the family as the place from which a patient exits; the patient who carries out a self-diagnosis; the receptionist who has the first contact with the patient once he/she decide to seek professional help; the doctor who accepts the patient handed over by the receptionist and who examines and treats the patient; and the family into which the patient returns after being treated and cured. At each of these points it is possible to differentiate the 'raw material - end product' aspects of the process: the patient leaves the family as its 'end product' and brings with him/her attitudes, habits, competencies and expectations acquired from the family into the process of assessing the meaning of a symptom; the patient enters the process as 'raw material' and after completing it and making a decision he/she becomes the 'end product' of that process; when the receptionist receives the patient, he/she become her 'raw material' and after dealing with him/her in terms of exploratory talks, consulting records and making an appointment, the patient becomes the receptionist's 'end product' and sees the doctor; the doctor receives the patient as 'raw material, deals with him/her by interview, examination, diagnosis and prescription of treatment and hand him/her over to the family as the 'end product'; the family receives the patient who then becomes its 'raw material' and who then undergoes the process of readjustment (or rehabilitation) to end as family's 'end product'. In this way the doctor-patient interaction is represented as a complex system including a number of factors. The various activities of each of these factors provide a good basis for the quality assessment of the parts of the whole process. The patient moving between the described parts of the system becomes exposed to a number of interaction activities, in all of which he/she is an active participant. Using the 'raw material - end product' concept for each step of this interaction it will be possible to establish the expected specifications and to measure it by using appropriate indicators and criteria.

DOCTOR - PATIENT INTERACTION

FAMILY (EP)	PATIENT (RM/EP)	RECEPTIONIST (RM/EP)	GP (RM/EP)	FAMILY (RM)
Values	Competence	Setting	Setting	Social support
Structure	Status	Records	Records	Skills
Roles	Personality	Diary	History	
	Symptoms		Diagnosis	
	Compliance		Treatment	
LEGIT-IMIS-ATION	SYMPTOMS DECISION	APPOINT-MENT	DIAGNOSIS TREATMENT MONITORING	LEGIT-IMIS-ATION

WELL ROLE ⟶ **SICK ROLE** ⟶ **WELL ROLE**

* EP=end product; RM=raw material

The most important concept involved in TQM is the role of each actor in assessing the state or condition of the received raw material before processing it and handing it on as the end product of that interaction. This is then repeated throughout the whole process and any mistake can be corrected at the spot where it has been noticed. The rule of a TQM process is that there are no failures in the output since the corrections are being made as a part of the production process.

By analogy, in the case of the doctor - patient example, the receptionist will be the first to assess the 'raw material' received from the family. If he/she notices that, for example, the patient lacks information about the operations of the general practice, he/she may remedy this by providing additional information to the patient. The doctor will assess the 'end product' of the receptionist, which now becomes the doctor's 'raw material'. If the doctor notices the receptionist's 'end product' is 'faulty' i.e. has not been properly prepared for the oncoming meeting with the doctor, he/she will have to compensate for this omission by additional preparations of the patient. During the process of interaction (contact, history, examination, diagnosis, treatment) this 'raw material' becomes transformed into the doctor's 'end product' which is returned to the family. Now it will be the family, which will assess the doctor's 'end product' in terms of defined specifications. If the family notices that the doctor's 'end product' does not meet the specifications, as for example, in the case when no preparations have been made for family support (resources, skills), the family will have a possibility to lodge a complaint to the proper authority and demand rectification of the omission.

If a setting does already have a quality management system in place, the role of health promotion and health education will be to ensure that the health-related specifications become a part of the general quality management system. If a setting does not have a quality management system, the health promotion and health education intervention can still be evaluated, using the TQM framework. In either case, it will be necessary to develop appropriate indicators and criteria, and ensure the data collection and analysis, and the feed-back mechanism for reporting and sharing information among all the participants, as well as the stakeholders is effective.

STANDARDS

The assessment of the quality of a product or service will only be possible if the expected and acceptable quality of the services provided can be defined. These expectations can be expressed in a set of standards and specifications.

The concept of "standards" has a specific meaning when related to the idea of measuring performance in terms of quality. In this context *standards apply to the requirements for the introduction and management of the quality assessment system in a setting.* These requirements are in general defined by a number of national or international bodies that are recognised as having the authority to certify such a quality assessment system in a setting. The standards are, therefore, only indirectly related to the quality of the product, but are directly related to the administrative system required for the monitoring and assessment of quality in a setting.

There are a number of ways the quality of a product or a service can be assessed. The method will depend on the conceptual framework one uses in defining the meaning of quality.

Quality has been considered as an expression of excellence and meeting some high specifications; it has been used to characterise consistency, fitness for purpose, value for money, meeting the expectations of the fund-giving bodies or as a means of transformation. In more general terms, quality is *"meeting the requirements of the customer".* In educational terms it needs to be recognised that in any process there will be a whole set of "qualities" which will have to be met to satisfy the needs of the consumer. This multiplicity of qualities will be of special importance in the case of a settings approach to health promotion and health education, with each setting having different specifications and consequently different qualities to be measured.

For some production processes and services there are set standards which are formalised and included in the standards set by recognised organisations or institutions. One of these, *The British Standards Institution*, Handbook 22 "Quality Assurance" (described in Bendell et al. 1993, Munro-Faure et al. 1993) provides a whole set of standards, such as:

- BS 4778: Quality Vocabulary
- BS 4891: A Guide to Quality Assurance
- BS 5233: Glossary of Terms used in Metrology.
- BS 5750: Quality Systems
- BS 5760: Reliability of Constructed or Manufactured Products, Systems, Equipment and Components
- BS 5781: Measurement and Calibration Systems
- BS 6143: Guide to Economics of Quality
- BS 7000: Guide to Managing Product Design
- BS 7229: Guide to Systems Quality Auditing

Another example of this kind of work is the research carried out at the University of Central England in Birmingham under the title 'Quality in Higher Education' (Harvey, et al., 1992).

An example of quality assessment of a service has been published by Cassam and Gupta (1992).

The role of external consultants

The introduction of a Quality Management System (QMS) into a setting is a complex procedure and has been the area of expertise of accredited management specialists, who act as external consultants to a setting. Their role is even more important if a setting aims at obtaining certification.

Within the general framework of the role of consultants (Hope, 1992) the specific role of a consultant as an enabler for a setting to introduce a QMS will consist of the following support:

- explanation of the requirements and advantages of a QMS for that setting;
- training of different levels of management in carrying out the necessary activities (preparing a policy statement, developing a QMS structure, meeting the required standards, specifications and procedures);
- establishment of documentation systems for quality assessment;
- role definition of various actors.

The consultants will act as a bridge between the setting and the certifying body and aim to ensure the success of the application for certification when all the standards are fulfilled. The consultant in some cases may be also an accredited assessor for the certifying body and be responsible for yearly monitoring of the activities in the light of the requirements of a QMS.

Certification

The basis for the introduction of QMS in settings which provide health promotion and health education as a part of their services is BS 5750 for services, developed by the Quality Management and Statistics Standards Policy Committee, which is identical with the ISO 9004-2 "Quality Management and Quality Elements - Part 2: Guidelines for Services", published by the International Organisation for Standards (ISO). The BS 5750 for services includes 12 parts which deal with all the basic elements involved in applying quality assessment and drawing inferences.

The introduction to ISO 9004 sets establishes the involvement of the members of the organisation to ensure the necessary quality of the services provided:

- managing the social processes involved in the service;
- regarding human interactions as a crucial part of the service quality;
- recognising the importance of a customer's perception of the organisation's image, culture and performance;
- developing the skills and capability of the personnel; and
- motivating personnel to improve quality and to meet customer expectations.

The introduction of a QMS into a service provider organisation should produce a competitive edge in a market economy. This can only be achieved if such a quality driven service is visible and formally recognised or *certified*. This can be achieved by registration against a specific Quality System Standard such as for example the BS 5750. The accredited assessment body should be consulted in choosing the appropriate Standard. There are a number of accredited bodies, some of which are specialised (for example UK Certification Authority for Reinforcing Steels - CARES) where others are of a more general character (for example British Standard Institute Quality Assurance - BSI, or Lloyds Register Quality Assurance Ltd - LRQA).

The concept of certification has been increasingly gaining in importance. This is especially the case in industry, where the idea is widespread that it will soon be possible to compete as a supplier only if an organisation is certified for quality. In services this is also becoming increasingly important, where the purchasers of services may favour providers of services certified for quality.

This will not, however, necessarily be the case, since management movements come and go, and there is no doubt that the quality movement has been somewhat of a crusade in management. Nevertheless, the concepts and procedures underlying quality management are so important that the shifts of fashion should leave its common sense core untouched. For health promotion and health education, its importance lies in encouraging the introduction of QMS in health planning, delivery of health services and health promotion and health education interventions, on the one hand, and making sure that quality management systems should, wherever possible, incorporate health promotion and health education aspects.

The requirements for certification are set out in each Standard and can be summarised as follows:

- quality must be management led. It has to include the understanding and meeting of customer needs; the understanding of the business processes; and investing time and effort to prevent errors;

- only senior management can change the philosophy and the culture of the organisation; they must ensure that the aims are understood by everyone; they must demonstrate their commitment in actions and words; they must encourage the full participation of all the employees in the efforts of achieving quality of services;

- the management has five key roles: (i) determine the aims of the business, its philosophy and policy for quality; (ii) develop the QMS to ensure this policy is understood and implemented at all levels; (iii) encourage every employee to become involved in implementing the QMS; (iv) invest in the necessary skills and resources to ensure the QMS is effective; and (v) take an active role in implementing and developing QMS.

BS5750

The main principle of BS5750, so far the most widely used standard, is that the set of standards should meet the needs and the interests of the organisation, as well as meeting the needs and expectations of customers.

The management should be responsible for introducing this system by setting out its policy, based on consultations with members of staff and taking into account the interests of the clients.

The implementation of the quality management system should ensure that the objectives related to quality are satisfied. The emphasis should be on problem prevention rather than problem detection after occurrence.

The management should plan and measure the quality related costs concerning the introduction and management of the quality system, as well as possible changes and improvements in the production process.

The management should introduce quality aspects into marketing, specifications and design, procurement, production and control of production, product verification. It should also be concerned with the measurement control, nonconformity and coercive action. Management should plan and control handling and post-production functions, quality documentation and control, personnel training, product safety and liability, and should be able to use statistical methods for the implementation of quality control systems.

Performance indicators need to be related to the objectives of the organisation under consideration. They can be broken down into input, process and output indicators and may also be categorised in terms of efficiency, effectiveness and economy. All performance indicators need to be related to the different types of interests of the stakeholders. In educational institutions, performance indicators for teaching and learning may include graduate destinations, degree classifications, value added, wastage and completion rates and student evaluations.

An important factor in the assessment of an educational institution is peer review, which can take three main forms: reputational studies, external examining and peer review based on a visit by a team.

Another way of assessing the performance of an educational institution is by inspection, which can include inspection surveys as well as informal inspections.

The certification of a quality management system in a setting, such as for example, an educational setting when applying the BS5750 standards, will require that the setting meets the following preconditions:

- production of a quality policy document signed by the top management of the setting;

- definition of the role of the personnel related to quality management including their responsibilities and their authority;

- verification of the resources and personnel, which includes monitoring the services and defining the resources for the implementation of quality assessment;

- selecting a management representative and his deputy with the responsibility for managing the quality assessment system;

- carrying out a management review with special reference to the quality system introduced; the required documentation; concern about purchaser satisfaction; publishing of the examination results; and the design of programmes related to the production process;

- control of the quality system with special reference to its functions; relevant factors; relevant activities; other factors affecting quality;

- review of the contracts, which should include the factors related to the purchaser-provider interface, enrolment of staff, introduction of processes assuring quality and the methods of assessment of the outcomes;

- design control which should be reflected in the planning and the development of programmes; definition of methods; selection of contents and building in of mechanisms necessary for peer or government reviews;

- document control which is related to the relevant quality issues; which should be approved by the certifying body; and which should include possibilities for modifications or changes;

- purchasing, which should be related to the defined specifications; it should be carried out from assessed sources;

it should define contractors and sub-contractors; and it should include the verification of products;

- product identification and traceability which should be reflected in the documentation concerning quality management;

- general and special process control which should include course planning, development, evaluation and review; timetabling; attendance; delivery; AV aids; accommodation; facilities; library;

- inspection, which should be concerned with incoming consumers; in-process inspection; final inspection and testing, as well as inspection of test records;

- equipment, which will include the inspection, measurement and testing of the equipment used; its condition and the appropriate inspections and tests;

- control of the product; with special reference to non-conforming products, services and the character of this non-conformity;

- corrective action which includes the mechanisms for complaints and comments, results of audit, as well as retention and success rates based on the analysis of the process;

- handling, storage, packaging and delivery of products which in an educational institution refers to student/trainee care, available instructions and health care, counselling, personal safety, accommodation and lodgings, etc.;

- quality records, which should include student and staff records;

- audit, which should be carried out internally and by external auditors; and which should be concerned with the training processes;

- training of staff, which includes the induction process, staff development and extensions, possibilities for retraining; mechanisms for staff relationship with the management through the process of communication;

- servicing of the institution which will include contract agreements, as well as support by students after completing their training;

- statistical techniques, which will be required for the analysis of performance indicators; drop-out rates; achievement records; purchaser satisfaction; as well as identifying the future trends in the institutional development.

IMPLEMENTATION OF QMS

The management responsibilities

The decision by a setting to integrate health promotion and health education into their daily activities will imply the introduction of a quality management system (QMS) into the monitoring and evaluation of the setting's activities. The main characteristic of a QMS in a service industry is that the focal point in the system is the customer. It also includes the management responsibilities and the personnel and material resources as well as the quality management structure.

The quality policy

The management is responsible for the provision of services to the customers. For this purpose it has to design a policy for satisfying the customers' needs and expectations. If the provision of services is based on the concept of quality, then the management has to undertake a commitment to quality management and introduce a *quality management system (QMS)*.

This commitment will be expressed in the *quality policy* which has to be produced by the top management. The quality policy will include:

- the service organisation's image and reputation for quality;
- the type of service to be provided (specifications);
- the objectives for the achievement of service quality (procedures);

- the approaches or methods used for the achievement of quality objectives; and
- the role of personnel responsible for implementing the quality policy.

Quality aims and objectives

The achievement of quality policy will require a clear statement of *aims* or goals of the service organisation, such as:

- effectiveness leading to customer satisfaction and consistent with professional standards and ethics;
- continuous monitoring and improvement of services;
- adjusting services to the needs of the society and the environment;
- efficiency in providing the services.

The achievement of these quality aims will depend on the selection of *objectives or specifications* including the following activities:

- clear definition of customer's needs which should include appropriate indicators and criteria related to quality assessment;
- application of appropriate procedures related to aims;
- preventive actions to avoid customer's dissatisfaction;
- optimising quality-related cost for the required performance and type of service;
- continuous review of service requirements and achievements to identify opportunities for service quality improvement;
- preventing adverse effects of the service activities on the society and the environment.

Quality responsibility and authority

The achievement of the stated aims by the selected objectives requires the establishment of a *quality system structure* to carry out effective evaluation and control of service quality intended to result in possible improvements.

The purpose of such a quality system structure is to provide a picture of the distribution of authority and role definition (job description) of the personnel in accordance with the requirements of the provision of services. The system should pay special attention to the qualitative and quantitative aspects of the personnel-supplier relationship at all interfaces within and external to the organisation.

Top management needs to ensure the development and smooth operation of the requirements for a quality system. The responsibility should be allocated to a *special person* or form a part of the overall role of a person. It is important, however, to understand the holistic character of the quality management approach. Quality depends not only on a designated person or on the performance of a part of the role of a person. It is the outcome of a *total commitment and aggregated performance* of all personnel, expressed in their commitment, motivation, involvement and networking. The main theme, however, is continuous improvement of services.

Management review

Management should make provision for *formal, periodic and independent review* of the quality system and their own responsibilities for its implementation, with a view to possible improvement. It should include a well structured and comprehensive *evaluation* based on the following information:

- findings of a service performance analysis: i.e. information on the overall effectiveness and efficiency of the service delivery process in achieving service requirements and customer satisfaction;

- findings of internal audits on the implementation and effectiveness of all elements of the quality system in meeting stated aims of the service quality;

- changes due to new technologies, quality concepts, market strategies and social or environmental conditions.

The outcomes of such reviews should be included into management policy and strategies for the future operation of services.

Personnel and resources

The management should provide the necessary conditions and opportunities for the implementation of a quality system based on the stated aims and objectives within a quality policy statement. These should include the needs of the personnel as well as the resources required for the provision of services.

Motivation

Creating structures and empowering personnel to participate in the QMS is not enough. Success also depends on motivating personnel so that they want to take on the responsibilities associated with QMS.

The achievement of this depends on taking into account a further development, generally known as *'quality management'*, which has been translated from its initial application in industrial production also into service areas. This has been extended to the idea of total quality management (TQM) which has had a strong support from major industries. It has also a number of critics, especially as far as TQM in smaller enterprises is concerned.

Whether the issue is QMS or TQM, the management needs to concentrate on the motivation, development, communication and performance of personnel, as follows:

- select personnel on the basis of competence to satisfy the job description;
- provide a work environment that fosters excellence and a secure job relationship;
- realise the potential of every employee by consistent, creative work methods and opportunities for greater involvement;
- see that all personnel feel that they have an involvement and influence on the quality of service provided to the customer;
- encourage contributions which enhance quality by giving due recognition and reward for achievement;
- periodically assess the factors which motivate the employees to provide quality service;
- implement career planning and development of personnel;
- establish planned actions for updating the competence and skills of the personnel.

Training and development

Education brings awareness of the need for change and provides the means of implementing it. The training elements include:

- training activities in quality management, including quality-related cost, and evaluation of the effectiveness of the QMS;
- training of personnel, which should not be limited only to those directly responsible for QMS;

- education of personnel about the organisation's quality policy, objectives and specifications for satisfaction of patients' needs;
- a quality-awareness programme which may include instructions and training courses for new entrants, as well as refresher courses for others;
- procedures for specifying and verifying that personnel have received suitable training;
- training in process control, data collection and analysis, problem identification and analysis, corrective action and improvement, team work and communication methods;
- the need to assess personnel requirements for formal qualifications and giving appropriate encouragement and support;
- the performance evaluation of personnel for the assessment of their needs for development and potential.

Communication

The service personnel in direct or indirect contact with customers (i.e. patients and their families) should have the communication knowledge and skills necessary to be able to provide a high quality of service. They should also be able to work as a part of a team within the organisation and be able to interact with other external organisations in the course of providing quality service to their customers.

A QMS depends on different groups of personnel with specific duties requiring the competence of the members in team work. A group can take the form of a quality improvement forum or quality circle, and members aim to improve quality of services by joint participation in the problem-solving processes.

Communication includes interaction within the management, between the management and employees, as well as among the employees. This can be enhanced through an effective information system and can include the following methods:

- management briefings;
- information exchange meetings;
- documented information;
- information technology facilities.

Material resources

The material required for the delivery of services may include:

- service provisioning equipment and stores;
- operational needs such as accommodation, transport, and information systems;
- quality-assessment facilities, instrumentation and computer facilities (hardware and software);
- operational and technical documentation.

Method of assessment

Evaluation of an activity related to the provision of services, based on the concept of quality, needs certain preparations. This is especially true for health promotion and health education services which have so far no generally agreed specifications and procedures, since there has been little evaluation in this area and the rare instruments have been concerned with the measurement just of efforts and outcomes.

The new organisational model of health promotion and health education based on a settings approach includes a great variety of different settings (i.e. school, hospital, family, etc.), which require the development of specifications and procedures for each individually, since there are few health promotion and health education specifications and procedures already available.

The development of specifications is closely related to the aims of the organisation or the intervention within an organisation. These aims will need to be differentiated on the following levels:

- organisational level - this will include the aims of the organisation in general as well as for its overall health promotional activities;

- process level - this will include the aims of the health promotion intervention;

- outcome level - this will define what kind of results are expected from the intervention.

The development of specifications for these three levels needs to reflect the relationship between them and the factors involved in evaluation, such as:

- aims - denote what is intended to be achieved;

- objectives - denote how it will be achieved;

- indicators - denote what will be used to assess the achievement;

- specifications - denote the acceptable level of quality and type of product;

- standards - denote the requirements for quality management.

Specifications

It is usual for specifications for the delivery of a service to be set by those responsible for such services and/or the professional bodies that are responsible for the activities of the staff providing the services. The approach to quality assessment is very similar to the established methods of evaluation in general. This will include the following steps:

Aims and objectives

The health promotion and health education intervention as a service provided by a setting needs clearly to define the aims in order to assess the outcomes. These aims should be closely linked to the achievement of standards and will represent the set specifications. Thc aims will have to be set on three levels:

- the organisational level;
- the process level;
- the outcome level.

Once these aims have been defined, the next step is to define the objectives, which will reflect the ways these aims are to be achieved. Each of the set aims may have several objectives. These objectives will represent the recognised procedures for the achievement of a specific aim and will include standard practices.

Indicators

The next step will be to choose which indicators will be used to assess the achievement of the set aims. They will also be used to assess the relationship between the aims and objectives selected, or in quality terms, between specifications and procedures - standard practices.

To be able to draw any conclusions from the measured achievements, they will have to be based on pre-set criteria which indicate what is and is not acceptable. This will show whether the achieved outcomes meet the set specifications and whether they can be defined in terms of optimal and minimal outcome or a lack of any noticeable change for better or for worse.

Data collection

Aims and indicators need to be translated into instruments, which will be used to monitor the processes and outcomes. These instruments can be in the form of existing records, specially designed questionnaires, aide mémoires for case studies or other tools for diagnosis and screening procedures.

CRITICISM OF QMS

The initial enthusiasm following the rediscovery of quality as an important selling point has been tempered by subsequent experiences and disappointments. Press reports about the need to promote the quality in industry have been countered by reports of disappointment due to the lack of noticeable benefits. The main complaints have been coming from small firms, which have found that there is a burdensome administrative commitment required by a quality management system (QMS)

Howe et al., (1993) describe the various doubts that the implementation has raised and discuss the problems that are being reported by those implementing a QMS in their enterprises.

One of the main problems seems to be associated with the urgent desire of some management groups to have the QMS used as a means for certification of the enterprise and, thus, to gain a competitive edge over the competition. The agencies involved in certifying an enterprise as having an approved QMS system, have set a number of strict preconditions and have introduced a system of monitoring the compliance with these conditions. As a result, some managers consider their enterprise to be successful once they have gained approval from the certifying agencies, so that QMS becomes and end instead of a means. This involves a considerable investment in time and labour and puts a great burden on the management and the staff. It is not unusual to find, when visiting an enterprise, that a number of employees are absent because they are attending various workshops and courses.

The emphasis on the process of acquiring and maintaining the QMS in operation can also represent a considerable burden on financial resources of the enterprise. This process has been developed in such a complicated way requiring such an amount of administration, that only the largest enterprises can cope with it, using internal resources. Most enterprises depend on external consultants, who help them in producing the policy statement, in introducing the monitoring instruments and evaluating the outcomes. An idea about the extent of this investment can be gained from the estimated expenditure amounting to 750 million dollars a year for external expert advice as quoted by Howe et al. (*Business Week*, 1991, Quality Issue).

In some enterprises, the emphasis on the processes (participation, responsibility) has been at the expense of giving consideration to the outcomes. There are instances where the managers are in no position to link the QMS directly to improvements of output or to the increase in the enterprise's financial gains. The main reason for this is meeting the standards has been done at the expense of setting the clear specifications of the end product. The enterprise may be producing a better quality of a product, but one which may be already obsolete in the market place. The quality has in this case been improved, but the product's market niche has been neglected. There is thus a difference between planning and designing the specifications of the product and ensuring that the product meets the quality standards.

The outcome of such criticisms has been a rethinking of the whole topic of quality as part of management activities. There are signs of some changes taking place at the grass roots: the focus is now shifting from the standards, set by the certifying bodies and emphasising administrative aspects, to the quality of people working in the enterprises.

When considering whether to apply the QMS to health promotion and health education activities within a setting, it is necessary to find out whether such a system already exists within a setting. *It will, therefore, be necessary to differentiate between the introduction of HP/HE into an existing QMS, or the introduction of quality aspects into an existing HP/HE system.*

There is a good chance that existing criticisms can be avoided, when applying QMS to settings involved with health promotion and health education. The members of many of the settings active in this area may not be interested in a formal certification of their quality management, even when they apply the principles of TQM to the assessment of processes and outcomes in the form of health gain. This would enable them to avoid bureaucratising the system and to reduce the administrative burden on the participants. On the other hand, it would give them all the advantages that such a quality management system can give.

The main danger from the introduction of QMS is that it may be limited to the managerial and administrative level of a setting, without ever reaching the level of consumers. The advantages can be considerable in the form of new approaches to evaluation and the accountability of the HP/HE activity. There could be also a gain in the form of an improved outcome, since in service industries any improvement in the process should constitute a direct improvement of the outcome in the form of a health gain for the consumer.

SUMMARY

The idea of assessing the quality of a product, as compared to limiting the approach to assessing the outcome, is new in health promotion and health education. The possibility of introducing quality assessment into the evaluation of health promotion and health education will require a modification of the indicators which have been used in the past. The introduction of health promotion and health education into existing quality management systems in various enterprises will require changes in the specifications used in these enterprises.

The important fact is that it is possible to apply the principles of quality management to the evaluation of health promotion and health education programmes, without necessarily applying for the certification of a quality management system by an external body.

In the case of an existing quality management system the introduction of health promotion and health education aspects will require, not only a change in the specifications but also a modification of the standards required for certification.

In general, it can be concluded that the introduction of quality aspects into health promotion and health education interventions and evaluation could represent a considerable improvement of both outcome and understanding.

AUDITING

Introduction
Professional Audit
Evaluative Audit
Summary

INTRODUCTION

The introduction of health promotion and health education activities into the auditing process, as well as the introduction of the auditing process into health promotion and health education activities is a relatively new idea. The former idea emerged when health promotion and health education activities switched from health problems, to settings with health problems, which brought about the need for a modification of health promotion and health education so that it fitted an organisational structure with its own system of evaluation, quality assessment and auditing. The latter idea became necessary with the growing demand for accountability of health promotion and health education activities, many of which did not start by defining their aims and, therefore, could not be evaluated.

The concept of auditing has been described in greater detail elsewhere (see Baric, 1994, Module 2, pp. 317-323). Audit has been defined as *the process of assessing an activity or performance against externally defined norms, indicators and criteria*. In general terms, it is possible to differentiate between professional audit and evaluative audit.

PROFESSIONAL AUDIT

There are a number of activities, especially in the service industry, which depend on a 'provider - purchaser' interaction, in which the process as well as outcome have been externally defined. Although relevant settings have a built-in system of accounting, quality assessment and evaluation, they are also subject to auditing by specially designated bodies, which have a formally established responsibility for monitoring and assessing the process and the outcome of such services.

Financial audit

The best known example of a professional audit *is the assessment of the financial activities of a setting in terms of accuracy of recording and justification of disposing of the income and expenditure.* This type of audit has a long history originating in the 16th century when it was known as 'an official systematic examination of accounts' (Medicom, 1991). The 'aims and objectives' on which an audit is based are usually defined in terms of an institution's plans concerning income and expenditure or a budget, which is approved at the beginning of the financial year and which needs to be followed in every detail. The 'indicators and criteria' for such an audit are provided by laws and regulations concerning the finances and accounts of an institution. In this way both the auditor and the auditee are quite clear about the existing expectations and need only to follow them.

Even this straightforward system of auditing has recently been undergoing certain radical changes. In addition to using the usual indicators and criteria based on the legal norms related to laws and rules avoiding criminal activities and enshrined in a number of laws and regulations, there is now a new concept of "green" audit. It adds to the usual indicators based on laws and regulations also the idea of environmental protection. Organisations are now being audited for irregularities in handling the finances, as well as for damaging effects their activities or products are having on the environment. In fact, auditing, like accounting is subject to changes in practice reflecting changing norms and values among the professionals involved.

Medical audit

Medical audit is an extension of the original concept of auditing. It is defined as *'the systematic critical analysis of quality of medical care..'* (Medicom, 1991, citing Marshal Marinker's 'Medical Audit in General Practice', British Medical Journal). Medicom (1991) produced a Study Book on Medical Audit in their series of books on 'Teamwork'. The book is written in two parts, the first part including a self-assessment exercise with background information covering the topic under consideration and the second part including a group work module consisting of a video programme and discussion material. It is especially designed for general practices and provides an opportunity for each member of the practice to study it individually.

The description of the medical audit (Medicom, 1991) quotes Metcalfe, who suggested that everyone in medical audit will be looking for something different: the government and the FHSA would probably see audit as a means of ensuring good services for the money paid; general practitioners may use audit to ensure that what they think they are doing is close to what they are in fact doing; and managers will probably try to identify the top and the bottom of a range of quality of services so that they can persuade those at the bottom to improve their services.

Medical audit can be applied to three different activities: it may refer to the collection of information about an aspect of medical care and its presentation to colleagues, after which recommendations and comments about the standards of performance are made, which is also known as 'peer review'; it may also refer to the educational process which relates to the identification of a problem in health care delivery that can then be rectified; it may also refer to 'practice audit' which is mainly concerned with data collection used for reports as required by the FHSA.

Below is an example of how the issues have been explored in one FHSA (Salford). In the course of discussions about the interpretation of the meaning and the aims of auditing general practices three levels of activity emerged:

Level 1 : This looks at what the practice is doing based on quantitative information, where examination of the data may indicate certain weak points in the system and can indicate where improvements are necessary;

Level 2 : This is concerned with the planning of change based on auditing clinical activities; this can be done with respect to a protocol or by just examining the activities in general; the outcome may be an improvement in clinical practice or an improvement in the protocol being used;

Level 3 : This is concerned with evaluating change and concentrates on an audit of critical or negative events occurring in a practice; it includes certain specified events, such as what preceded a maternal death, a child admission to hospital for asthma, etc; it explores the input prior to the event with the aim of deciding whether anything could have been improved at the time; this, however, does not cover auditing ‘avoidable’ events that may lead to future litigation.

The main reason for auditing is to improve the provision of services and to meet patients’ expectations based on the DoH document “The Patient’s Charter” (see Baric, 1994, Append 5.) Issues connected with auditing are of great importance at the time when GP contracts are discussed and revised, including GPs’ commitments to auditing their practice and their activities.

The Medicom (1991) book refers to the ‘audit cycle’ as developed by Baker and Pressley (“The Practice Audit Plan”). The cycle includes three stages: deciding what should be happening; studying what is actually happening; and introducing necessary change. It is based on collecting the relevant data about effort, efficiency and effectiveness in the provision of care. The main characteristic is confidentiality concerning the data, with special reference to the need for reporting, which should not allow for identification of individual patients. Such an audit will require additional resources in terms of time and equipment. Economy of efforts can be achieved by role differentiation between the members of the practice, which should be based on the existing competence and skills of each member in data collection and analysis.

The introduction of the concept of a ‘health promoting general practice’ (Baric, 1994, pp. 347-394) will result in redefining many of the aspects of the existing medical audit including quality assessment. This quality assessment process needs to include the evaluation and auditing of the practice as a setting, the job satisfaction of the staff as well as the health gain of the patients. It should also include the links of the practice with other relevant institutions in the community for the purpose of providing continuous care of the patient.

Health promotion and health education audit

The reform of the NHS in the UK has resulted in a number of Department of Health documents which have been concerned with the establishment of specifications related to the delivery of the health care. One such document, based on the Citizen's Charter, is concerned with the rights and duties of patients, which have been given in the "Patient's Charter" (Baric, 1994, Appendix 5).

The rights and duties defined in the 'Patient's Charter', as well as in the DoH document "The Health of the Nation" (Baric, 1994, Appendix 4), provide an adequate basis for auditing health promotion and health education activities, by using as indicators the stated rights and duties of patients. Although so far there has not been a specific auditor designated to audit the performance of various health promotion officers and health promotion units, this possibility could arise as the result of an increased demand for accountability in health promotion services, corresponding to general accountability in the provision of health care.

The basis for auditing health promotion and health education activities in the present situation is provided by the wide range of professions and occupations, actively involved in providing health promotion and health education services. At present the concept of auditing health promotion and health education activities, without taking into account the settings in which they occur, is not sufficiently developed for application in practice. Therefore, most of the auditing of health promotion and health education activities will form a part of auditing the activities of the settings in which it takes place. For example, auditing health promotion and health education in general practice will need to form a part of auditing that general practice. It thus includes health promotion and health education indicators and criteria into the overall assessment of the general practice.

EVALUATIVE AUDIT

There are situations where there is an obvious need for accountability and which would require an evaluation of a specific activity or programme, but where it is not possible because the programme in question does not have any defined aims and objectives on which an evaluation could be based. In such cases it is possible to carry out a special variety of evaluation known as 'shadow evaluation' (Rossi & Freeman, 1993) in which aims and objectives are assured. Another means of meeting the need for accountability is by evaluative auditing, which can be defined as *the assessment of a programme against some generally agreed upon specifications and using indicators and criteria relevant to these agreed expectations.*

Evaluative auditing applies the same approach as general evaluation with a number of specific modifications. It is possible, for the sake of convenience, to distinguish a number of distinctive stages in evaluative auditing, although in some cases the stages can become merged.

Aims and objectives

Where a programme or activity does not have any explicit aims, and for that reason an evaluative audit is being used, the aims will have to be set by the evaluator. If existing expectations are used, then an ordinary audit is possible, but if an attempt is made to assess the actions and programmes of health promotion and health education, going beyond these stated parameters, the evaluative audit will have defined the 'expected aims'. These can then be used as the basis for evaluative audit.

The same process will apply to the definition of objectives. These can be assumed from the examination of the programme activities and related to the aims.

Once the aims and objectives have been identified, then it will be easy to select the appropriate indicators and agree about the acceptable criteria for the establishment of positive or negative outcomes.

Method

Evaluative audit will depend on the methods used to establish the existing expectations in terms of aims. This can be achieved *internally* by analysing the objectives (activities, programmes) existing in the setting and deriving the assumed aims, which should reflect the reasons for the objectives.

Another way of establishing aims 'after the event' is to survey the various stakeholders. These can be subdivided into groups of individuals with common knowledge or expertise. The method of 'group interview' can then be used for each of the subgroups. There are several varieties of group interviews (Denzin & Lincoln, 1994) ranging from highly structured to free and unstructured ones:

- *focus group* interviews, which are formal and take place in a selected setting in which the role of the interviewer is directive and the questions are structured; such interviews are used for exploratory pre-test of instruments and situations;

- *nominal group* interviews, which are set in formal settings, the role of the interviewer is directive, questions are structured, and the use is exploratory or for pre-testing;

- *field (formal) group* interviews, which are set in prearranged and organised settings, but are carried out in the field, the role of the interviewer is somewhat directive, the questions are semistructured, and it is used for descriptive and in-depth studies;

- *field (natural) group* interviews, which takes place in informal or spontaneous settings, the role of the interviewer is moderately non-directive, the questions are very unstructured, and the use is for exploratory and ethnographic studies;

- *brainstorming*, which takes place in formal or informal settings, the role of the interviewer is non-directive, the questions are very unstructured, and it is used for exploratory purposes.

The method of group interviews will depend on the characteristics of the group members. To establish opinions about the possible aims within a setting, a number of groups may be involved:

- the group of *stakeholders* (authorities, professional organisations, grant giving bodies, etc.), who may provide the 'official' opinion about the expectations related to roles and the activities within a setting;

- the group of *experts or professionals* (the most knowledgeable people in the area, including professional experts such as teachers, doctors, other academics and specialists), who may provide a 'professional' opinion about the role and the activities of the setting;

- the group of *employees* (managers and workers), who may find themselves in the situation of defining in words what they are doing and why they are doing it in a particular way;

- the group of *consumers* (clients, patients, pupils, students, family members, etc.), who will be able to provide information about their interpretation of the setting is all about, what it is doing and what it could do in addition to improve their actions or programmes.

The interviewer needs to combine the skills of interviewing with the skills of running a group. The expertise required consists of the ability to listen, prompt and summarise individual statements and to be flexible, objective, emphatic, persuasive and a good listener; he/she should also have the skills to manage a group by preventing one person or a small coalition from dominating the group, encouraging reluctant members to participate, and to make sure to obtain the opinions of the whole group concerning the entire topic. The interviewer thus combines the role of the directive interviewer with the role of the group moderator. He/she must be simultaneously concerned with the questions and answers, as well as the processes of group dynamics.

To avoid the effects of group dynamics on the process and outcome a version of the *Delphi method* is often used (Scriven, 1991). This approach is based on the important role of the moderator who should be equal in expert knowledge to the respondents. The method of approach is to select groups of experts (stakeholders), but to avoid putting them in a face-to-face situation, thus avoiding irrelevant influence from group effects, where one person may sway a group's views. Instead, the mediator sends out a set of questions or statements and collects the answers from the respondents, asking them to provide the reasons for their choices. The mediator examines the answers, feeds them back to the group members with the respondents' explanations. This can be repeated several times until a consensus emerges. Each member has time without any external pressure to reconsider his/her statements. Such an approach is useful for obtaining expert opinions in deciding about the important points or in setting future trends of a programme. It has proved very effective in predicting change and in identifying solutions to problems.

In a group interview, discussions need to be continued until some agreement about the aims in the setting has been reached. This may require a number of meetings and good communication within the groups if the aims are to be shared and acted on.

Outcome

The outcome should be a consensus of opinions, within the groups involved in the exercise, about the aims of a programme or a setting. A possible way of keeping the group discussion on track is to relate the proposed aims to the existing objectives or activities within the setting. This should produce 'realistic' aims to be achieved by the objectives (or activities) pursued in the setting or in the programme.

Another way of focusing the group's attention on the topic under discussion is to ask the members to illustrate the proposed aims using the possible indicators to be used in the measurement of such aims. Once the indicators have been agreed upon, the next step should be to reach an agreement on the criteria for success or failure.

The outcome of the group activity should be the possibility of defining the aims, describing the objectives, selecting the indicators and reaching agreement on the criteria for an evaluative audit of a health promotion and health education activity as a special programme or as a part of a setting's activity.

SUMMARY

Auditing an activity or a setting can be defined as the process of assessment against some external norm (legal, moral, religious, professional, etc.). The auditor usually has a recognised formal status and the auditee accepts the process of auditing as an integral part of procedures a setting or a programme.

Professional audit is concerned with settings or activities that are formalised and have institutionalised norms or expectations. There are situations where normal evaluation is not possible because the setting or the programme does not have set aims which would provide a basis for the evaluation. In such instances it is possible to assess the activities of a setting or a programme by using evaluative audit, which applies special methods of defining the aims 'after the event' and then carries out the process of assessment.

It should also be noted that the process of auditing has attracted the attention of writers of computer software dealing with these issues. For example, GFQ Software (address: D-55595 Spabrücken - Schöne Aussicht 15, Germany) has produced software for auditing the environmental and health outcomes of various programmes. These are based on German laws and regulations, but could be adapted to the needs of any other country. These developments are part of the new recognition of the important contribution auditing makes to health promotion and health education activities.

APPENDIX 1

SUMMARY

Second Evaluation of the Implementation of the Global Strategy for Health For All 2000

WHO EURO 1994

Reproduced with kind permission of the WHO Regional Office for Europe, from *Implementation of the global strategy for health for all by the year 2000. Second evaluation. Eighth report on the world health situation.* Copenhagen, WHO Regional Office for Europc, 1994 (WHO Regional Publications, European Series, No.52)

INTRODUCTION

In 1978, a conference on primary health care was held in Alma Ata, then in the Soviet Union, which resulted in the publication of the Alma Ata Declaration, signed by all the Member States. One of the commitments of the Member States was to strive to achieve "Health For All by the Year 2000".

In 1990-91, in line with the timetable agreed by the Member States, a large-scale evaluation of the Health For All strategy was made in each country of the European Region. The findings of the evaluative report were presented to the Regional Committee in 1991. The summary of the final report is presented in this Appendix.

In the preface to this report, Dr Asvall, WHO Regional Director for Europe, provides the background to the changes occurring in Europe and comments on the findings.

The evaluation shows that, on balance, health in the European Region improved in the 1980s. Member States have increased life expectancy advance towards the elimination of some infectious diseases, reduced mortality from most of the leading causes of death, and reduced infant and maternal mortality. Progress in promoting lifestyles conducive to health is moderate: the growing trend in most countries towards non-smoking is the most dramatic and visible change. Progress towards healthier environments is also moderate, although food safety is a cause for concern. Work to reform health services is wide-spread but progress towards high quality and efficient care is far from what it could be. There is no real progress as yet towards the primary target for health for all - equity. On the contrary, there is a widening gap between the northern and western and the central and eastern parts of the Region. Because of this health divide, many targets have not been achieved for the Region as whole. Closing this gap as far as possible - at least to the level of the differences that existed at the beginning of the 1970s by raising the level of health of the appropriate population groups, is the task for the coming decade.

After the end of the Second World War, Europe was a relatively quiet place, a Region where political boundaries were sharply drawn and where individual countries maintained a slow and steady pace, each seemingly content with its particular approach to social development. In the late 1980s, however, a process of change started, slowly at first and then rising to a crescendo. Now political change of enormous magnitude is under way in the countries of central and eastern Europe. At the same time, most countries' economies are facing problems and unemployment is rising to levels last seen during the great depression in the 1930s.

Since the Regional Office of WHO started working with the new democratic structures that emerged in central and eastern Europe, evidence has accumulated that the fundamental approaches laid down in the European strategy for health for all in its 1991 update indeed provide the best framework for the analysis and choices that countries have to make. It is also becoming evident that the countries in transition need to clarify their priorities for development for themselves and their international partners. So far, the debate in these countries has not adequately addressed the fundamental issues that influence risk factors to health or the quality of the health service systems.

The serious health problems of these countries can be addressed in new and imaginative ways by bringing together a much wider array of partners who can contribute to better health development. Unfortunately, data gathered since the 1990-91 evaluation indicates a deterioration of the health status, at least in some vulnerable groups, and particularly in the countries of the former USSR. This is related to acute shortages of vaccines, essential drugs and financial resources in general.

This report provides a summary of general changes in health in the European Region and the summary of specific changes related to each of the 38 WHO targets agreed upon in 1984.

SUMMARY OF GENERAL FINDINGS

The second evaluation of the strategy of Health For All is of particular importance, both for the WHO Regional Office for Europe and for the Member States, as both are halfway between the adoption of the regional targets in 1984 and the common goal of achieving them by the year 2000. With a good overview of developments in the 1980's that were related to health for all, goals, actions and achievements can now be critically reviewed and evaluated.

The evaluation was carried out in two sections, the first one dealing with the assessment of the situation and the second one with statistical indicators. In this way, the evaluation included qualitative data, as well as statistics, which enabled comparison of the development between various Member States. The method of expert judgement and qualitative information was used in descriptions where numerical information was lacking.

Demographic situation

The population of the WHO European Region was 842 million people in 1990, and is expected to increase slowly (at an annual rage of about 0.5%) to some 884 million in the year 2000. This increase will take place mainly in the former USSR and Turkey, since population growth in all other sub-regions has practically ceased. Austria, Germany, Hungary, Sweden and some other countries will probably experience a decrease in the population.

Fertility rates have dropped everywhere in the Region, although they are recovering slightly in some northern countries and in Germany. Reproductive behaviour now shows a common pattern throughout the Region. Most countries have a fertility level below the replacement minimum. Marriages are becoming less frequent and non-marital cohabitation, with less intention to have children, is increasing. Divorce rates are increasing steadily and births out of wedlock follow the same trend and represent more than 40% of all births in Denmark and Sweden. These developments indicate a fundamental social trend which is spreading widely. The implications for health need to be considered in assessment, not only of social health and wellbeing but also of the adequacy of health and social services.

The population in the European Region continues to age. Between 1980 and 1990 the very old (80 years and over) increased from 16 million to 21 million, while the population aged under 20 years decreased by 6 million. This process will continue with a notable increase of population in the group aged 60-79 years. The process of structural ageing, however, is less advanced in Turkey and the former USSR. This points to the differences in the countries' main health problems. The economically active population is also ageing, although this is not evident from the proportion of this large age group.

This process has a number of important consequences. Young people are growing up in smaller families than ever before. The ratio of active middle-aged people to people in need of support is declining and may reach critical levels, a trend which is already putting additional pressure on the health and social services in some countries. Postponing death in ageing populations has been associated with increasing expenditure on health and social services. In some countries there is also increasing concern about the quality of life of people with major diseases and in advanced age.

Migrant populations are usually mentioned only in passing, but they account for a significant proportion of the total population in many countries. It is frequently assumed that restrictive measures will halt immigration. Migration has continued, however, and is expected to increase significantly. The social integration of migrant groups already poses a considerable burden, particularly when they are detached from the rest of the population and concentrated in certain geographical areas. In general, immigrants have poorer health than indigenous population. Their access to and use of health services is lower; their educational level is also lower and they are more likely to engage in behaviour that endangers their health. As immigrants now constitute a sizeable proportion of the population in some countries (for example, Monaco 66%, San Merino 42.7%, Israel 42.5%, Luxembourg 23.8%, Switzerland 16.7%, France 11.1%, UK 8.7%, etc.), the inequities from which they suffer could negatively influence the overall trends in, for example, infant mortality, accidents, homicides, etc. Immigration also has consequences for housing and nutrition. The data mentioned gives an idea of the situation in the early 1980s. Immigration to the Region as a whole, and particularly to Israel, has increased since then. Emigration from the central and eastern parts of the Region has increased sharply and is likely to continue as long as the social and economic crises lasts.

Economic development

Economic output per head, as measured by GNP, has increased in all countries for which data are available except Poland. These increases have not occurred at an equal pace and, the higher the initial level, the greater the increase. Differences in wealth between countries have increased, although they are more moderate when adjusted for purchasing power. The rich have, therefore, become richer and the less affluent relatively poorer. There are indications of a similar pattern, both in regions and in social groups in countries. Further, problems of social deprivation have increased. In addition, the recent economic breakdown in the central and eastern parts of the Region has resulted in the cancellation of programmes for disease prevention, health promotion and social support. Even before that, however, such programmes rarely had adequate support in terms of finance, personnel and political will.

The existing trend towards increasing inequities in health has continued. Although several countries have started programmes to alleviate the effects of socio-economic deprivation, real improvements are unlikely unless this issue is placed firmly on the political agenda and widely discussed. To facilitate this development, health authorities could commission and support surveys of the health situation in different social and geographical groups in relation to economic deprivation.

Employment

In the European Region, at least, employment is not so much a matter of subsistence as a pre-requisite for a dignified and meaningful life. Fulfilling and rewarding employment is a major factor in good health. Unemployment is associated with over use of health services, destructive and aggressive behaviour, suicide and homicide. Unemployment is a major and increasing problem in the Region. Some of the countries with the highest unemployment in the Region are (estimate for last available years 1989 and 1990): Spain 17.3%, Ireland 16.7%, ex-Yugoslavia 14.1%, Italy 12.%, Belgium 10.1%, UK 5.8%. These figures do not give an accurate picture of the situation in central and eastern parts of the Region, where there is not only unemployment, but also the under-use of skills and time, non-registered unemployment of young people and relatively low rates of participation by the eligible population in the labour force. In addition, the labour force's low mobility, with very limited experience of job loss, retraining and job search, is a serious problem in the central and eastern countries but also in other Member States of the Region. Under the prevailing conditions, the European Region will become less and less dependent on unskilled work than other parts of the world.

In view of the rising proportion of women entering the labour force, greater efficiency in industry and the widespread introduction of computers in administration, unemployment could be one of the important health hazards of future years.

After the cold war

The increasing efficiency of nuclear as well as conventional weapons are a terrible threat to humanity. Peace and the absence of the threat of hostilities are, therefore, the most important pre-requisite. With the end of the cold war, the fear of war has markedly decreased. Nevertheless, hostilities between ethnic and religious groups have erupted in some countries where they were previously under control and have continued in several others. There is no reliable account of the direct and indirect toll in human suffering as a result of these conflicts.

The end of the cold war also started a process of fundamental socio-economical change in the central and eastern parts of the Region. For many people, the threat of an uncertain future has replaced the threat of war. Large sectors of the population have suddenly been reduced to the poverty level, and there has been acute shortages of food and medical supplies. These obvious needs give rise to a spirit of international solidarity, and support was provided to countries struggling with transitional problems. The greatest need, however, is hope for the future based on real opportunities and sustainable development. Technical assistance and effective cooperation in all areas, including health, are the means being established to achieve this goal.

Reform of health services

At the end of the 1980s and the beginning of the 1990s, many countries in the Region changes their health care system and others expressed their desire to do so. Efforts are now directed towards deep and widespread change and the driving force for such change comes from the health services themselves. Awareness is growing of the importance of efficient, equitable and high quality services.

The developments in the 1980s have provided us with three important lessons on health services:

- countries are moving towards more decentralisation as a means of improving health care systems; the role of the central government is shifting towards the making of policy and strategy, and its functions towards deciding on and controlling expenditure through large scale economic mechanisms;

- internal market mechanisms and competition are seen as additional resources for improvement; they are compatible not only with global budgeting and general taxation, but also with insurance schemes;

- health and welfare are resources, not areas of unproductive investment; they are as important as any other national resources; investment in them should, therefore, be on a par with that in other sectors; this requires well informed political decisions and managerial judgements; this also means that health must be on the political agenda, regardless of the direction of reforms.

Long-term trends in health

Any consideration of long-term trends in health should take a broad view. Many health assessments rely on mortality rates to make valid comparisons of health. Overall mortality rates have continued to decrease and there is no reason to doubt that this decline will continue.

The reasons for this decline in mortality rates are only partly understood. The main contributing factors have been general improvement in economic and living standards, whereas effective health care services have made a relatively small, although important, contribution to the decline in mortality rates.

Prevention has had an important effect in reducing mortality in infants and children and make outstanding contributions to the marked reduction, even the elimination, of several infectious diseases. The reduction of mortality in infancy and childhood has been due largely to immunisation programmes against particular infectious diseases. The reduction in mortality in middle-aged and elderly people has been much smaller, because some causes of mortality have increased and others have decreased.

Future improvements in life expectancy will come increasingly from reductions in mortality in middle-aged and even the elderly. In many northern European countries, mortality during infancy and childhood is so low that further reductions will be very difficult and expensive.

More effective health care can result from further advances in science and drugs, and from giving appropriate treatment to all who might benefit from it.

Primary prevention has been successful where it has depended on health care technology (e.g. immunisation) but less so where it has depended on changes in people's lifestyle (as in reducing tobacco consumption). Issues on which the government can legislate (e.g. industrial and domestic air pollution) have also seen improvements. For example, government legislation on providing seat belts and wearing them has achieved high rates of compliance in most countries and contributed to the reduction of mortality from motor vehicle accidents.

Evidence is increasing that screening and early treatment reduce mortality from several types of cancer, including cancer of the breast and the cervix, and that screening for hypertension helps to reduce mortality from cardio-vascular diseases. The improvement in screening techniques and extensive programmes for early detection and treatment of disease may be expected to reduce significantly mortality in the near future.

The rate of further economic progress is difficult to predict, although any improvement could affect the life expectancy of the population. Higher standards of living can offer greater choice of lifestyle, including health-damaging behaviour. Giving people more control over their living and working environments, however, could improve the quality of life and increase the level of health by enabling people to make healthier choices.

SUMMARY OF FINDINGS FOR EACH TARGET

Health for all by the year 200

Equity in health

Target 1: By the year 2000, the actual differences in health status between countries and between groups should be reduced by at least 25%, by improving the level of health of disadvantaged nations and groups.

Equity cannot be measured with only one indicator. Disparities in rates of infant mortality by social group decreased in some countries. Several countries reported a decrcase in differences in the availability of health services. Nevertheless, differences in mortality within and between countries are tending to increase, particularly as a result of the slower pace of development in the central and eastern parts of the Region. In general, inequities are increasing or persisting more often than they are decreasing. Monitoring of inequities should be significantly improved.

Adding life to years

Target 2: By the year 2000 people should have the basic opportunity to develop and use their health potential to live socially and economically fulfilling lives.

In most European countries, attempts to increase health potential are related to support for disadvantaged groups. Progress has been made in adopting legislation, policies and programmes for such support. Estimates of perceived health vary widely. There is concern that negative trends in human contacts and social networks may be undermining progress towards better social health.

Better opportunities for the disabled

Target 3: By the year 2000 disabled persons should have the physical, social and economic opportunities that allow at least for a socially and economically fulfilling and mentally creative life.

While more legislation has addressed the disabled and the attitude of the public is becoming more favourable, activities are usually limited to financial support, sheltered work and the like. Quantitative data to measure progress are scarce, but a qualitative assessment shows some progress towards this target.

Reducing disease and disability

Target 4: By the year 2000 the average number of years that people live free from major disease and disability should be increased by at least 10%.

More countries are reporting on the prevalence of chronic diseases. Estimates of their prevalence vary considerably and time trends are not available. Life expectancy free from disability shows differences that are difficult to interpret. The achievement of this target does not seem likely.

Elimination of specific diseases

Target 5: By the year 2000 there should be no indigenous measles, poliomyelitis, neonatal tetanus, congenital rubella, diphtheria, congenital syphilis or indigenous malaria in the Region.

Many countries have formulated immunisation policies and begun to develop programmes to achieve the target. Only half of the countries, however, have set objectives and defined evaluation mechanisms.

Progress towards eradicating specific infectious diseases has been fairly good, particularly over the past 2-3 years. The target is likely to be achieved. Nevertheless, most recent data show an increase in the incidence of infectious diseases in some central and eastern European countries.

Life expectancy at birth

Target 6: By the year 2000, life expectancy at birth in the Region should be at least 75 years.

Twenty countries, with about 45% of the Region's population, have already achieved target 6 or will do so by the year 2000. Eight countries in the central, eastern and southern parts of the Region, with 54.4% of the population have poor prospects of reaching the target. Assuming that the trends for 1980-89 will be roughly the same in the 1990s, the average life expectancy for the whole Region is projected as being close to, but still less than 75 years by the year 2000. The chances of reaching the target depend almost completely on the progress made in the central, eastern and southern parts of the Region.

Infant mortality

Target 7: By the year 2000, infant mortality in the Region should be less than 20 per 1000 live births.

The average infant mortality in the Region is close to the target. Around 1989 the average for 99.6% of the population was about 22 per 1,000 live births. Four countries, with 45% of the population, still have an infant mortality rate about 20. Romania, the former USSR and the former Yugoslavia are likely to reduce this figure to below 20 by the year 2000. Turkey is expected to reach 25 by that time.

Maternal mortality

Target 8: By the year 2000, maternal mortality in the Region should be less than 15 per 100,000 live births.

By 1989, 24 Member States, with 51% of the population of the Region, had reached the target. The average for 28 countries, with 93% of the population, was about 25 maternal deaths per 100,000 live births. The chances of the whole Region reaching the target by the year 2000 depend mainly on improvements being made in Romania, Turkey and the former USSR.

Diseases of the circulation

Target 9: By the year 2000, mortality in the Region from diseases of the circulatory system in people under 65 should be reduced by at least 15%.

By around 1989, the average cardio-vascular mortality for 27 countries with 60% of the Region's population was about 14%

lower than the 1980 level. This represents considerable progress. On a country-by-country basis, the reduction of cardio-vascular mortality by 15% has been, or will be achieved well before the year 2000 in 19 Member States with 44% of the total population in the Region. Five countries with 45% of the Region's population, however, show an increase.

Cancer

Target 10: By the year 2000, mortality in the Region from cancer in people under 65 should be reduced by at least 15%.

Only six countries, with 3.7% of the Region's population, are likely to achieve the target. Another nine countries have decreasing trends in cancer mortality, but these are insufficient to reach the target. The remaining two-thirds of the European population is experiencing cancer mortality. Lung cancer is the main cause of this increase. The Region is not moving towards the achievement of target 10.

Accidents

Target 11: By the year 2000, deaths from accidents in the Region should be reduced by at least 25% through an intensified effort to reduce traffic, home and occupational accidents.

The average age standardised mortality from external causes for 27 countries, with 60% of the Region's population, was reduced by 11.5%, from 63.4 per 100,000 in 1980 to 56.1 around 1989. The cumulative reduction of 25% for these countries should be reached around the year 2000. About 40% of this reduction is due to a decrease in mortality from traffic accidents, largely because of successful preventive measures. In countries with

36% of the population in the Region, however, mortality from accidents is still rising.

Suicide

Target 12: By the year 2000, the current rising trends in suicides and attempted suicides in the Region should be reversed.

Some evidence points towards positive changes in mortality from suicide. The average mortality for 25 countries representing 55% of the European population, peaked around 1984 and is now showing a slight downward trend. This target is, therefore, likely to be achieved.

Lifestyles conducive to health

Healthy public policy

Target 13: By 1990 national policies in all Member States should ensure that legislative, administrative and economic mechanisms provide broad intersectoral support and resources for the promotion of healthy lifestyles and ensure effective participation of the people at all levels of such policy-making.

Support for legislative and administrative intersectoral measures to promote healthy lifestyles is increasing. More emphasis, however, is needed on linking intersectoral policy developments with economic mechanisms and developments. This is a particular challenge in the central and eastern countries of the Region, which are moving from centrally planned and state-owned enterprises to privatised firms and market economies.

Social support systems

Target 14: By 1990, all Member States should have specific programmes which enhance the major roles of the family and other social groups in developing and supporting healthy lifestyles.

Welfare services to raise the abilities of families to lead healthier lives have been extended. Less developed are efforts to adjust such services to the changes in the structure, functions and mobility of families that are taking place all over the European Region. Partial compensation for these shortcomings comes from fast developing systems that give social support for health through non-governmental organisations such as groups of patients, consumers and local health initiatives. The most outstanding success is the overall self-help movements in many western European countries. They have reached a level of progress that probably meets the expectations for this issue in the early 1980s.

Knowledge and motivation for healthy behaviour

Target 15: By 1990, educational programmes in all Member States should enhance the knowledge, motivation and skills of people to acquire and maintain health.

Educational programmes for health have increased and the approaches used have changed. There has been a shift towards developing the skills needed in particular social settings such as schools and workplaces; this is linked to the shift from health education to health promotion. Health education infrastructures have been strengthened, but coordination is weak. In general, people's levels of health knowledge and awareness are high in subjects such as smoking, alcohol and nutrition. It is important to estimate people's motivation and skills to maintain health, but information on these is not generally available. While there is evidence of progress, the level of actual achievement cannot be estimated.

Positive health behaviour

Target 16: By 1995, in all Member States, there should be significant increases in positive health behaviour, such as balanced nutrition, non-smoking, appropriate physical activity and good stress management.

The availability of data on dietary and smoking patterns in Europe is improving. This is not yet the case for physical activity and stress management.

The proportion of fat in people's diet continues to increase in most countries of the European Region; few remain below the recommended level. The prevalence of over-weight and obesity, particularly in middle-aged women and predominantly in the south and east of the Region, is very high. Only seven countries have so far adopted comprehensive policies on nutrition along the lines suggested by the World Food Conference in 1974.

Overall tobacco consumption has continued to decline in 13 countries and is stable or increasing in the others. Smoking prevalence is still very high, although there are encouraging signs of a decrease in smoking among young people of both sexes.

There is evidence of slow progress towards the target.

Health damaging behaviour

Target 17: By 1995, in all Member States, there should be significant decreases in health-damaging behaviour, such as over use of alcohol and pharmaceutical products; use of illicit drugs and dangerous chemical substances; and dangerous driving and violent social behaviour.

The extent of alcohol-related problems is serious; most are linked to normal drinking. Alcohol policies thus have to be more comprehensive.

Information on drug abusc is improving. In countries where drug abuse 'epidemics' started long ago, the problem seems to be stabilising. Countries with little experience of drug problems are now increasing concerned. Policies are being reoriented towards demand reduction.

On balance, there is evidence of positive developments towards the target. Further improvements are needed, however, in the formation base and policies that support the progress.

Healthy environment

Environmental health policies

Target 18: By 1990, Member States should have multisectoral policies that effectively protect the environment from health hazards, ensure community awareness and involvement, and support international efforts to curb such hazards affecting more than one country.

Most countries are strengthening their mechanisms for internal coordination on environment and health. Further, the number of agreements between countries that have been made or signed shows that countries in the European Region recognise the importance of international cooperation on this issue. The general public's understanding of the significance of the relationship between environmental pollution and health is increasing substantially, but there is still concern that environmental protection may be jeopardised for reasons of economic development and employment. While there is evidence of progress towards the target, the target as a whole has not been reached.

Monitoring and control mechanisms

Target 19: By 1990, all Member States should have adequate machinery for the monitoring, assessment and control of environmental hazards which pose a threat to human health, including potentially toxic chemicals, radiation, harmful consumer goods and biological agents.

Systems for monitoring the quality of drinking-water, food and ambient air are improving, but only rarely are they linked directly with health. They are normally used to control pollutant emissions. The general increase in public concern for the environment has been combined with the growth of a belief in the public's right to know about environmental hazards to health.

Knowledge about relationships between environmental conditions and health is not sufficiently established. There is evidence of progress towards the target, particularly recently, but as a whole it has not been reached. The information base on the environment and health needs to be strengthened, and capacities for environmental monitoring and assessment should be improved.

Control of water pollution

Target 20: By 1990, all people of the Region should have adequate supplies of safe drinking-water, and by the year 1995 pollution of rivers, lakes and seas should no longer pose a threat to human health.

Overall, 94% of the population of the Region have a piped water supply, although the corresponding figures are lower in rural areas. There is some concern about the contamination of drinking water from chemical dumps. Countries with old water supply systems have problems with leaking pipes.

As to the adequacy of drinking-water supplies, the target has, therefore, almost been met, but there is insufficient information to assess safety. Action against the pollution of surface waters has increased, although new concerns have arisen.

Control of air pollution

Target 21: By 1995, all people of the Region should be effectively protected against recognised health risks from air pollution.

In general, the decrease in particulate matter and sulphur dioxide in the atmosphere has levelled off. A good start has been made in phasing out lead in petrol, but the increasing use of cars has inhibited any overall decrease in nitrogen oxide concentrations. The quality of air in many large cities continues to cause concern. Health risks associated with indoor and outdoor air pollution continue to be identified. The European Region is moving towards the target but is unlikely to reach it by 1995.

Food safety

Target 22: By 1990, all Member States should have significantly reduced health risks from food contamination and implemented measures to protect consumers from harmful additives.

Changes in agricultural practices and an increase in mass catering have not reduced risks from food contamination. Many countries have experienced epidemics of food contamination with *Salmonella spp.* In the last few years, mainly from poultry, with a threefold increase of suspected cases in six years. Some countries have reported an increase in infections with *Campylobacter spp.* With the exception of most central and eastern countries in the European Region, toxic chemicals in food have decreased and the use of persistent pesticides has been reduced. The target has not been reached, however, and improvements are needed in control procedures, reporting systems and personnel training.

Control of hazardous wastes

Target 23: By 1995, all Member States should have eliminated major known health risks associated with the disposal of hazardous wastes.

The 1980s saw an increase in the amounts generated of municipal and hazardous waste, but this has been accompanied by an increased awarcness of and concern about its safe disposal on thc parts of governments, industry and the population. Appropriate means of disposal are being developed. Adherence to international agreements on the transfrontier movement of hazardous waste has increased. There is concern about earlier and some current dumping of chemical waste. The European Region is moving towards the target but is unlikely to reach it by 1995.

Human settlements and housing

Target 24: By the year 2000, all people of the Region should have a better opportunity of living in houses and settlements which provide a healthy and safe environment.

The quality of housing as measured by heating and sanitary facilities, continues to increase. In most countries of the European Region, the average space per person is also increasing, but the number of people living in substandard dwellings remains high and homelessness persists. Healthy housing is attracting greater attention, and standards are being raised. The Region is moving towards the target, as better opportunities for most people are established, but substantial groups have not yet benefited from this improvement.

Working environment

Target 25: By 1995, people of the Region should be effectively protected against work-related health risks.

The number of accidents at work continues to fall but notifications of occupational diseases are increasing, although it is difficult to know the extent to which this reflects a true increase in incidence. Occupational health services still vary in extent and scope of responsibility, but they cover less than 50% of all employees in the European Region. Work hygiene services are not linked with health services. Protection against work-related health risks will not be achieved by 1995.

Appropriate care

A system based on primary health care

Target 26: By 1990, all Member States, through effective community representation, should have developed health care systems that are based on primary health care and supported by secondary and tertiary care as outlined at the Alma Ata Conference.

The Region has shifted towards arrangements for health care that favour primary care, but countries need to build on previous achievements in primary health care in a changing situation. Political opinion is also moving in this direction, although the target has not been reached in a literal sense. Countries are experimenting with different schemes in line with the notion of primary health care. Major changes in health systems are in train in the central and eastern Member States of the Region.

Resources for and content of care

Target 27: By 1990, in all Member States the infrastructures of the delivery systems should be so organised that resources are distributed according to need, and that services ensure physical and economic accessibility and cultural acceptability to the population.

Target 28: By 1990, the primary health care system of all Member States should provide a wide range of health - promotive, curative, rehabilitative and supportive services to meet the basic health needs of the population and give special attention to high-risk, vulnerable and underserved individuals and groups.

The levels of staffing and coverage of health systems remain high. Interest has increased in ensuring equity in the availability and accessibility of a wide range of health services, and the continuing reforms of health systems aim at a more rational examination of needs. Nevertheless, measuring equity is not easy when so many definitions are used. Despite progress towards greater accessibility of services, neither target can be regarded has having been achieved.

Care providers and community resources

Target 29: By 1990, in all Member States, primary health care systems should be based on cooperation and team work between health care personnel, individuals, families and community groups.

Target 30: By 1990, all Member States should have mechanisms by which the services provided by all sectors relating to health are coordinated at the community level in a primary health care system.

Progress towards cooperation and coordination in the provision of health services based on PHC is mixed. Interest in, and concern about, this issue have increased. Nevertheless, community participation is not sufficiently stimulated in many countries; health system managers at the local level give more time to technical and financial matters. The trend towards decentralisation is clear but decentralisation does not ensure community participation. There is little evidence that the targets have been achieved.

Quality of services

Target 31: By 1990, all Member States should have built effective mechanisms for ensuring quality of patient care within their health care systems.

Target 38: Before 1990, all Member States should have established a formal mechanism use of health technologies and of their effectiveness, efficiency, safety and acceptability, as well as reflecting national health policies and economic restraints.

Quality assurance has reached the political agenda in many countries. A number of approaches are seen; that of defining and collecting the minimum sets of data required for quality assurance purposes is gradually being adopted, although not systematically. The indicators used cannot always detect the relationship between the outcome of care and quality assurance of activities. Systematic technology assessment remains rare. Progress has been made towards target 31, but the available data do not indicate that these targets have been attained.

Research and health development support

Research strategies

Target 32: Before 1990, all Member States should have formulated research strategies to stimulate investigations which improve the application and expansion of knowledge needed to support their health for all developments.

Strictly speaking, only two countries have reached the target in the sense that they have a research policy for health for all. Many others have general research policies or explicit research priorities that reflect the priorities established in the Regional

Office's policy. Research activities supporting health for all, however, are common and some countries have introduced changes in their research administration and funding mechanisms that are likely to benefit such research.

Policies for health for all

Target 33: Before 1990, all Member States should ensure that their health policies and strategies are in line with health for all principles and that their legislation and regulations make their implementation effective in all sectors of society.

All Member States have endorsed the regional policy for health for all; in many, it was discussed and approved by the parliament. Several countries have developed national policies and strategies for health for all; decentralised responsibilities for health, however, forbid these in some countries. The outlook for the implementation of the regional policy is varied. Most northern and western countries in the European Region reported good progress in putting its principles into effect; others cannot overcome tradition and the financial constraints on providing services outside hospitals. In central and eastern countries, programmes related to health for all were not really implemented in the past and present economic conditions do not offer much hope of implementation in the near future.

The target can be regarded as having been met in respect of policy formulation and endorsement, but the comprehensive implementation of health for all principles should be further pursued.

Planning and resource allocation

Target 34: Before 1990, Member States should have managerial processes for health development geared to the attainment of health for all, actively involving communities and all sectors relevant to health and, accordingly, ensuring preferential allocation of resources to health development priorities.

In many countries, the insufficient implementation of health policies is related to inadequate management. Not only the central and eastern countries of the Region, but also many others have introduced health reforms in which managerial changes are key elements.

Financial constraints and concern about the health of the whole population are major trigger factors. Expenditure on health has tended to increase, but varies widely between countries. In much of the Region, health expenditure account for less than 5% of the gross national product. Some progress has been made in involving communities and other sectors, mainly at the local level. Despite this progress, however, the target has not been achieved.

Health information systems

Target 35: Before 1990, Member States should have health information systems capable of supporting their national strategies for health for all.

Current or planned changes in information systems result mainly from reforms in the management and financing of health services. Although changes in line with health for all are taking place, most of the countries of the Region still cannot provide comprehensive information support to health for all policies.

Even if information is generally available, the resources and trained personnel required to analyse it from the perspective of health for all are insufficient. Many countrics prepare or plan to prepare public health reports. Target 35 has not been completely achieved.

Human resource development

Target 36: Before 1990, in all Member States, the planning, training and use of health personnel should be in accordance with health for all policies, with emphasis on the primary health care approach.

Target 37: Before 1990, in all Member States, education should provide personnel in sectors related to health with adequate information on the country's health for all policies and programmes and their practical application to their own sectors.

The health for all movement has influenced the training of health personnel. Important documents on education policy have been issued. The changes that have taken place mainly affect postgraduate training and the medical professions. Activities to education people in health-related sectors about health for all have been few. There is little evidence of positive developments in the planning and use of health personnel. Large differences remain in the availability of personnel within countries. Ratios of health professionals entering the labour force annually to the total population also vary greatly. Shortages of nurses and other care personnel are almost ubiquitous. Despite progress in this are, the targets have not been achieved.

References

1. *Global estimates and projections of population by sex and age: the 1988 revision.* New York United Nations 1989.
2. Tabah, L., *World demographic trends and their consequences for Europe,* Strasbourg Council of Europe 1990.
3. *Demographic yearbook 1983.* New York United Nations 1985.
4. *Demographic yearbook 1989.* New York United Nations 1991.
5. Beaglehole, R., International trends in coronary heart disease mortality, morbidity and risk factors. *Epidemiological reviews* 12:1-15 (1990).
6. Modell, B., & Bulyzhenkov, V. Distribution and control of some genetic disorders. *World health statistics quarterly,* 41: 209-218 (1988).
7 Bytechenko, B., *Development of the EPI in Europe - programme situation and functions.* Copenhagen, WHO Regional Office for Europe, 1991 (document ICP/EPI 026/12).
8. *National health policy of Turkey.* Ankara, Ministry of Health, 1993.
9. *Health for all in Wales. Health promotion challenges for the 1990s.* Cardiff, Health Promotion Authority for Wales, 1990.
10. Tsouros, A., ed. World Health Organization Healthy Cities project: a project becomes a movement. Review of progress 1987 to 1990. Copenhagen, FADL, 1991.
11. *The challenge of health. The new role of sickness funds and health insurance schemes. International AOK/WHO Conference.* Hamburg, AOK Hamburg 1989.
12. *Investment in health. Proceedings of the International Conference on Health Promotion, Bonn, 17-19 December*

1990. Bonn, Wissenschaftliches Institut der Arzte Deutschlands, 1990 (documents EUR 14281 EN).

13.*Nutrition policies in central and eastern Europe: report on a consultation*. Copenhagen, WHO Regional Office for Europe, 1991 (document EUR/ICP/NUT 133/BD/2).

14.*Measuring obesity - classification and description of anthropometric data*: report on a WHO consultation on the epidemiology of obesity. Copenhagen, WHO Regional Office for Europe, 1988 (document EUR/ICP/NUT 125).

15.*Food and nutrition policy in Europe: report on a WHO conference*. Copenhagen, WHO Regional Office for Europe, 1991 (document EUR/ICP/NUT 133).

16.*Tobacco: supply, demand and trade projections, 1995 and 2000*. Rome, Food and Agriculture Organization of the United Nations, 1986 (Economic and Social Development Paper, No. 86).

17.Nutbeam, D. et.al. The lifestyle concept and health education with young people. Results from a WHO international survey. *World health statistics quarterly*, 44: 55-61 (1991).

18.*It can be done: a smoke-free Europe,* Copenhagen, WHO Regional Office for Europe, 1990 (WHO Regional Publications, European Series, No.30).

19.*Environment and health*. The European Charter and commentary. Copenhagen, WHO Regional Office for Europe, 1990 (WHO Regional Publications, European Series, No.35).

20.*Guidelines for drinking-water quality*. Vol. 1: recommendations. Geneva, World Health Organization, 1984.

21.*Post-Water-Decade strategies*: report on a WHO subregional consultation. Copenhagen, WHO Regional Office for Europe, 1990 (document EUR/ICP/CWS 015).

22.*The state of the environment*. Paris, Organisation for Economic Cooperation and Development, 1991.

23. *Air quality guidelines for Europe.* Copenhagen, WHO Regional Office for Europe, 1987 (WHO Regional Publications, European Series, No. 23).
24. *Second International Mediterranean Conference on Tourist Health*, Rimini, Italy, 15-18 March 1989. Copenhagen, WHO Regional Office for Europe, 1989 (document EUR/ICP/CDS/ 038).
25. *Evaluation of the strategy for health for all by the year 2000. Seventh report on the world health situation. Volume 5. European Region.* Copenhagen, WHO Regional Office for Europe, 1986.
26. *Alma-Ata 1978: primary health care.* Geneva, World Health Organization, 1978 ("Health for All" Series, No.1).
27. Van Oyen, J.H. Health for all in Europe: an epidemiological review. Copenhagen, WHO Regional Office for Europe, 1990 (document EUR/ICP/HSC 013(6)/BD/1).
28. Bollini, P., & Mollica, R.F. Surviving without the asylum. An overview of the studies on the Italian reform movement. *Journal of nervous and mental diseases,* 177(10): 607-615 (1989).
29. Blendon, R.J. et.al Satisfaction with health systems in ten nations. *Health affairs*, Summer 1990, pp. 185-192.
30. *Changing health care in the Netherlands*, Rijswijk, Ministry of Welfare, Health and Cultural Affairs, 1988.
31. *Working for patients.* London, H.M. Stationery Office, 1989.
32. *Crossroads. Future options for Swedish health care.* Stockholm, Federation of Swedish County Councils, 1992.
33. Saltman, R.B., & von Otter, C. Public competition versus mixed markets: an analytic comparison. *Health policy,* 11(1): 43-45 (1989).
34. Hakansson, S. et.al. *The Leningrad experiment in health care management 1988.* Copenhagen, WHO Regional Office for Europe, 1989 (document SRR/MPN 501).

35. Harrison, S. et.al. *The dynamics of British health policy*. London, Unwin Hyman, 1990.
36. Harrison, S. *Managing the National Health Service: shifting the frontier?* London, Chapman & Hall, 1988.
37. Krans, H.M.J. et al, ed. *Diabetes care and research in Europe: the St. Vincent Declaration action programme*. Copenhagen, WHO Regional Office for Europe, 1992 (document EUR/ICP/CLR 055/3).
38. *Developing quality of care through information systems: hospital infection surveillance as a model*. Copenhagen, WHO Regional Office for Europe, 1990 (document EUR/ICP/CLR 049).
39. *Research policies for health for all*. Copenhagen, WHO Regional Office for Europe 1988 (European Health for All Series, No. 2).
40. *Priority research for health for all*. Copenhagen, WHO Regional Office for Europe, 1988 (European Health for All Series, No.3).
41. *The health of the nation: a strategy for health in England*. London, H.M. Stationery Office, 1992.
42. United Nations Development Programme. *Human development report 1992*. Oxford, Oxford University Press, 1992.
43. World Federation for Medical Education. The Edinburgh declaration. *Medical education*, 22: 481-482 (1988).
44. *Ministerial consultation for medical education in Europe*: report on a WHO meeting. Copenhagen, WHO Regional Office for Europe, 1989 (document EUR/ICP/HMD 115(S).
45. *European Conference on Nursing*. Copenhagen, WHO Regional Office for Europe, 1989.

APPENDIX 2

A Guide to Using Epi Info 6: A Word Processing, Database and Statistics System for Epidemiology on Microcomputers

The Division of Surveillance and Epidemiology
Epidemiology Program Office
Centers for Disease Control and Prevention
Atlanta, Georgia, USA

in collaboration with
the Global Program on AIDS
WHO, Geneva, Switzerland

Introduction

A very useful tool for research in the field of health is a set of computer programs called Epi Info 6. It has many advantages: it can run on widely-available IBM compatible machines; it is easy for beginners to use; it is health-oriented, having been initially created, with the collaboration of WHO, for the specific use of public health workers; above all, it is free, and users are encouraged to make copies to distribute to others.

Health researchers can obtain a copy of Epi Info and its accompanying manual by applying to the Division of Surveillance and Epidemiology, Epidemiology Program Office, Centers for Disease Control and Prevention (CDC), Atlanta, Georgia 30333, USA, or to the appropriate disease surveillance and epidemiology centre in their own country. In the UK, for example, it is available from the Communicable Diseases Surveillance Centre, 61 Colindale Avenue, London NW9 5EQ. There will probably be a charge for the printed copy of the manual. Since the program disks may freely copied and distributed, it is a good idea to check for viruses.

The notes in this appendix are intended to provide a simple introduction to Epi Info's capabilities. For detailed and advanced work with the program, it is necessary to be able to refer to the manual, which is approximately 600 pages long when printed, and is not easy reading! The version described here is Epi Info 6, since the system has been constantly revised since it was first produced in the Epidemiology Program Office of the Centers for Disease Control and Prevention (CDC), USA. Version 5 was produced by the CDC and the Surveillance, Forecasting and Impact Assessment Unit, Global Programme on

AIDS, World Health Organisation (WHO), Geneva, Switzerland. Version 6 (available 1994-95) was largely again the responsibility of the CDC. The main features of all versions are similar.

Epi Info 6 is described as a word-processing, database and statistics system for epidemiology on microcomputers. It can, however, be used for designing and carrying out a questionnaire-based study on any subject, not only in public health, although its examples and advice are all geared to the health research field.

Epi Info consists of a set of programs, which can be used together to carry out tasks, including a word processor, a data entry management program, an analysis program, a program that offers advice on research design and so on. The beginner does not need to know how all these programs work, but advanced users may want to customise the programs for their own purposes, and guidance is given on this in the manual.

New users, including those relatively new to using computers, benefit from the clear instructions provided by pull-down menus, with alternative keyboard entries. These make it simple to choose the required actions, whether it is writing a memo, getting advice on designing a questionnaire, printing a questionnaire, entering data or carrying out an analysis.

Epi Info as a tutor

One of the excellent features of Epi Info is its value as a tutor. A combination of a thorough and well-explained set of entries in the Help screen (press <F1> for help) and a series of tutorials on aspects of the system, together with worked examples, can be used to provide instruction in many aspects of elementary epidemiological research. Even if your interest lies in conducting survey research that is not specifically epidemiological, the principles covered in the guidance still apply, although the illustrative examples may be less relevant.

Inexperienced researchers are therefore advised to work through the tutorials and examples before using the programs for their own work. Experienced researchers will also find it helpful to take a quick trip through what is offered.

Epi Info does not give guidance on how to use computers, so if you are a complete beginner, it will be necessary to familiarise yourself with your computer and, in particular, with the file-handling features of DOS. The notes in this appendix assume that the reader has this basic knowledge.

Installing Epi Info on your machine and getting started

Epi Info 6 will run on a 386 IBM-compatible microcomputer with PC-DOS or MS-DOS operating system (Version 2 or higher), although a 486 is better; 512K bytes of RAM , although 640K is better; one floppy disk drive, although a hard disk is very much better. The system does not use Microsoft Windows©, but can of course run under windows as a non-Windows program. A graphics board is necessary to produce graphs. A wide range of printers is supported.

The printer for output can be specified during installation. In addition, a printer can also be selected within the word processing program (EPED) and the statistical and record producing program (ANALYSIS).

The programs cannot be run from the original floppy disks, since the files on it are compressed. They need to be expanded and placed on the hard disk of your machine or on formatted floppies. To install the programs on a machine with a hard disk, place the first Epi Info disk in your floppy disk drive, for example, drive A, and type A:INSTALL at the C:\> prompt (or whatever your hard disk prompt is). The installation program guides the user through the actions needed. It also offers the possibility of copying the disks. Epi Info can be run from floppy disks, although this is less satisfactory. In this case, the installation program will expand the programs from the original Epi Info disks and put them on new disks, ready to be run, so enough formatted floppy disks of 720K capacity or above, to provide about 6 megabytes of disk space for the whole installed system, will be needed.

Some of the programs respond to a mouse, and future versions will be totally "mouse adapted", so the mouse, if available, should be activated. The programs also run successfully through keyboard entry.

Type and enter 'CD\EPI6' at the C:\> prompt, to get into the Epi Info directory, and then type and enter 'EPI6' to run the program. (What you are expected to type here is printed between single quotes.) The introductory screen with pop-up menus gives the user all the information needed to get started. To exit from any program to this menu screen or to return to DOS from Epi Info, press the <F10> key, or use Quit from the File menu. Help on various functions is available by pressing the <F1> key. This help key is context sensitive, and comes up with the assistance most likely to be needed at a particular point.

Epi Info can best be learnt in stages through trying out its various functions. The manual is exhaustive and covers all aspects, including some that would not be relevant to a beginner.

The set of programs included in Epi Info

EPI6 -- This is the main menu, giving access to the rest of the programs in the suite. It offers an editor/viewer, programmable functions for menu choices, and a facility for displaying help files with hypertext (selected text items leading to others).

EPED -- A word processor for general text production or for creating questionnaires. Within EPED is an "assistant" program, EPIAID, which gives guidance on text preparation, building questionnaires and designing research studies, in the first instance for epidemiology, but also for other surveys.

ENTER -- Produces a data file automatically from a questionnaire created in EPED (or in ASCII form in another word processor). Data entered into a questionnaire form a database file. This file can be revised after records have been entered.

CHECK -- Improves the ease and accuracy of data entry, through setting up ranges, legal values, automatic coding, skip patterns, and other automated features.

ANALYSIS -- Produces a wide range of statistical results from the data files. Its capabilities are described in detail later.

CSAMPLE -- This performs analyses of surveys of a more complex design than that assumed in ANALYSIS, including cluster sampling, stratification and weighting.

STATCALC -- Calculates statistics from table values entered from the keyboard, including calculations for single and stratified 2-by-2 tables, sample size, and single and stratified trend analysis. It is useful for demonstrations in teaching.

EPITABLE -- An epidemiological calculator, which is a late addition to Epi Info, offering many statistical functions and graphs.

EPINUT -- A program for nutritional anthropometry (specialised).

EXPORT -- This exports Epi Info files into 12 other common database and statistics program formats.

IMPORT -- Brings files from other programs into Epi Info.

MERGE -- Questionnaire files in Epi Info or other programs may be in varied formats. This program combines differing data files.

VALIDATE -- Compares two Epi Info files for discrepancies.

Help Files -- The contents of the manual are contained in Help files available by pressing <F1>.

Sample Programs -- Numerous examples are worked through.

Tutorials -- EPED, ENTER and ANALYSIS can be learned through tutorials.

Utility -- A program called REC2QES can reconstruct a questionnaire from an existing Epi Info data file.

This suite of programs, used together, provides a very powerful tool for carrying out research projects. It offers a means of starting at a fairly simple level and developing to quite a high level of complexity.

The opening screen and tutorials

The title or opening screen, to which you can return by pressing the <F10> key, after using a program or getting into difficulties, has a ribbon menu along the top of the screen identifying the activities available: Programs, Tutorials, Examples, Manual, File and Edit. Click on the mouse or strike a key when the cursor is on an item to produce a pop-up menu.

The Programs menu offers access to the programs described in the previous section. It is possible to find out in advance a great deal of information about using each program by using the <F1> (Help) key. The help is in general extremely good, and this is a possible way of beginning. Using this method does, however, take some time to grasp how to carry out practical tasks.

A better approach is to take the time to go systematically through the Tutorials menu: Making a Questionnaire, Entering Data, Analysing Data Part 1, Analysing Data Part 2, which deals with more complex methods, and an example called 'An Epidemic', which works through a specific case. (Note that SetUp, in this menu, just reports on the system, and is not concerned with printers.) The first three tutorials provide a very good feel for the way in which the system as a whole works and what it can do.

In order to get additional guidance on using the word processor, EPED, press <F1> for help once you are in the EPED program, or follow the tutorial provided in EPED itself.

The pop-up menu of the item 'Examples' lists miscellaneous aspects of Epi Info, such as dealing with matched case-control data, generating artificial data and producing mailing labels.

EPED - the word processor

To produce a document, or to design and produce a questionnaire, select EPED from the opening menu. A work space for the document appears on the screen. The word processing function is a relatively basic one, as compared with some sophisticated dedicated word processing programs, but possesses the most important functions, such as full screen entry and editing of text, automatic formatting of text during entry through word wrap (that is, continuously entered text is automatically divided into lines), cutting and pasting of blocks of text, and finding and replacing of text through commands. Flexible tab settings, automatic setting of tabs in columns in a table, top, bottom, right and left margin settings, bold, italic, compressed, underlined, superscript and subscript text, and the use of non-English characters are available.

In the EPED entry screen, the 10 function keys and 10 <Ctrl> function keys execute commands or pop up a screen menu offering other available commands. As usual, the <F1> key provides the help menu, and the <F10> key leaves the program and returns to the opening title screen. If you have been entering material on the screen since the file was last saved, a prompt reminds you to save the file before leaving EPED, so there is no risk of losing work. Always leave EPED through using <F10>, and do not just switch off the machine.

In order to produce a text file, a word processing mode needs to be chosen. One mode is screen entry with word wrap (WW), in which the program automatically starts a new line when required. In word wrap mode, the length of the line already set is 65, which is appropriate for a standard A4 document, although this width can be changed. If you want to control the line breaks and to use the whole width of the screen (80 characters), the modes to use are text (TXT), which produces a text without word wrap, or questionnaire (QES) mode. How to design a questionnaire is discussed below. To set the mode, press the <F6> key, to show the SET menu, and use the space bar to toggle among settings.

The cursor can be moved through the text using arrow keys or the mouse. <Backspace> and <Delete> keys can be used to correct errors. Finding and replacing text uses <Ctrl-F6> and <Ctrl-F7>. There are two methods of dealing with whole blocks of text: block commands through keyboard entry or through commands contained in the Block menu, which is reached by pressing <F8>.

To prepare a document, type it in the form in which you would like it to appear, using <Enter> to insert a blank line between paragraphs, tabs for indents, and text effects such as bold, underline and italics to add emphasis. Simple boxes can also be used to highlight text. To draw a box on the screen using single lines, press the <Scroll Lock> key and then draw the box with the up, down, right and left arrows. This produces a single line box. Pressing the <Home> key and making the box in the same way will produce a double line box.

Save the document at any time - but certainly before you exit from the program - by pressing the <F9> key. A window asks for a file name, as well as the disk on which the file will be stored. The file name must be in the DOS form of eight or fewer characters. The saved document can be subsequently viewed, edited or printed.

To print a document, press <F5>, and follow the menu.

This file, or any other saved text file, can be opened by pressing <F2> and choosing from the list of files in a directory.

For any user with WordPerfect word processing software, it is useful to know its files can be converted and used directly in the program. Short cut keyboard commands similar to those of the word processing program WordStar are provided, but these do not have to be used, since most functions can be carried out by using the menus.

If you are familiar with an existing word processing program, you may want to use it to create the document. In this case, the text should be saved in ASCII format (standard international character code of 128 characters), and then opened as though it were an EPED file. This is possible because EPED files are themselves in ASCII form. If your file contains non-ASCII characters, there is a menu command to deal with the conversion. Non-English characters are also available by pressing the <Alt> key (for lower case characters) and the <Alt> < Shift> keys (for upper case characters) and cycling through a set of characters to get the one required.

To get the feel of EPED, use the interactive tutorial. Press the <F3> function key to run EPIAID and choose the word processing tutorial from the pop-up menu. This provides five lessons:

- The basis of word processing
- Creating a document
- Retrieving and editing a document
- Using find/replace and cursor movement commands
- Using block commands.

To quit EPED, press <F10>.

EPIAID as an assistant

EPIAID provides a set of guides for the novice researcher. It is one of the most valuable features of the system. The EPIAID main menu offers the following research topics, in addition to the EPED word processing tutorial already mentioned: writing a memo in a specific form; making a questionnaire; and developing a study design.

The memo preparation gives guidance on preparing a memo in a particular form used by the Centers for Disease Control and Prevention, Atlanta, but the form can be tailored to fit the requirements of other organisations, although this is best left to a more advanced user.

Developing a study design is particularly important as a first step in research. EPIAID's approach is to prompt the user to decide whether the study is case-based or exposure-based, and whether there will be a comparison group. If there is a comparison group, a case-based study, of those individuals exhibiting the item in question such as a particular illness, becomes a chase-controlled study and an exposure-based study, of those people exposed to a risk, becomes a cohort or follow-up study. The decisions made during the prompting of the study design program can be recorded as text, and serve as the basis for a description of methods used in the final research report.

The guidance on making a questionnaire in this menu is based on developing a mock questionnaire related to an epidemiological study of foodborne-illness. The approach adopted in EPIAID is to encourage the user to proceed backwards, from the topics and items needed for the study, to the actual questions to ask. This is an absolutely vital piece of advice in order to avoid the over-lengthy and badly focused questionnaires that are far too frequent.

More general guidance on making a questionnaire can be obtained from the tutorial provided in the EPI6 opening screen.

Making a questionnaire

It is important to realise that the ENTER program uses the questionnaire file that you design, in order automatically to create a data file. The first ten non-punctuation characters of the type at the beginning of each question are taken by ENTER to make a variable name. ENTER is able to discard some non-significant words. For example, if you type 'Age' as the question, the program will just choose this as the variable name. If you type 'What is your age?', the program discards 'What' and calls the variable 'ISYOURAGE'. A neater way of getting the program to use the word or set of words you want is to enclose it or them in curly brackets. Thus, 'What is your {age}?' will provide the variable name AGE. Care in wording the question is, therefore, desirable.

Having gone through the EPIAID guidance on questionnaire design, a researcher will have an idea of the questions needed and the order in which they should be asked. Epi does not give guidance at this level, but can to some extent shape design by providing nine ready-made field types. These are as follows:

- *text field* - this is indicated by a continuous underline with a maximum length of 80 characters;

- *numeric field* - this uses # to represent expected numbers; the maximum length is 14 characters, counting a decimal point as one character;

- *uppercase field* - all entries between < (less than) and > (greater than) symbols will be converted to uppercase;

- *yes - no* - this is a one-character field in which only 'Y' for yes, 'N' for no or the space bar or enter key (representing missing data) are accepted;

- *data field* - this can be in one of four forms, including standard US and European;

- *phonenumber* - this is a local phonenumber entered as a set of digits, 3 followed by 4;

- *long-distance phonenumber* - as above, but with a long-distance prefix;

- *today's date field* - this can be either today's date or the date of the last change of the record (both provided automatically by the computer's system date);

- *identify number* - provides an automatically incremented identity number.

The total length of a questionnaire may be up to 500 lines long.

To begin making a questionnaire, run EPED from the EPI6 menu. Press <F6> to see the SETUP menu, and from this choose QES from the WW/TXT/QES modes, mentioned earlier.

Give the questionnaire a title (one or more lines), and centre it by pressing keys for <Ctrl> <O> (letter O, not zero) <C> before the first character of each line. Entering questions can be made easier by using a menu of the field types already described. The procedure to get the pop-up menu is a little complicated: press the control key and the key for Q at the same time, then press Q on its own. The selection of field types from the menu is made, as usual, by moving the cursor to the choice and pressing the enter key. The field is inserted at the point where the cursor is placed in the text. Ordinary word processing functions are available within the questionnaire mode.

To print the questionnaire, if required, the file containing it must be saved. The menu must end in .QES. The <F9> key saves and <F5> gives a pop-up menu. If you wish to print the file currently on the screen, select PRINT FILE NOW and press the enter key. It may be that the printer needs some adjustment before it will work. Margins can be set by using the <F6> (Set) menu.

Most questionnaires, however, will be filled in on the screen, either directly or transferred from paper. Epi Info also gives assistance in this tedious task, by means of the program ENTER.

Entering data

As data are entered into a questionnaire, a database with the same name as the questionnaire file and with the suffix .REC is formed, using automatically generated field names as already described. This file may be browsed, searched for specific items, and manipulated, like any other database.

Advanced users may like to know that databases can be linked together in hierarchical form, to allow variable numbers of records to be associated with a 'parent' file.

To enter data, run ENTER from the main menu. An ENTER menu will appear. Choose 2 for a new data file. In the space for '<data file> .REC', type the prefix part of the name of the questionnaire. Suppose you have created a questionnaire on smoking among school children called 'Smokers.ques'; type 'Smokers'. When asked for the name of the questionnaire file, type 'Smokers' again. Press the enter key.

Fill in the blanks in the form. When the message 'Write data to disk? (Y/N)' appears at the bottom of the screen, answer 'Y'. The record will be saved and a new form will appear. If you realise you have made a mistake, reply 'N' and the cursor moves again to the first field in the questionnaire, so that the entry can be revised.

During data entry, a number of commands can be used:

- *backspace* - deletes the character to the left of the cursor;

- *right or left arrows* - move cursor one character to right or left;

- *up or down arrows* - move one field back or forward;

- *page up or page down commands* - move a page back or forward;

- *the home or end keys* - move to the first or last entry field in the questionnaire.

The insert, delete and <F10> (exit) keys work as usual.

In order to denote missing data, press <Enter> to produce a blank field.

It may be necessary to alter a record already saved. To do this, it is necessary to search the database for the record. Press <Ctrl-F> and then type in the item to search for, in order to list relevant records.

If there are several records, move through the list and choose the one you want. The record can be modified, or marked for deletion pressing <F6>. <Ctrl-N> is used if searching or editing is finished and new records are to be entered.

Advanced searching is possible using 'fuzzy' searchers, where only part of a clue word is known and * is used to stand for the unknown; for example, 'Robert*' turns up both 'Roberts' and 'Robertson'. A 'soundex' (= 'sounds the same') search is also available, but must be programmed in.

Sometimes it is not the single record, but the whole structure of the data file that needs revision, perhaps because you need to add new questions to a questionnaire that you have been using. ENTER can detect the changes and produce a data file in new format.

The main features of ENTER that have been described can be identified (along with some more advanced features) in the ENTER main menu, which reads as follows:

1. Enter or edit data.

2. Create new data file from .QES file.

3. Revise structure of data file using revised .QES.

4. Reenter and verify records in existing data file.

5. Rebuild index file(s) specified in .CHK file.

At the bottom of the ENTER screen, special function keys are listed.

A subsidiary program to make data entry easier is CHECK. This program should be used, if needed, before any entries are made. It checks for errors during the data entry process, does automatic coding of entries, and skips entries in parts of the questionnaire if certain conditions are met. After designing the questionnaire, make a .REC file, but do not enter anything yet. Run the CHECK program. The questionnaire appears on the screen, with a set of function keys on the bottom line. These cover a number of possibilities for checking on entries as they are made:

- *range checking* - to make sure that the entry is within certain bounds (<F1> <F2>);

- *legal values* - acceptable entries (<F6>);

- *must enter* - does not allow a blank (<F4>);

- *repeat* - automatically copies entry in last record (<F3>);

- *conditional jumps* - skips entries as appropriate (<F7>);

- *linked fields* - places a linked entry in field (<F5>);

- *automatic coding* - jumps to a linked field from an entry (<F8>);

- *edit field* - allows editing of CHECK's commands (<F9>).

CHECK can be used to control entries in even more complex ways. The aim is to make the lengthy and difficult task of creating the database easier and more accurate, so the need for CHECK can be judged on this basis.

Data can be incorporated in a database directly, from an already created database. This can be accomplished by reading-in a database from another program.

Epi Info 6 can import files in:

(1) fixed-length card format;
(2) comma-delimited format with string or text fields enclosed in quotation marks;
(3) Lotus.WKS and .WK1 files;
(4) DBASE II, III, IV files directly.

The procedure is to make a questionnaire in the exact format needed to fit the incoming file, and then to create a .REC (database records) file in the way already described. The command line entry:

IMPORT STUDY.DBF STUDY.REC 4

will import a DBASE file (denoted by 4, as in the above list) called STUDY.

Epi Info files can also be exported to other programs in a wide range of formats.

Still another means of incorporating data into an existing database is through merging it with another Epi Info file with the same structure. This is accomplished by using the CONCATENATE option in the program MERGE. This produces a third file (given a new name) from the existing files. (It is also possible to join dissimilar files and update files through using MERGE, but this is a little more complicated).

Analysing data

Once a database contains enough data, its contents can be analysed. The program to do this is called ANALYSIS. The program incorporates two tutorials that show what can be done; it is strongly recommended that the user goes through them.

ANALYSIS runs by commands; these are entered on the command line, rather than by means of menu items. There are about 60 commands to carry out the ANALYSIS functions. Not all of these are of immediate importance to a beginner, but they are not complicated to use, so it is possible to develop expertise in using ANALYSIS in easy stages.

The first step in using ANALYSIS is to make a database active. The command 'Read' is entered on the command line, that is, after the prompt EPI>. A directory of files appears and the one that is wanted can be selected. It is also possible to go straight to that file by entering its name (without the .REC) as the second word after 'Read'.

This is the pattern for all the commands: first the command, then the object(s) to be worked with. For example, 'Freq Sex' should produce a frequency table for the variable sex, that is, the number of cases for females and males is given, together with the percentages and cumulative percentages. To produce tables counting records in which the values fulfil criteria for two fields at the same time, use the command 'Tables', followed by the variables, e.g. 'Tables Sex Ill'. This command, followed by more than two variables, will produce a stratified table, where the variables after the first two serve as the basis for dividing the tables into levels (strata).

Commands available can be combined into a program, which is merely a file created by a word processor and saved under your file name (let's say 'Whatever') with the suffix .PGM. Then all that is necessary is to type on the command line 'Run Whatever.PGM'. An example, showing the format, is given in the manual (P122):

```
READ DISEASE
SELECT MONTH = 07
SORT DISEASE RECNUM
ROUTE PRINTER
SET PAUSE = OFF
LIST DISEASE RECNUM AGE SEX COUNTY
TABLES DISEASE COUNTY AGE SEX
ROUTE SCREEN
ECHO (The tabulation is complete. Returning to DOS).
QUIT.
```

The key <F2> lists all commands available in ANALYSIS. The commands include a set for program operations and file manipulations. Certain operations can also be performed on records, either checking records (such as LIST or SELECT) or using variables within each record (such as +, -, <, >, IF, COMBINE) to allow for arithmetic and logical operations.

The statistics available are as follows:

- FREQ
- MEANS
- REGRESS
- MATCH
- OUTPUT FREQ
- SUMFREQ
- TABLES
- MATCHED
- OUTPUT TABLES
- SUMTABLES

ANALYSIS also has the following commands for producing graphics:

- BAR
- PIE
- HISTOGRAM
- LINE
- SCATTER

For anyone with some prior knowledge of statistical analysis, the commands are fairly clear, especially if the user has been through the ANALYSIS tutorials. In addition, there are explanations of all the commands in the manual. Some commands, such as MEANS, get detailed treatment. MEANS provides the equivalent of:

For Normally Distributed Data (parametric tests)
ANOVA (for two or more samples)
Student's t test (for two samples)
For Data not Normally Distributed (non-parametric tests)
Kruskal-Wallis one-way analysis of variance (for two or more samples)
Mann-Whitney U Test = Wilcoxon Rank Sum Test (for two samples)

The uses of these different tests is described in the section on statistics in the manual.

The ANALYSIS program performs statistical calculations that assume the data come from simple random (or unbiased systematic) samples, but in many survey applications, more complex sampling strategies, where only part of the sample is random, are used. A program called CSAMPLE offers a means of dealing with the more complicated analysis required.

Three of the features CSAMPLE takes into account are:

- Cluster sampling
- Stratified sampling
- Unequal sampling rates

The procedures available in CSAMPLE cannot be explained in detail in these notes, but are well illustrated by an example in the manual, a WHO Cluster Survey of Vaccination Status. Working through the example will help to show what this more specialised program can do.

Both ANALYSIS and CSAMPLE carry out their calculations on a pre-existing database. Sometimes, however, it is desirable to carry out statistical analyses on data entered directly on the screen. This can be useful when you have a small amount of data that can be entered from the keyboard or when it would be helpful to demonstrate an example for teaching purposes. The program to do this is STATCALC.

STATCALC offers the following choices:

- Tables (2x2, 2xn)
- Sample size and power
- Chi square for trend.

An additional resource, EPITABLE, offers new statistics to extend ANALYSIS, including vaccine efficiency, screening statistics, random numbers and probability statistics. The help file (<F1>) contains full documentation on this program, recently added to the Epi Info suite.

Making a report

For easy reading of tables in a report, it is sometimes necessary to modify their layout and printing. Sometimes you will need to insert text to explain tables. The tables themselves can be altered in a number of ways through commands from within ANALYSIS itself. An example is 'SET PERCENTS = ON' or 'OFF', which controls the presence of percentages. The TITLE command allows labelling of tables. To give a well presented picture of the data, however, use the REPORT command.

First use EPED (or any word processor) to make a file to describe the report. This serves as a template to tell ANALYSIS how to print a report of the statistical results. It is best to give the file the suffix .RPT. The first line is in the form: #USES <variable name> <variable name> etc. Various symbols (described in the manual) tell ANALYSIS where and how to print out tables. The use of this report generator is not very intuitive, but a little practice can improve on what ANALYSIS would produce.

Obviously, a report can contain more than a set of tables linked by a few lines of text. The final form of a full descriptive report can be quite elaborate, and include the statistical report as only part of the whole. EPED can be used to prepare the whole document (as described at the beginning of these notes) and print it out, but it may be desirable to use another word processor to achieve desk-top publishing standards.

Epi Info at advanced level

Epi Info is an excellent resource for the researcher, and has been developing, by improvement and addition, over a number of years. Only some of the most important of its features have been described here, especially those which a beginner would need to understand in order to get started.

The more the suite of programs is used, the more its remarkable capabilities emerge. A further step for a user who has become confident with Epi Info is to start customising menus and procedures using the shell program, EPIGLUE. A researcher can also improve speed and ease of use by employing macros for frequent procedures, that is, sets of key strokes recorded and then played back when required. The menu for macro use can be found in the <F4> TXT menu in EPED.

A skilled programmer in Pascal or C++ can extend Epi Info for special purposes, and guidance on this is given in the manual.

Overall, Epi Info has very great value as a public domain system, appropriate for social and epidemiological research from the simplest to the most complex levels. Any health promotion/health education researcher is advised to obtain it if possible.

REFERENCES

Allport, G.W. (1969) **Pattern and Growth in Personality**, Holt, Reinhart and Winston, London

Anderson, S.B. et.al (1975) **Encyclopedia of Educational Evaluation**, Jossey-Bass, San Francisco, USA.

Babbie, E., (1989) **The Practice of Social Research** (5th edn), Wadsworth Publishing Co. Belmont, California.

Bailey, N.T.J. (1951) "On Assessing the Efficiency of Single Room Provision in Hospital Wards", *Journal of Hyg. Camb.* Vol. 49, pp. 452-457.

Bailey, N.T.J. (1952) "Operational Research in Hospital Planning", in *Operational Research Quarterly*, Vol. 8, pp. 149-157.

Bakke, E. Wight, (1950) **Bonds of Organisation,** Harper and Row, New York.

Baric, L. (1968) "An introduction to operational research in health education" in *Int. Journal of Health Education*, Vol.XI, No.2, pp. 50-61.

Baric, L. (1969) "Recognition of the 'at risk' role", *Int. Journal of Health Ed.* Vol 12 No 1.

Baric, L., McArthur, C. & Sherwood, M. (1976) "A Study of Health Educational Aspects of Smoking in Pregnancy", *International Journal of Health Education* 19, 1-16pp.

Baric, L., & McArthur, C. (1977) "Health Norms in Pregnancy", *British Journal of Preventive and Social Medicine*, 31, 30-38pp.

Baric, L. (1979) *"Levels of Uncertainty and Health Action"* in Bell,Ed. **Uncertain Outcomes**, MTP Press, Lancaster, 1979.

Baric, L. (1989) "Evaluation - A Tool for Planning, Management and Auditing HP/HE Interventions" in *The Journal of the Institute of Health Education,* Vol.27, No.2.

Baric,L. (1991) **Health Promotion and Health Education - Problems and Solutions**, Module 1, Barns Publications, Hale Barns, 2nd edition 1991.

Baric,L. (1994) **Health Promotion and Health Education in Practice -The Organisational Model**, Module 2, Barns Publications, Hale Barns, WA15 OHS.

Baric, L. (1995) "The Singer or the Song - HP/HE vs. Healthism", *Journal of the Institute of Health Education*, to be published.

Becker, M.H. (Ed.) (1974) "The Health Belief Model and Personal Health Behaviour", *Health Education Monographs*, Vol.2 No.4.

Becker, M.H. (1986) "The tyranny of health promotion", *Public Health Review*, 1986,14, pp.15-25.

Bell, C.R (Ed.) (1979) **Uncertain Outcomes**, MTP Press Ltd., Lancaster.

Bendell, T., Kelly, J., Merry, T., & Sims, F. (1993) **Quality : Measuring and Monitoring**, The Sunday Times Business Skills, Century Business, London.

Bernstein, L., Freeman, H. & Ross, P. (1985) **Collecting Evaluation Data**, Sage Publications, London.

Bradford Hill, A. (1961) **Principles of Medical Statistics**, The Lancet Ltd.London

Campbell, D.T., & Stanley, J.C. (1968) **Experimental and Quasi-Experimental Designs for Research**, Rand McNally., Chicago.

Carley, M. (1981) **Social Measurement and Social Indicators**, George Allen and Unwin, London.

Carlisle, E. (1972) "The Conceptual Structure of Social Indicators" in Shonfield, A. & Shaw, S. (eds) **Social Indicators and Social Policy**, Heinemann Educational Books, London.

Carlyon, W.H. (1984) "Disease prevention - health promotion: bridging the gap to wellness", in **Health Values: Achieving High Level Wellness**, 8 (3).

Cartwright, A. (1967) **Patients and their Doctors, A Study of General Practice**, Routledge and Kegan Paul, London.

Cassam, E., & Gupta, H. (1992) **Quality Assurance for Social Care Agencies**, Longman, Harlow.

Checkland, P., & Scholes, J. (1990) **Soft Systems Methodology in Action,** Wiley, New York.

Churchman, C.W., Ackoff, R.L., & Arnoff, E.L. (1957) **Introduction to Operation Research,** Wiley & Son, New York.

Cohen J. (1964) **Behaviour in Uncertainty**, George Allen & Unwin, London.

Cohen J. (1972) **Psychological Probability**, George Allen and Unwin, London.

Cook, T.D., & Campbell, D.T. (1979) **Quasi-Experimentation : Design and Analysis Issues for Field Settings**, Houghton-Mifflin.

Cook, T.D., & Gruder, C.L. (1978) "Metaevaluation Research" in *Evaluation Quarterly*, 2:5-15.

Deming, W.E. (1986) **Out of the Crisis**, Cambridge University Press, Cambridge.

Denzin N.K. Lincoln Y.S. (1994) **Handbook of Qualitative Research**, Sage Publications, London.

Department of Health/ NHS Management Executive (1991) **Assessing Health Care Needs**, DoH, London.

Department of Health (1992) **On the State of the Public Health 1991**, HMSO, London.

Department of Health (1992) **Health of the Nation**, The White Paper, HMSO 1992, London.

Doll, R. Hill, B.A. (1950) "Smoking and the carcinoma of the lung" in *Brit. Med. Journal*, Vol.2 p.739.

Doyal, L., & Gough, I. (1991) **A Theory of Human Need,** Macmillan Education Ltd, London.

Duckworth, E. (1965) **A Guide to Operational Research**, Metuhen & Co. Ltd, London.

Dunn, W.L. (ed) (1973) **Smoking Behaviour, Motives and Incentives**, V.H.Winston & Sons, Washington.

Etzioni, A., (1993) **The Spirit of Community**, Touchstone Press, New York.

Euroqol Group (1990) "Euroqol - A new facility for the measurement of health-related quality of life", *Health Policy 16*: pp.199-208.

Feigenbaum, A.V. (1991) **Total Quality Control**, McGraw Hill, Maindenhead.

Fellner, C.H., & Marshall, J.R. (1970) "Kidney Donors" , in J. Macauley and L. Berkowitz (eds) **Altruistic and Helping Behaviour**, Academic Press, London.

Fitz-Gibbon, C.T., & Morris, L.L. (1987) **How to Design a Program Evaluation**, Sage Publications, London.

Fitz-Gibbon, C.T., & Morris, L.L. (1987) **How to Analyze Data**, Sage Publications, London.

Francis, V. Korsch, B.M. & M.J.Morris (1969) "Gaps in doctor-patient communication: patients' responses to medica advice", *New England Journal of Medicine*, 280, pp.535-540.

Frank, A.W. (1991) "From Sick Role to Health Role : Deconstructing Parsons" in Robertson, R. and Turner, B. (eds) **Talcot Parsons: Theorist of Modernity**, Sage Publications, London.

Freidson, E. (1961) **Patient' View of Medical Practice**, Russell Sage, New York.

Galtung, J. (1980) "The Basic Needs Approach" in K. Lederer (Ed) **Human Needs**, Gunn and Hain, Cambridge, Mass.

Galtung, J. (1982) "Why the concern with ways of life?" in I. Miles and J. Irvine (Eds) **The Poverty of Progress**, Oxford Pergamon Press.

Glass, G.W., McGaw, B., & Smith, M.L. (1981) **Meta-Analysis in Social Research,** Sage Publications, Beverly Hills, California, USA.

Glasser, B.A. (1958) "A Study of the Public Acceptance of the Salk Vaccine Programme", *American Journal of Public Health*, Vol. 48, pp. 144-146.

Goodall, J.W.D. (1951) "Single Room in Hospital: Estimate of the Medical Need", *Lancet*, 1, 43.

Guba, E.G., & Lincoln, Y.S. (1989) **Fourth Generation Evaluation**, Sage Publications, London.

Gudex, C., Kind, P. (1988) "The QALY Toolkit", *Discussion Paper No.38,* Centre for Health Economics, Health Economics Consortium, York.

Guetzkow, H. (1962) **Simulation in Social Sciences**, Prencie Hall Inc. Englewood Cliffs, New York.

Greenhalgh T. (1995) "Scourge of Women in the West", *The Times,* 10th Jan 1995.

Hamilton, D. et.al (1977) **Beyond the Numbers Game**, Macmillan.

Harvey, L., Burrows, A., & Green, D. (1992) **Criteria for Quality**, Quality in Higher Education Project, Baker Building, The University of Central England, Birmingham, Perry Barr, Birmingham, B42 2SU.

Heinzelmann, J. (1962) "Factors Influencing Prophylaxis Behaviour with Respect to Rheumatic Fever: An Exploratory Study", *Journal of Health and Human Behaviour,* Vol. 3, No.2.

Henerson, M.E., Morris, L.L., & Fitz-Gibbon, C.T. (1987) **How to Measure Attitudes**, Sage Publications, London.

HMSO (1970) **Classification of Occupations**, Office of Population Census and Surveys, London.

Hochbaum, G.F. (1958) **Public Participation in Medical Screening Programmes**, Dept. of HEW, USPHS, publication 72 (mimeo).

Hochbaum, G.F. (1958) **Public Participation in Medical Screening Programmes**, Dept. of HEW, USPHS, publication 72 (mimeo).

Hochbaum, G.F. (1960) **Behaviour in Response to Health Threats**, Dept. of HEW, USPHS, (mimeo).

Honzik, M. P. (1988) "Value and Limitations of Infant Tests" in Oats,J.ed., **Early Cognitive Development**, Open University set book, Croom Helm, London.

Hope, P. (1992) **Making the Best Use of Consultants**, Longman Group UK, Harlow.

Howe, R.J. Gaeddert, D., & Howe, M.A. (1993) **Quality on Trial**, McGraw Hill, London.

Hudson, J., & McRoberts, H.A. (1984) "Auditing Evaluation Activities" in Rutman **Evaluation Research Methods**, Sage Publications, London.

Hunt, M.S.(1988) "Subjective health indicators and health promotion", *Health Promotion*, Vol3.No1, Oxford University Press, Oxford.

Hunt, S., & McKenna, S. (1992) "Do we need measures other than QALYs?" in A. Hopkins (ed) **Measures of the Quality of Life**, Royal College of Physicians, London.

Hunter, J.E., Schmidt, F.L. & Jackson, G.B. (1982) **Meta-Analysis : Cumulating Research Findings Across Studies**, Sage Publications, Beverly Hill, CA, USA.

Ikard, F.F., Green, D.E., & Horn, D.A. (1969) "A Scale to Differentiate Between Types of Smoking as Related to Management of Affect", *International Journal of Addiction*, 1969, 4 (4), pp.649-659.

Illich, I. (1975) **Medical Nemesis - the expropriation of health**, Calder & Boyars, London.

Ishikawa, K. (1976) **A Guide to Quality Control**, Asian Productivity Organisation, Tokyo.

Ishikawa, K. (1985) **What is Total Quality Control? The Japanese Way**, Prentice Hall, London.

Kegeles, S.S. (1959) "An Interpretation of Some Behavioural Principles in Relation to Acceptance of Dental Care" in **Proceedings of the 1959 Biennial Conference of State and Territorial Dental Directors with the Public Health Service and the Children's Bureau**, USPHS, Pub. No. 698, pp. 29-30, Gov. Ptg. Off. Washington, D.C.

Kennedy, I. (1981) **The Unmasking of Medicine**, George Allen & Unwin, London.

King, J.A., Morris, L.L., & Fitz-Gibbon, C.T. (1987) **How to Assess Programe Implementation**, Sage Publications, London.

Kurtz, I. (1987) "Health educators - the new puritans", *Journal of Medical Ethics*, 1987, 13, pp. 40-41.

Lapin, L.L. (1988) **Quantitative Methods for Business Decisions with Cases**, Harcourt Brace Jovanovich, New York.

Lancaster, K. (1966) "A New Approach to Consumer Theory", *Journal of Political Economy*, 1974.

Lawson N. (1995) "Poor people, poor diets", *The Times*, 24.1.1995.

Light, R.J., & Pillemer, D.B. (1984) **Summing Up : The Science of Reviewing Research,** Harvard University Press, USA.

McArthur, C., Waldron, E., Dickenson, J. (1958) "The Psychology of Smoking", *Journal of Abnormal Psychology*, 1958, 57 (2), pp.267-275.

McCall,R.B. (1988) "Towards an Epigenetic Conception of Mental Development in the First Three Years of Life", in Oats,J.ed. **Early Cognitive Development**, Open University set book, Croom Helm, London.

McKeown, T. (1976) **The Role of Medicine: Dream, Mirage or Nemesis?,** Nuffield Provincial Hospital Trust, London.

McKeown, T., & Lowe, C.R. (1977) **An Introduction to Social Medicine**, Blackwell Scientific Publications, London, 2nd edn. 2nd printing.

Medicom (1991) **Medical Audit**, Study Book, Teamwork Series, Medicom UK, Kingston upon Thames.

Meltzer, N.J. (1953) "A Psychological Approach to Developing Principles of Community Organization", *American Journal Public Health,* Vol. 43, No.2.

Miles, M.B., & Huberman, .M. (1984) **Qualitative Data Analysis: a Sourcebook of New Methods,** Sage Publications, London.

Miller, D.C. (1991) **Handbook of Research Design and Social Measurement** (5th ed), Sage Publications, London.

Møller, C. (1987) **Personal Quality**, Time Manager International A/S, Denmark.

Morris, L.L., & Fitz-Gibbon, C.T. (1987) **How to Present an Evaluation Report,** Sage Publications, London.

Morris, L.L., Fitz-Gibbon, C.T., & Freeman, M.E. (1987) **How to Communicate Evaluation Findings**, Sage Publications, London.

Morris, L.L., Fitz-Gibbon, C.T., & Lindheim, E. (1987) **How to Measure Performance and Use Tests,** Sage Publications, London.

Munro-Faure, L., Munro-Faure, M., & Bones, E. (1993) **Achieving Quality Standards**, Institute of Management, Pitman Publishing, London.

Noak, H., & Abelin,T. (1987) "Conceptual and Methodological Aspects of Measurement in Health and Health Promotion" in Abelin et.al (eds.) **Measurement in Health Promotion and Protection**, WHO European Series No.22, Copenhagen.

OECD (1988) **Performance Indicators in Higher Education - a Study of their Development and Use in 15 OECD Countries**, OECD, Paris.

Parlett, M., & Dearden, G. (eds) (1977) **Introduction to Illuminative Evaluation : Studies in Higher Education,** Pacific Soundings.

Parsons, T. (1951) **The Social System,** The Free Press: NewYork.

Patton, M.Q. (1987) **How to Use Qualitative Methods in Evaluation**, Sage Publications, London.

Phillips, B.S. (1976) **Social Research**, Macmillan Publishing Co., New York

Piaget, J. (1926) **The Language and Thought of the Child**, Harcourt Brace, New York.

Polgar, S & Thomas, S.A. (1991) **Introduction to Research in the Health Sciences**, Churchill Livingstone, London.

Posavac, E.J., & Carey, R.G. (1985) 2nd edn. **Program Evaluation : Methods and Case Studies**, Prentice-Hall Inc. New Jersey, USA.

Patching, D. (1994) **Practical Soft Systems Analysis**, Pitman Publishing, London.

Rose, G. (1992) "Strategies of Prevention: The Individual and the Population", in Marmot & Elliott (eds.) **Coronary Heart Disease Epidemiology**, Oxford University Press, Oxford.

Rosenstock, J.M., Derryberry, M., & Carriger, B.K. (1969) "Why People Fail to Seek Polio Vaccination", *Public Health Reports,* Vol. 74, No.2.

Rosenstock, J.M., Hochbaum, G.M., et.al (1960) **Determinants of Health Behaviour**, White House Conference of Children and Youth.

Rosenstock, J.M., Hochbaum, G.M., et.al (1960) **The Impact of Asian Influenza on Community Life: A Study of Five Cities**, USPHS, Publication No. 766.

Rosser, R., Watts, V., (1972) "The Measurement of Hospital Output", *International Journal of Epidemiology 1*: pp. 361-368

Rosser, R., Kind, P. (1978) "A Scale for Valuations of States of Illness: Is there a consensus?" *International Journal of Epidemiology 7:*, pp. 347-357.

Rossi, P.H., & Freeman, H.E. (1985) **Evaluation: a Systematic Approach** (3rd ed), Sage Publications, London.

Rossi, P.H., & Freeman, H.E. (1993) **Evaluation: a Systematic Approach** (5th ed), Sage Publications, London.

Royal College of Physicians (1989) **Medical Audit**, Report of the Royal College of Physicians, London.

Rufford, N. (1995) "China moves to ban babies with defects" in *The Sunday Times*, 5.2.95. p17.

Rutman, L. (1984) **Evaluation Research Methods**, Sage Publications, London.

Scriven, M. (1991) **Evaluation Thesaurus** (4th edn), Sage Publications, London.

Sen, A. (1985) **Commodities and Capabilities**, Elsevier, Amsterdam.

Senge, P.M. (1990, 1993) **The Fifth Discipline: The Art and Practice of the Learning Organisation**, Century Bussines, London.

Skrabanek, P. (1994) **The Death of Humane Medicine - and the Rise of Coercive Healthism**, The Social Affairs Unit, St Edmundsbury Press Ltd., Bury St Edmunds, Suffolk.

Smith, A. (1968) **The Science of Social Medicine**, Staples, London.

Smith, M.L., Glass, G.V., & Miller, T.I. (1980) **The Benefits of Psychotherapy : An Evaluation**, Johns Hopkins University Press, Baltimore, USA.

Smith, N.L. (1981) **Metaphors for Evaluation**, Sage Publications, London.

Stecher, B.M., & Davis, W.A. (1987) **How to Focus on Evaluation**, Sage Publications, London.

Stouffer, S.A. et.al (1949) **The American Soldier**, Princeton University Press, Princeton, USA.

Strauss, A., & Corbin, J. (1990) **Basics of Qualitative Research**, Sage Publications Inc.

Stufflebeam, D. (1980) **Evaluation Standards**, McGraw Hill, New York.

Stufflebeam, D. (1981) "Meta-Evaluation : Concepts, Standards and Uses" in Berk, R. Ed. **Educational Evaluation Methodology : The State of the Art**, John Hopkins, Baltimore, USA.

Suchman, E.A. (1967) **Evaluative Research, Principles and Practices in Public Service and Social Action Programs**, Russell Sage Foundation, London.

Suchman, E.A. (1969) "Social Factors in Illness Behaviour", *Milbank Memorial Fund Quarterly*, 47 (Part II) 85-93pp.

Susser, M.W. & Watson, W. (1962) **Sociology in Medicine**, Oxford University Press, London.

Toh, R.S., & Hu, M.Y. (1991) **Basic Business Statistics : an Intuitive Approach**, West.

Townsend, P. & Davidson, N. (1982) **Inequalities in Health - The Black Report,** Penguin, Harmondsworth.

Walton, M. (1989) **The Deming Management Method**, Mercury Books, Gold Arrow Publications, London.

Webb, E.J. Campbell, D.T. Schwartz R.D. Sechrest, L., (1971), **Unobtrusive Measures**, Rand McNally, Chicago.

WHO (1978) **The Alma Ata Declaration** in Alma Ata 1978 Primary Health Care, Geneva, WHO 1978 "Health For All".

WHO (1980) "Development of Indicators for Monitoring Progress towards HFA 2000", Report of the Programme Committee of the Executive Board, EB67/12 Add.1, WHO, Geneva.

WHO EMRO (1981) **Basic Indicators for Member States**, WHO EMRO, Alexandria.

WHO EMRO (1984) **Report of the Working Group on Concepts and Principles of Health Promotion**, Copenhagen.

WHO (1986) "The Ottawa Charter for Health Promotion" in *Health Promotion No.1*, 1986, pp. iii-v.

WHO (1993) **Health Promotion in the Work Setting, Report of the Conference, Cologne, 1991**, Verlag für Gesundheitsförderung, G. Conrad, Gamburg, Germany.

Willer, D. (1967) **Scientific Sociology**, Prentice Hall Inc. New York.

Williams, G. (1984) "Health promotion - caring concern or slick salesmanship", *Journal of Medical Ethics,* 1984, 10.

Wilson, R.N. (1963) "Patient/practitioner relationship" in Freeman, H.E., Levine, S. & Reeder L. (eds) **Handbook of Medical Sociology,** Prentice-Hall, Engelwood Cliffs, NJ.

Wurman, R.S. (1991) **Information Anxiety**, Pan Books.